A MEMOIR

BLACKLISTED

D. L. JANNEY

E F LEE
PUBLISHING

© 2017 by D. L. Janney

All rights reserved. No part of this publication may be reproduced, distributed, or transmitted in any form or by any means, including photocopying, recording, or other electronic or mechanical methods, without the prior written permission of the publisher, except in the case of brief quotations embodied in critical reviews and certain other noncommercial uses permitted by copyright law. For permission requests, write to the publisher, addressed "Attention: Permissions Coordinator," at the address below.

E F Lee Publishing, LLC
265 Main Street #663
Danbury, CT 06813
www.efleepublishing.com
info@efleepublishing.com

Ordering Information: Quantity sales. Special discounts are available on quantity purchases by corporations, associations, and others. For details, contact the publisher at the address above. Orders by U.S. trade bookstores and wholesalers. Please contact E F Lee Publishing Distribution: Tel: (888) 286-5212; or visit www.efleepublishing.com.

Cover photo courtesy of Fabrizio Gianni

Design & Layout by Michael Shaker

Printed in the United States of America

1. Non-fiction 2. Biography & Autobiography 3. Fashion

Second Edition

ISBN: 978-0-9974678-2-6

*I would rather be a real nobody,
than a fake somebody.*
-ANONYMOUS

*The best things in life are the
most difficult.*
-ANCIENT GREEK SAYING

To thine own self be true.
-WILLIAM SHAKESPEARE

*It is not only the things we choose
to do that define us, but the
things that we choose not to do.*
-ANONYMOUS

ACKNOWLEDGEMENTS

I am eternally grateful for the love and support of my beautiful wife Susie and all of my incredible children: Marit, Kasen, Gretchen, Ingrid, Kristofer, Nicholas, and Jeremiah. A special heartfelt thanks to Lee and Judy (aka Grammy and Papa) for "saving us" time and time again. Your love and support in times of our greatest need will never be forgotten. A very special thanks to Michael for believing and taking action to produce the book you now hold in your hands.

FROM THE AUTHOR

The book you now hold in your hands is my story. The names have not been changed and there are no innocents to protect...the innocent need no protection. My intention was to write a memoir that takes the reader to a place that they have never been, to live in the mind of another. I hope that you find something to take with you as you follow my journey. Thank you.

1

COLD STREETS OF NEW YORK

Everything was gray...; the sky, the sidewalk, the steel and concrete buildings, the ashen faces of the people rushing by me with wide eyes and downturned mouths. My head and body felt dreamlike, as if they were not my own. The cold air pushed hard and biting from the East River through my thin wool overcoat. The heavy box trucks lumbered down the broken road, each bump they hit thudding in my chest. A giant heart seemed to pump inside my body, without feeling and without warmth. I was hollowed out and empty...bone weary from everything and nothing at the same time. I had been trying for two long months, searching for an agency that would give me a chance, send me on a few appointments to get some work. So far, I had not even had a *near miss*. With every rejection my face had grown hot and red with embarrassment. I had mumbled "thanks" to no one and then found my way to the elevators that would deposit me back on the cold New York streets. Ford, Zoli, Wilhelmina, and Elite had rejected me more than once, each for a different reason.

Joey Hunter at Ford had not gotten specific; I had been sent to see him by a friend of the woman that suggested I go to NYC to model six months ago. He seemed agitated that I was even sitting in his smoky, dimly lit office. It was two in the afternoon, but the dark, heavy wooden slats of his blinds were pulled down, blocking almost all the sunlight from the bright winter day. He leaned back in his studded leather chair behind his massive mahogany desk. There was an old black rotary phone among the clutter of papers and glossy eight by tens of young women smiling. I got the feeling that I was cutting into his time *interviewing* Eileen's new female prospects. His walls were covered with neatly framed magazine covers showing the beautiful women of Ford. He leaned far back in his padded leather chair with the brass studs on the cushioned arms and said to me between puffs of his cigar with a supercilious look of the most judging form of condescension;

"You'll never be in the top five percent of the modeling business. The lower ninety-five percent don't make a living; they just tell everyone that they are models while they go to school or wait tables in Midtown. And then they tell everyone who will listen to them that they are just waiting tables until they get their big modeling break. Kind of pathetic, don't you think?"

I stared Joey in the eye for a moment and thought, *why does he need to say this?* He could have said; *You're not Ford material*, or, *Why don't you get some good pictures and come back?* but to say I will never make it in modeling? Who the hell is he with his wide collared beige golf shirt and fat paunch pushing his pants and shirt out over the front of his wide white belt? Man, he got way too much pleasure popping my fragile balloon of hope.

I wanted out of his stuffy office. I wanted to get back to the street so that I could breathe. I knew that he was right; I had little or no chance to make it in modeling. What burned me up inside is that people think they can say the nastiest things to you if you come to them looking for a job. Joey acted as if I should have bowed down to him for the pearls of wisdom that he doled out between clouds of foul cigar smoke. Well, not me. Forget that. Especially if you're not even giving me a chance. Keep your stupid theories and predictions to yourself; let me figure it out on my own. After all, what do you care? I will never be sitting in your crappy power office again.

I could feel the frustration and anger rising up inside of me like hot water in a pot coming to a boil too fast. I had visions of grabbing him by the shirt. Power does not equal intelligence or wisdom, but everyone with even a modicum of each think that they can say whatever they want to the weak and poor, their successful lives and fat bank accounts proof to the world that they are someone to be listened to, a wise and significant human being. Not me. If you're smart, you're smart. If you're stupid then you will always be stupid. No amount of money or power will ever change my mind. I know that this goes against all that the world was built on. I decided not to take Joey's words to heart, no matter what his credentials were. I'll store this in my memory to motivate me when I feel like giving up. He won't tell me how to feel about myself, ever.

Jan from Elite was a different sort. He was a quiet man in his early thirties with puffs of blondish-red hair in the middle and sides of his head. His skin was the color of a sun-bleached seashell, pinkish-white. He wore jeans and short sleeved shirts, both which didn't seem to fit quite right, as if his body did not work with western style clothes. He had the look of a man that was never good at sports; any sport. He seemed to love being in charge of the men's division at Elite and took his job very seriously. His meekness turned to power when he realized that a few words from him could determine the fate of a hopeful male model. I met Jan on a busy Tuesday morning when four other models were waiting in the small, glass walled reception area. The walls were covered with framed pictures of past and present female models on the covers of Vogue, Cosmo, Mademoiselle, Elle and Marie Claire. Jan looked carefully at my book the first time I met him and diplomatically told me that my pictures were no good, *but* that I may have a good look. He told me to get more pictures. I agreed with him about the book's being worthless, but knew that I couldn't get any more pictures to show him unless I took them myself, and I didn't have a camera or any money to pay someone to take my picture.

    I returned to Elite three more times after that Tuesday morning, twice with some really bad pictures that Lou and his girlfriend, Ginger, took of me on a cold Wednesday night in what he called his studio, but was really just an old barn. Ginger had played makeup artist. She covered my face with foundation, working especially hard on erasing the dark circles beneath my eyes with a bottle of liquid foundation and a dirty looking triangular makeup sponge. The results had been some really bad close-up black and white pictures with the light shining white and bright from behind my head and the makeup accentuating the wrinkles around my eyes. I looked much older than my nineteen years. I never showed them to anyone and let Lou keep all of the copies for his photography business, but I later got a few decent color photos from outside his Weston house. I wore jeans that were close to being too small and a borrowed denim jacket with the red baseball cap that I wore every day at Monmouth College. Lou didn't like them because he thought they were not *professional* looking, but I thought they showed some of my personality. The pictures were not bad, and I thought I almost looked like a model.

Jan really wanted to find a place in his growing men's agency for me, but without some good pictures to show the owners of the agency, he wasn't willing to take the risk of signing me. I almost felt that the rejections were harder on him than on me. I knew he wasn't going to sign me, so I wasn't surprised when he flatly told me that I was not really ready to be a model for Elite. My mind was working as he spoke and I agreed with Kyle...I was not right for Elite.

Zoli had been an intimidating experience, with its dark wood paneled waiting room and corporate-like atmosphere. It was filled with pictures of serious dark haired models with chiseled features, each one lit more dramatically than the last. I had noticed that none of them looked like me; wet, slicked back hair, oiled torsos, or fine Italian suits covering fit bodies. They were all either tanned or Sicilian.

I had known I would be rejected before I had a chance to show my portfolio to a booker. I was broad shouldered, 6'1", with arms like braided whipcords. My eyes were a color green that I had never seen before, looking more like a husky's eyes than a human's. Icy and cold and deep set behind high, sharp cheekbones marred by a childhood scar from a run-in with a nursery school bully and a large wooden construction block. The incident left me with two deep scars at the outside edge of my right cheek. An *equal sign* that marked my imperfect face. Other scars sat upon my face, but required closer investigation. The equal sign jumped right out at you; no one ever missed it. It never bothered me. I always liked scars; thought they were cool. They were a visual reminder of past events etched into my skin. It did not occur to me until I started trying to model that there were adults who survived childhood with unscarred faces. Perfectly smooth faces and bodies, without blemish.

My arms and legs were covered with scars, but they weren't noticeable unless you looked closely. The one exception was the north-south slash starting above my right collarbone and ending four inches lower. It was pointed at the top and bottom and about a half inch wide in the middle. It had healed up fast and flat to my skin, the pinkish-red color the only clue to the casual observer that the scar even existed.

I had never had stitches due to being raised as a Christian Scientist. I was convinced that the deep gash healed as well as it did because of that fact. I seemed to always stop bleeding fast and heal quickly, even when my toddler brother got a hold of my dad's hatchet and swung it down on me when I was tied up playing Indian in the woods of Wisconsin. I saw Jayson standing above me with the hatchet held in his two tiny fists raised above his head. At the last minute I lifted my head up from the ground to avoid the blow, but he caught me on the back of the head with the sharp end of the hatchet. There was a lot of blood, but it stopped quickly after matting the hair at the back of my head in the cold fall weather. My brother Stokes took one look at the mess and puked in the leaves while Dad played with the cut and decided to shave my head around the crown and put three pieces of white tape to hold the gash together. He was proud of his handiwork and referred to it repeatedly as a butterfly dressing. I knew that my dad made it worse and that I would have to deal with the repercussions of a bald spot in the back of my head for the first half of my sophomore year in high school. I never really trusted my dad to do the right thing in any situation, and this time was no different. Unfortunately, my dad was the biggest human being I had ever seen, and he took the term *might makes right* to a whole different level. On a physical level, going against my dad was a suicide mission at best. I was the second born in a family of six. I quietly defied my dad most of the time, but when I slipped and put my thoughts into words and directly confronted my dad, the backlash was always swift and unpredictable.

I spent the next six months trying to comb my long seventies styled hair over the three inch round bald spot that Dad had created around the wound. I was made fun of by most of the students that sat directly behind me, but I have to admit, I did look like a monk with a really bad haircut.

When I got the chance to show my book to the receptionist at Zoli, she looked at the cheap, oversized portfolio with a smile-sneer and said to me in her Long Island, nasal toned voice: "I'm sorry, we're not taking any new models at our agency at this time. Thanks for coming by." I nodded my head and reached across her desk to retrieve my book. I was okay with the rejection; it's not like she said, "What are you thinking? A model? Seriously?" I knew that

I would never be with an agency like Zoli; it wasn't me, it was them.

I was feeling down and more foolish than ever. My life seemed an ocean of nothingness; nothing on the shore of the past, nothing on the horizon of the future. I looked down at the cracked and dirty sidewalk as I turned without purpose to cut west on 58th Street towards Park Avenue and start my walk back to Grand Central Terminal. The icy wind cut into my face and through my old Levi's.

A voice broke the silence, "Hey! Are you a model?" I turned to see two men who had watched me as I walked past them on the sidewalk.

"What?" I asked, confused and caught off guard.

"A model," he repeated as he pointed to the over-sized portfolio beneath my right arm. "You're carrying a portfolio. You must be a model."

"Well, not exactly. Is it really that obvious?"

"Yes," the taller one replied matter-of-factly, as if he knew me.

"Do you have an agency?" he continued with a large, ultra-white smile.

"No. I've been rejected by all of the agencies. I'm thinking of calling it quits," I said self-consciously, as my words slowed and my eyes turned back towards the ground.

"Don't," he said with some urgency. "I think you can make it. You've got an unusual look, but that can work to your advantage. My name is Ron and this is Marcus," he said with another thousand-watt smile.

There was an awkward pause as I looked at the pair, trying to work out their connection to each other and at the same time ask myself why they would want to help me.

Ron broke the silence and said, "Marcus is my brother,"

as he turned towards Marcus and made a slight bow, at which point Marcus burst out laughing;

"Yeah, we're brothers," he said hoarsely as he put his hands on his knees and forced out a laugh laced with scorn.

They didn't look like brothers to me. Ron was too blonde and too tan for early March while Marcus was pale with bad skin and was dressed worse than I. Marcus was thin while Ron looked as if he spent most of his time in the gym when he wasn't taking protein supplements.

Ron continued where he left off, "I was a model in the seventies. I think I can help you."

No sooner had he spoken those words than I started to walk away. Something wasn't right and the word "help" always seemed to come with strings attached. I wasn't sure how he could help me, anyway.

"Wait!" he called out, "I'm going to give you the name of a men's agency in New York."

I stopped walking and turned half way around to listen to him.

"The Agency is Legends and the head of the agency is Paul Rackley. He knows me. You should go there now. It's on 32nd Street, near Park Avenue."

"I've never heard of them," I said flatly.

"I know," he replied, "They just started. Paul used to work for Zoli's."

"Okay, thanks for the tip," I said without emotion as I turned again to walk away.

"No, wait! Listen to me. You should go there now. And when they take your picture, hold your chin down. It will help to hide your jaw."

"Why would I want to do that?" I asked, getting uncomfortable with the conversation again.

"Trust me, it doesn't look good in pictures. Your jaw looks like it could overshadow your face."

"Thanks," I said, unsure of how to take the information that Ron had just shared with me.

"Good luck," they both said at the same time, as Marcus laughed too hard while I walked away.

"You'd better hurry," Ron added. "They close at five."

The agency was on the other side of Grand Central and the sun was dropping fast with the temperature. I made a half-hearted decision to make the walk to 32nd. The walk took longer than expected and I was cold from the strong wind pushing up from the south. The sidewalks were almost empty as I turned west onto 32nd Street. I found the street number on the side of the building near the new glass and gold toned metal door and opened the heavy door with the smooth handle. The new lobby was brightly lit and empty except for a large black man with an ill-fitting uniform sitting at a curved, golden desk at the other end of the lobby. The walls were covered with large floor-to-ceiling mirrors and the ceiling was the same shiny gold-toned metal as the desk. I glanced in the mirrored wall at my face. It was red and blotchy from the cold and my hair was flat on one side and sticking up on the other. I did my best to push my hair down with my hand as I walked towards the desk.

"Who are you here to see?" the security guard with the wet-looking afro sticking out from the black-brimmed chauffeurs hat asked as I approached the large desk.

"Paul at Legends," I said quietly as I looked him in the eye.

"Eighth floor. Sign in," he said as he pointed to a huge book that was filled with signatures on the raised counter above his desk. "You'd better hurry, they leave in a few minutes."

I scribbled my name and the time in the wide paged ledger and quickly said, "Thanks," as I sprinted towards the large golden-doored elevators. I stepped through the open doors and pushed the number eight. Thirty seconds later the elevator doors opened to the dimly lit lobby of the Legends agency. I walked over to a young receptionist who ignored me, knowing that acknowledging my existence would allow me to speak to her. I stood in front of her small, sleek desk until she lifted her head slowly and deliberately from the work in front of her.

She spoke with irritation in her voice; "Appointments are over," she said without changing her expression. She was almost beautiful with her pale skin, dark hair, and brown eyes.

I absently studied her face for a moment before asking her, "Is Paul Rackley here?"

She looked at me with more focus, shook her head and rolled her eyes back with exasperation; she seemed to be working out in her head whether I knew Paul, or simply knew his name and that he was the head of the agency.

"He's gone for the day. Let me see your book," she said with a mixture of heat and ice.

I handed her my book over the top of her slim desk and took a seat on the long orange couch without arms. Her body language and tone of voice let me know that this was going to end soon with me heading for the elevators.

She feigned a look of interest as she rapidly flipped through the pictures in my portfolio. After less than a minute she closed my book without picking it up and pushed it to the front edge of her desk with her index finger.

"You're not right for our agency. Sorry," she said contemptuously while looking intently at some papers stacked neatly on her desk.

Again I felt the blood rush to my cheeks as I forced out a "Thanks." I picked up my book from her desk and headed over to the elevators ten steps away. The rejection felt worse coming from a receptionist her age in the lobby of an agency that I had never heard of. It seemed a desperate attempt to find any agency that would represent me, and this time I had failed before I even met any booker in the back. I mumbled, "Thanks," again to the girl who had already forgotten my existence.

As I was opening the large glass door a man with a rumpled shirt and a brown cardigan walked out from around the glass block wall and said quietly, "I'm Paul," as he looked directly at my face.

"Hi, I'm Daryl," I responded tentatively.

"What are you doing here?" he asked with a serious expression pulling at his brow.

"Trying to get someone to look at my book."

"Let me see it."

I handed him my book. He sat down on the couch and thumbed through the plastic covered pages thoughtfully as he looked up at me several times.

"Why do you want to be a model?" he asked as he looked up from my portfolio.

"To earn some money," I replied earnestly.

"It's not that easy. Your book *is* terrible, but the pictures don't really look like you."

I was puzzled by his comments.

He continued calmly as he held my book on his lap, "Are you in school?"

"I left college after the fall semester. I'm taking some time off to try to get some work as a model."

"Where are you from? You don't sound like you're from New York."

"I'm from Illinois, near Chicago."

"Ahh that explains it. You should really go back to school. I don't like to see anyone leave school to become a model. It's better to finish college and then try modeling. That's what most of the guys do. How old are you anyway?"

"Nineteen."

"Wow," he said quickly as he looked up at my face, "That is really young. I don't know any models who are that young. Are you sure you know what you're getting into?"

"No," I said honestly, "I don't. Do I have an agency?"

"Yes," Paul answered with some hesitation as he nodded his head as if to convince himself. "I think you have a chance. Come back Monday at nine. We need to get you some better pictures."

"Thank you Paul, really. I'll see you then," I said as my insides jumped with a rush of hope.

I walked to the elevators at the same time as Paul and we rode down to the street level together. He headed west while I headed to the east. He turned and called out from twenty feet away; "I really do hope you go back to school."

I hesitated for a moment on the wide sidewalk and took in his words. I wouldn't mind going back to school, but to do that I needed money, and modeling could make me enough to go to a good school, not a shit hole like Monmouth College. I had an agency. I guessed that meant something.

2

A ROOM OF MY OWN

The air of Grand Central Terminal was thick with the smell of the damp, unwashed bodies of the homeless as I pushed open the heavy glass and brass framed doors from street. All of the heavy wooden benches were filled with homeless men and women, either sleeping or slumped over their plastic garbage bags and shopping carts filled with all their worldly possessions. I looked over at a large group packed together on the heavy wooden bench furthest from the doors, near the oversized cast iron radiators. A few of them returned my gaze with blank, empty stares. I had noticed that the standard reaction to the homeless from the people going to work on the trains was to pretend they did not exist; literally that they were not there.

I thought back to one of my first train trips to the city from Westport when I saw a white-bearded homeless man lying on the three steps in the narrow passageway between the 42nd Street subway and the filthy men's bathroom in the station. I stopped amid the surging stream of people and bent over to take a closer look at him. Staring closely at his drawn face that looked as if it was frozen, I could see his teeth pushing out from under his lips. His face was a gray-blue color that I had not seen before. He was blocking one of the frosted glass swinging doors, and several people had stepped over him to get to the bathroom. I was certain he was either dead or close to it, so I quickly walked back to the round information booth with the clock on top and found a round-bodied police officer leaning on the counter with a coffee in his hand. I told him about the homeless man and then hurried back while the policeman walked slowly with his coffee still in his hand. When he arrived he pushed the man's foot with the sole of his boot, but the homeless man didn't move. He then called for help on his big police radio and stood guard with his back to the man as he directed those trying to use the door away, telling them to use the other bathroom entrance. I turned and headed for the subway, glancing back once over my shoulder at the scene. Although it was unpleasant, I found that no strong emotion hit me. Silently I wondered why.

I checked the schedule above the ticket counters and purchased a one way off-peak ticket to Westport. The smell of freshly baked croissants and strong coffee filled the warm air as I walked past Zabar's to the right of the ticket counters. It had been nine long hours since I'd eaten a cheap, late breakfast special at the tiny coffee shop near the station. Eggs, rye toast and home fries cost me a dollar ninety plus tax. I bought a can of Coke and went below the station to wait for my train. I looked up at the schedule, 6:07. Twenty seven minutes to wait. I sat on the plastic scoop seats bolted in a row to each other and the floor and placed my backpack under the seat.

I looked up to people watch and noticed a dark-haired beauty with a tailored blue suit and a soft-sided briefcase. She was in her late twenties, her white silk blouse open at the neck, and her straight black hair lay flat on her shoulders. She was a beauty and appeared to have a playmate's body beneath her suit. My mind pictured her in a white bra and panties complete with the same high-heels she was wearing with her suit. She glanced over at me and we caught each other's gaze for a moment—1, 2, 3—and then she quickly looked away. She had taken a quick look at my clothes and guessed me to be as broke as I was. I had no money. I wondered if that might change now that I had an agency.

I looked up at the clock with the Roman numerals and decided to see if gate 112 was open yet. I slung my backpack over my shoulder and walked to the gate, checking the sign at the entrance to the train platform to make sure that "Westport" was on the list of stops. I walked past ten Metro North cars until I saw the non-smoking cars. The platform echoed with loud, screechy sounds of trains coming and going...smoke and steam seemed to hang in the air like fake clouds. The first non-smoking car was full, so I continued to walk until I reached one with open seats. The car was brightly lit and I could see into the glass windows, but those inside couldn't see out to the darkened concrete platform area. I took a seat facing the back of the train with my back against the front end of the car. I watched as fewer and fewer people walked into the train with their brief cases and wrinkled dark colored suits. I was invisible to them. No one looked at me and no one nodded as I watched from my seat against the wall. I did not stare at strangers in the traditional sense, only looking intensely for a moment and then looking away before they noticed me. I was always looking to see what was going on around me, from the trash on the floor to the smeared glass of the long rectangular windows, to the people sitting with hard-set mouths and knit brows. I was constantly looking from curiosity as well as from an incessant need to understand...the need to understand that which could not be understood. I rarely talked to anyone unless they spoke to me first; I always had the feeling that they had no interest in me, so why bother with a banal conversation about the usual stuff. *Where are you from? Are you in school? What are you doing in New York...?* Most of the time I bored myself with my thoughts, so why would others want to know what I thought? I pulled a hard covered book that I borrowed from the Pequot Library from my backpack and settled in to read *Lady* by Thomas Tryon. The words of the story pulled me back in time. Gradually I stopped feeling my arms, my head, and my thumping heart and simply watched the story unfold in my mind, forgetting the one person that brings me all the pain: myself.

Saturday morning brought more gray skies with a cold, steady wind that came up from the south. The Saugatuck River was filled with chunks of ice covered with snow floating motionless in the dark, briny water. The house sat high on Riverside Road, halfway between the Post Road in Westport and the Saugatuck Railroad Station. I rented a room in the rundown white colonial from the eighteen hundreds with crooked and broken black shutters. A clear view of the Saugatuck River was the house's only good feature.

My small room was without heat and the cold came in through the one leaky window and rolled down from the doorless attic stairs, which sat in the corner of my 5' x

8' room. I thought about putting my bare feet on the cold wood floor several times before following through. I had nowhere to go and not much money to spend, so I crawled back into bed after using the bathroom off the kitchen. The rent was 180 dollars per month for the old sewing room/closet at the top of the back stairs. It was more of a hallway to the open-timbered attic where all of the past and present renters kept the items that were too big for their rooms. The room was only a place for me to sleep. Two adults couldn't stand on the floor between the child's dresser and the single bed. The broken-back cot was pushed against the corner facing the door that led to the narrow stairs with a left turn at the bottom. My feet hung over the end when I slept on my stomach. Soon after moving in I asked the curly-haired woman that rented me the room if I could borrow some of the furniture I had seen sitting in the dusty attic. She said she didn't care and I pulled down a small child's dresser, a small legless homemade cupboard with one door, and a fold up cot with a lumpy mattress that same day. I found a small table and wobbly ladder backed chair that I placed facing the window to use as a desk for writing. The room was not good, but for 180 bucks a month it was all mine. I could lock the door when I was asleep and lock the door when I left for the day with a small combination padlock.

3

INVISIBLE BOY

When I went to Monmouth College, few people thought of me as smart, let alone gifted. Within a few weeks most people knew me as the good-looking freshman that had a big smile and broad shoulders. Girls approached me to talk and would ask me to take a walk with them or escort them back to their rooms after a party; no one thought of me as smart. I never made a big issue of it and let it slide; I liked being thought of as good-looking more than smart, anyway. Since I had arrived in Connecticut, I had found that everyone thought of me as a handsome slacker that relied on his looks instead of his brains. It was inconceivable to them that I was a very smart young man that just happened to be good-looking. Even marginally intelligent people seemed to believe that they were much smarter than I was, using this belief as a way to put me in my place; to put me down by questioning my intelligence.

They had tested my IQ in the middle of fourth grade and I had been placed in a special program at another school for gifted kids from the district. I never found out the exact number for my IQ, but I know that I was the only fourth grader at Paddock Elementary School who was chosen to enter the new program for special kids. The IQ cut-off for the program was 134, which was at the low end of the highly gifted spectrum. Above that was exceptionally gifted and then genius.

My brother was in the same program that had started the year before called Special Opportunity. Our fifth grade teacher, Mr. Englehart called it Special Op. It was located at Pleasant Hill Elementary School. Of the twenty-two students in the Special Op fifth grade class, I was perhaps the least gifted and was in awe of some of the things that came out of the mouths of my hyper-intellectual classmates. We had no curriculum and no grades. We were allowed to do whatever we wanted, except in science. Mr. Englehart would sit Indian style on his large wooden desk and talk to us about whatever science news or project that was on his mind for at least an hour a day. The rest of the time we were basically on our own; we were even allowed to set our own recess.

I remember one winter day when there was over a foot of freshly fallen snow on the ground and Tina decided to have the whole class go outside and play a game that she had invented in the snow. It was a type of logic game that had to do with moving caribou across a sheet of paper strategically. Tina told us how to line up and she used the snow as the paper; we were the Caribou. We bundled up and stayed outside for over an hour. I glanced over after thirty minutes of playing in the snow and noticed that the classrooms facing the playground had students faces looking at us from the large windows with amazement. They seemed shocked that we were allowed to play in the freshly fallen snow while they were stuck indoors studying.

Mr. Englehart did not give us grades, he would instead write paragraph after paragraph about how we behaved socially and psychologically. He wrote things like *Daryl does not take failure well* or, *Daryl has a tendency to lose his temper*, or, *Daryl does not play well with others*. He took me out in the hallway during one frustrating episode when I lost my temper and told me to count to ten and take deep breaths. I tried, but it never seemed to work.

I became more and more alienated as the year wore on, and I was the least popular member of the class after losing my temper and threatening to beat the shit out of Tom. He had stolen my bright red backpack and made fun of it to the other kids, saying that it looked like a *canned ham* and then pretended to climb the cast iron drain on the side of the school to jump with his *red parachute* as he pointed at me and laughed. The exchange ended with Tom flinging the backpack into the snow behind me when I demanded he give it back. I knew Tom was afraid of me one-on-one, but he knew I wouldn't smash his face in front of everyone, especially if they were already laughing at me.

It was the first time that I realized how foolish my *giant of a dad* was in using his strength to intimidate people as an adult. It was at this time that I realized that beating someone up means you lose more than you win.

All of the adults in my life, including my dad, saw me as a serious kid with a permanent scowl who was smart and could remember things. In sixth grade I was chosen to tutor second and third graders in speed reading and walked the halls without a pass. The kids that I became friends with outside of special op saw me as an *egghead* who could also do sports. Within six months I was more out than in according to my erudite classmates in special op. They saw me as the least talented of the smart kids, and, to be honest, I had to agree with them. It didn't help that I wished more than anything that I was not a part of the bullshit special op program to begin with. If I could have found an easy way to get back into the mainstream classes, I would have done it in a second, anything closer to normal was fine with me. There was only one girl who was even close to attractive in the class: Tina. She was the tallest person in the class and could sing like a bird. I asked her to go roller skating with me in the sixth grade and, to my surprise, she said yes. I met her at the Orbit roller rink carrying my black leather skates with the red wheels over my right shoulder. I helped her lace up her beige rental skates and was feeling happy that she came. After once around the wood planked rink, I thought I heard someone calling my name; the next time around I saw six kids from my class leaning over the four foot concrete block wall that separated the rink from the carpeted area yelling at me, laughing, and calling me Derwood. Of course, Tom was in the lead. I tried to pretend that it didn't bother me, but when Tina started to laugh along with them, I knew that she had told them about our date and was as responsible for the situation as Tom.

Sixth, seventh, and eighth grade were all a blur of being with the same people who spent most of their time making fun of me and feeling as different as anyone can feel. I was the butt of any and all jokes. I was happy to start high school and become quietly invisible in the massive midwestern school, William Fremd High School.

4

THE FIRST...

It was around nine when I awoke again, and the bright winter sun painted color into the gray morning. I was naked under the covers and stood up on the cold floor and quickly pulled on a pair of ripped jeans and an old crew neck sweatshirt. I listened at my door at the top of the stairway to hear if anyone was in the bathroom near the back door to the kitchen. It was quiet, so I moved down the stairs with my head bent to the left to avoid the low ceiling before the left-hand turn at the bottom of the stairs. The small bathroom was empty, and the mirror was fogged up with steam from the shower and the floor was wet. The lockless door, allowed my roommates to come in while I showered to brush their teeth or take a leak, without even knocking. I quickly showered and combed my hair straight back with a black comb with missing teeth. My hair was long over my ears and had no real style. I didn't have money for a haircut. I used a pair of borrowed kitchen scissors to chop around my ears. That made it look only slightly worse. I wiped the steam from the mirror with my hand and stared blankly at my reflection.

My eyes were green and cold...not the big, inviting blue eyes that I saw on models and the actors on television. My cheekbones lifted sharply from my square jaw, sitting high, giving the illusion that my eyes were set even deeper than they were. My eyes had half-moon dark patches below them. They looked fine above my dark skin, though they would have looked unhealthy above a pale cheek. Stokes, my pale-skinned older brother, often said that I had a *dirt tan* because I stayed tan even in the dead of winter. I tanned easily in the summer without trying. Years of gymnastics had left my shoulders broad and well muscled, with lean, corded arms. It was difficult for me to roll dress shirt sleeves to my elbows because of my oversized forearms. I did not have a deep chest and was very aware of this flaw when being asked to do photos without a shirt, something I had only done once. I got some attention at Monmouth College from the girls when my 150-pound body filled out to 175 before I left for New York, but I never felt I had a great body; lean and strong, yes, but not great. I must be around 180 now. I quickly pulled my sweatshirt on and took the stairs two at a time and pushed open the door to my room.

The possibilities of a Saturday always got me down. I would spend time missing the family life I never had and think about how empty my life was. Sundays were even worse. I secretly prayed that Sunday was removed as a day of the week. It was a sad day full of guilt from Mom. She would phone early on Sunday morning to ask if I was going to *Saint Mattress*, and then laugh at her own joke. When you are young and alone and know that you are basically a *fuck-up* in the eyes of your family, Sunday becomes a *special* day to wallow in self-pity. Sometimes I would wake early and lie in bed with my heart beating fast and hard in my chest as my feet sweat under the covers; feeling guilty for not making my way to church in downtown Westport. Other Sundays I would dress in second-hand clothes bought from the huge Goodwill store on Riverside Avenue and silently sit through the one-hour church service, feeling sleepy and guilty at the same time. I tried to listen intently to the service and be moved and inspired by the words of the first and second readers, but my mind would not cooperate. It was always drifting off; thinking about semi-nude women with ripe breasts and flawless skin. Beautiful faces with sweet expressions, or about my first girlfriend.

Her name was Jeanne. She was a senior at Monmouth College when I was a freshman. She was a student teacher at the Monmouth grade school while she finished up her class work at the college. I remember one Spring morning waking up while Jeanne came back into her apartment-like room fresh from a hot shower, her blond hair wet and combed straight back onto her shoulders, her pale skin flushed red from the heat of the shower. I rolled over in bed to get a better view of her in the soft light of morning. Unaware that I was awake, she opened her towel with her left hand and reached for her wool skirt with her right hand. She quickly pulled on her skirt and zipped up the back and sat topless on the corner of the queen size bed to pull on her sheer pantyhose. The morning light allowed me to see clearly what I couldn't see at night when we made love. Her shoulders were slender, but strong. When she turned back towards the closet to grab a blouse I was able to see her full, upturned breasts with nipples the color of ripened wheat on a September afternoon. She noticed me watching her dress. She turned away shyly and covered her breasts with her blouse. I reached out for her hand and said, "Please, don't. I love looking at you." She blushed a deeper red and looked towards the floor; for a beautiful woman, she was very shy.

I met Jeanne at a party at the TKE house when my tactless, drunk roommate walked across the crowded dance floor and said to her; "My roommate is *totally* in love with you. Would you *please* talk to him so he will shut the hell up about wanting to meet you?" He demanded more than asked. She blushed slightly and looked towards the ground as I made my way across the dance floor to apologize for Mark's behavior, knowing what he had said without hearing his words.

Jeanne met me halfway across the dance floor with a red Solo cup in her hand. We awkwardly introduced ourselves as I apologized for Mark's rude behavior. Almost immediately the noise of the party melted away until it was just Jeanne and I standing alone in the middle of the dance floor, looking into each other's eyes and talking. From that moment on we spent almost all of our free time together until she left school to start teaching and I went off to camp in Missouri I came back in June to see her one more time while she packed to leave for good. Jeanne was secretly embarrassed that she was in love with someone so young and suggested we *take a break*. I never saw her again.

5

NORTHERN COMFORT

I looked into the small dresser for something to wear; I pulled out some khaki pants and a light blue button-down shirt that was only slightly worn at the collar. I grabbed my wool overcoat and put on my knit cap and headed out the back door. The cold of the day felt good as it bit into my face and filled my lungs with chilled air, waking me up and adding texture to a day that seemed to be without hope. I passed by the Goodwill with the high ceilings on the Saugatuck River and onto downtown Westport, absently looking at the lights that still hung on the naked branches of the trees that lined Main Street. I stopped at the lone payphone that sat at the corner convenience store and put in a quarter and called Barbara.

"Hello?" She answered quietly as if someone was listening.

"Hey," I said.

"Hey."

"How are you doing?"

"Okay," she said quietly.

"What's wrong?"

"Mike came by the house last night. He was wasted and crying, and he kept telling me that he wanted to get back together."

"Really?" I said with irritation "What the fuck is wrong with that guy?" I spat out.

"I know," she quietly sobbed, "Everything's okay. He didn't even wake up Sean or Jessica. They aren't even going to know who he is when they get older. I'm really glad that it will all be over with him soon. One of my friends said that he's probably going to jail for dealing. That will give me a break from him."

"Did you call the police?"

"No," she said quietly, "They already know about him. It wouldn't do any good anyway; they just talk to him. He went to school with some of them. I'm going to my parents' condo anyway. They won't be back from Florida for another two months."

"Really?"

"Yeah. They said I could stay there with Sean and Jessica until they get back. Hey, can you wear those tight jeans that you wore last week tonight?" she asked, changing the subject with her soft voice.

"Okay." I said, feeling my stomach jump at her words and tone, "You really think about stuff like that?"

"Ye-ah," she said seductively "I want to get you into bed and take those pants off."

I thought back to other nights with Barbara and replied, "Okay... see you at seven."

I hung up the phone and looked at all of the expensive foreign cars driving by me and parked along Main Street.

I had always had a thing for Chevies and dreamed about a convertible SS Malibu all through High School.

No one wanted to have an American car in Westport; it was strictly BMW's, Porsche's and Mercedes'. I knew that I had little chance of buying a foreign car, I was not even sure if I could make rent this month...and the food situation was a whole different story. Fear sat in the pit of my stomach as I wondered what was going on tonight at Monmouth College or at my house in Palatine. My dad was a deep con grifter who borrowed money from everyone he met—from our church, school, coaches...basically, everyone whom we came into contact with. It was all to be used for business investments, but for some reason, none of the money ever made its way back to the investors. I learned early on that the men at Klimmers Hardware Store didn't think much of my dad. They would laugh at me when I went in to buy things for Dad and put it on his charge account. I thought that he sent Stokes and me into stores because he was lazy. It took me a few years to realize that that was only part of the reason. Although Dad was a hulk of a man more suited for work as a contractor, he constantly tried to recreate himself as a sophisticated businessman, complete with a gold Rolex and a gold Cross pen to accent his custom suits. He never finished high school but viewed himself as a businessman with enough brains and sophistication to compete with the best.

I silently walked back to 82 Riverside, staring at the clouds as they lit up from the sinking winter sun above the glassy surface of the river.

Barb picked me up at 7:00 from the side of the house in her Volvo station wagon that her printing tycoon father had given her when he bought a newer model. She was wearing a long navy wool coat that smelled of cigarette smoke. I leaned over to kiss her on the lips and grabbed the shoulder and arm of her coat and pulled her close to me, out of her seat and onto my lap. She grabbed me in much the same way and kissed me hard on the mouth, reaching around my waist and pulling herself close and tight to me. We didn't look like a match, but there was something about her that attracted me like gravity; a pull that I could not resist.

We first slept together at her parents' luxury condo after meeting at a church event. The next morning she rolled over and looked sleepily at me in the early light that spilled into the large master bedroom with dark furniture and white carpet and drapes, and asked me, "How did you know I wasn't some dirty girl?" with a crooked smile pushing at the right corner of her lips. Barbara spoke slowly as if she had been drinking, and in no hurry to let the words escape from her mouth.

"I don't know. I just knew I guess. What kind of freaking question is that?"

She looked at me with that wry half-smile again and reached under the covers to grab me by the waist and pull herself closer to me.

We arrived at a biker bar in the crappy area of Fairfield on the Bridgeport line at 7:30. Barbara sat close to me, and we leaned towards each other as if we secretly wanted to become one. We never spoke of it; it just seemed that way. Barbara introduced me to her friend JC, a full faced, solidly built guy with unfortunate fat lips. He wasn't fat, but his face was bloated and looked as if it belonged on a much heavier man. He looked at me with a mixture of suspicion and interest through heavy-lidded eyes as puffy as his lips. It was obvious to me that he liked Barb and was silently wondering where the hell I came from as if I had cut in line in front of him at the grocery store. I did what I always did and tried to ignore the tension that couldn't be ignored. The three of us laughed and drank beer as JC recounted stories from when he and Barb had partied in high school. Although they were both only twenty-four, the stories seemed to come from a time long ago. JC was with a few other friends that were introduced to me, but they didn't talk to me. JC asked me if Barb and I were dating, and it occurred to me that Barb hadn't told him about our relationship. Things wound down quickly between JC and me once I answered his question. By ten everyone was ready to call it a night. I was amazed at how old her friends seemed, their faces worn and wrinkled from heavy drinking and smoking, from years of no exercise and long work days spent on their feet. They worked hard for every dollar that they made. JC had been a mechanic for eight years. I had not yet worked a full-time job for more than a few months. I couldn't relate to their lives, and Barb wanted to be just like them.

 I spent the night at the condo with Barb and woke up to see little Sean and Jessica crawling around the soft comforter on the king sized bed, snuggling near their mom. The walk-in closet in the master bedroom was literally three times larger than my room. I reached for my shorts that were in a pile on my side of the bed and pulled them on. I looked back at Barb, nude and motherly, stroking little Jessica's blond hair as she rested her head in the crook of one of Barb's long arms. Her dark nipples were visible above the white comforter.

"You're okay with them seeing me, I mean in bed, with you?" I asked as I sat back down on the edge of the bed.

"Yeah, it's okay. They don't really understand that we are sleeping together. Jessica doesn't even remember Mike; we've been apart since she was six months old. Sean doesn't understand and sometimes asks about Mike, but that happens less and less as time goes on."

I pulled my jeans on and walked downstairs to the kitchen to see what was in the refrigerator. It was stocked with food. I grabbed a yogurt, wolfed it down, then poured a big glass of fresh squeezed OJ from Stew's and drank it. I had never met Barb's mom or dad, but I knew that one thing we had in common was that we all hated Mike. He was a full-time douchebag who thought he was much tougher than he actually was; the type of guy that you just want to disappear, knowing that nothing good would ever come from him. I wasn't sure if they would think any better of me, a nineteen-year-old with a part-time job trying to break into the modeling business; not exactly a blueprint for success. Barb represented security for me, and her warmth and genuine kindness melted something inside me; she made me feel things that I wanted to keep buried. It wasn't quite love, but it wasn't something that I wanted to give up anytime soon. Right now Barb was all that I had, and I thought that I could see in her eyes that look that let me know that she knew something that she would never say out loud; that I would break her heart. I knew that she was a soulful, warm, beautiful, kind woman and that she loved me. Barb offered me warmth, security, and unconditional love...but I needed a soul as tortured and complicated as I was if I were ever going to tear down the icy walls surrounding my heart. Good luck with that one.

The rest of Sunday was burned by playing with Sean and Jessica and getting an early dinner at the Sherwood Diner. I paid for half, even though Barb insisted on paying with her dad's money. Jessica fell asleep in her car seat while Barb drove me to the other side of town and dropped me off around 6:00 at 82 Riverside Avenue. I felt empty and cold as I waved to her as she quietly pulled away from the curb and drove away.

6

A BIG MISTAKE

I slipped in noiselessly through the side door and had started to open the board and batten door to the back stairs when Sofie turned around from the sink and said with a casual purposefulness,

"Hey. How's it going?"

I turned around carefully and faced her, the thin board and batten door still propped open in my right hand. She was wearing her go-to outfit; sheer white v-neck t-shirt with what looked to be a sheer, white bra and fitted khaki pants belted with a thin, worn black leather belt and black high top Keds shoes with white laces. I concentrated on not looking at her clearly visible nipples and instead looked at her face. She had full lips and a high bridged nose that suited her face, big blue eyes with thick lashes, and thick dark eyebrows. Her hair was a mass of cascading red curls that fell below her shoulders. Her teeth had been braced straight as a teenager, but she had a crooked lipped smile when she laughed. Her voice was mid range but went straight through her nose, giving it a nasal sound as if she was always blocked up with a cold or had sinus problems. She looked very much like one of the sisters of Ruth in Cecil B. DeMille's movie The Ten Commandments.

"Hey," I said, caught completely off guard. "I'm okay. How are you?"

"Not so good," she said as she looked down and dried her hands on the front of her khakis. "You know what happened last week can never happen again. Right?"

"Okay," I said without much emotion, as my throat tightened involuntarily. "I think that's a good idea. It was a mistake, right?" I said, trying to find the right words to make what was unfixable right.

"Yep," she said flatly with her lips pulled tight over her teeth, "a fucking big mistake."

I couldn't tell if she was pissed that we had been together or embarrassed because of our age difference.

I shrugged my shoulders and turned to climb up the narrow back stairs to my room as I silently prayed that she wouldn't follow me to talk about what she meant, why she said it, and how upset she was. She was intriguing and fairly cool, but at ten years older than me, I could see that she could be a real pain in the ass if she didn't get her way. She was a grown woman who bossed people around for a living, I didn't want to be part of her world. Besides, the age difference really was a problem for me. I heard the way that she talked to her assistant and the short Mexican women with stained aprons that came into our crappy kitchen on the weekends to help her cook for her catered events. The mistake she was upset about was sleeping with her on a quiet weeknight when the other tenants were out of the house.

We started talking in the kitchen about why I came to

Westport and we never took our eyes off of each other. She was dressed in her work clothes and I was barefoot in jeans and a stained gray t-shirt. We moved closer and closer to each other as we talked until I was standing less than a foot away from her as she leaned back on the sink cabinet while we kissed, a wet, sloppy, *I have no idea what the fuck I'm doing* kiss. She looked up at me with a surprisingly neutral gaze and reached behind me and pushed her long-fingered hands into my back pockets. I don't know why it happened. It felt all wrong. She walked past me and grabbed my hand and led me into her room off the kitchen. I stood in her doorway for a moment, hesitant, and then walked through without talking. It was as if I were being pulled through her doorway by a wire attached to my chest. I ended up standing in the middle of the floor in her mess of a room with a queen-sized mattress on the floor. She reached behind me, latched the door and walked over to the bed and swept the fashion magazines off the un-made bed and onto the floor. She pulled her t-shirt over her head, unclasped her opaque white bra, pulled her khakis and underpants off at the same time, then kicked them into a pile of clothes already on the floor. I quickly followed her lead and ended up naked standing on the bare wood floor with her hips pressed up against pressed up against mine. She tilted her head back for another kiss; it was wet and warm and a little too sloppy. We had sex while the old television blasted the Johnny Carson show. She left the lights on as we kneeled together onto the bed and started to explore each other's naked bodies. There was no furniture in her room; all of her clothes were stuffed into the closet and spilling onto the floor. I found myself staring at and then touching a scar that went from her pubic line to her sternum. It was the biggest scar I had ever seen, raised and wide and a shiny dark purple; the stitch lines and needle holes scarred along the length every quarter inch; a scar like a ladder up her abdomen.

I found myself wondering what could have caused such a scar. It intrigued me and repulsed me at the same time. We made love, and it was over before I knew it. I became repulsed by what I had done, feeling sick to my stomach, but I felt some strange duty to not rush out the bedroom door and run up the stairs to my room. Sofie was wide-awake and reading as I drifted into an anxious sleep in her brightly lit bedroom. I fell asleep for over an hour while she read one of her magazines. An MTV video was blaring on the television as I awoke, forgetting where I was. I looked over at Sofie's nude body covered to the waist by a sheet and suddenly I wanted to go again. She was indifferent to my advances and simply spread her legs slightly and dropped her magazine to the hardwood floor as I moved over her. Her lack of interest only got me more excited. She was dry and it did not seem like it was going to work, but soon we were going again. For some reason, it lasted less than the first time. I had no idea whether she enjoyed it or not. I felt even worse than before, weightless and floating as if I didn't exist. I spent the rest of the night in her room with a burning deep in my chest. I slipped out noiselessly before the sun came up the next morning. Sofie snored in a tangle of sheets on her mattress. The peaceful image of her nude body stayed with me, scar and all.

I sat on the edge of my bed and listened for any indication that she was coming up the narrow back stairway to my room. Soon I heard her worn out Honda Civic start and the wheels crunch on the gravel driveway and squeak like a chirping bird when they hit the pavement. I started to relax and lay down on my narrow bed. She was gone. I got undressed and into my cold bed with the layers of sheets and old cotton blankets. Sleep did not come easily as random images and thoughts of Sofie and Barbara rushed back and forth in my head. It didn't matter if my eyes were opened or closed.

7

A SLIPPERY SLOPE

Monday morning came, and I made my way to the Saugatuck train station to catch the 7:08 Express. I made it to Grand Central in just over an hour and got off the train feeling tired and hungry. I was too nervous to eat, so I grabbed an orange juice and drank it down fast while walking south to the agency on 32nd Street. I got to the shiny glass and gold building at 8:55 and took the elevator up to the eighth floor.

"I have a nine o'clock appointment with Paul," I said quietly to the same young receptionist who had rejected my portfolio so casually on Friday.

"Oh," she said flatly without looking up at me. "Have a seat," as she motioned with her right hand towards the couch that seemed to rise up from the carpeted floor.

I sat close to the glass wall. Within a minute a slim man with a clear acrylic clipboard with a few sheets of paper came out from behind the wall with a swish-of-a-walk and said; "Daryl?"

"Yes," I said as I started to stand up. "That's me," I

extended my right hand to him which he looked at, raised his eyebrows and ignored.

"Come with me," he said without looking at me, as he turned sharply on his heel and swished past the glass block wall.

He sashayed along while talking over his shoulder at me. We ended up in an area with a grouping of round Plexiglas topped desks and a long Plexiglas half wall shelf filled with the cards of the male models that Legends represented. I got that sick, empty feeling in my stomach, and wondered what the hell I was doing there as my heart started to race. All of the cards looked better than any of the photos that I had, and all of the guys looked better than I did.

"Hello Daryl," Paul said while extending his right hand for me to shake.

"Hi, Paul," I said while meeting his hand with mine and giving his hand a firm squeeze while looking directly at him.

"So... you decided not to go back to school?" he asked with an ironic smile.

"Not yet, anyway," I replied with a soft laugh.

"Okay!" he said emphatically with some degree of resolve as he pushed himself back from his desk, "*Now* we need to get you some new pictures for your book."

"Great," I said. "What do I need to do?"

"Well first I am going to send you to Ken Haak. He doesn't live far from here. Bruce Weber was Ken's assistant and most of what Bruce does now he learned from working for Ken. Although I have to admit, Bruce's work is slightly more commercial than Ken's."

I had seen photographs done by Bruce Weber in GQ

magazine. I heard from other models that he also shot all of the Ralph Lauren and Calvin Klein campaigns. Every model that I spoke to thought Bruce was the Francis Ford Coppola of the modeling world.

"I told Ken about you this morning, and he's expecting you around ten. You can leave now and walk to his studio. It's on Thirty-fourth Street, off Park. Come back to the agency when you're done and we can talk about how it went."

"Will do," I said with as much confidence as I could muster. "Thanks for giving me a chance, Paul," I added with an optimistic tone and a doubting heart. I hoped that things would work out, but I had no idea what to expect.

"Just get some good pictures to put in your book," he said with a smile as he turned back to the work at his desk.

I soon arrived at Ken's brownstone on the East side. I pushed the old brass doorbell and heard a loud ring from behind the door. The heavy door swung open slowly, and a small old man with white hair and heavy framed glasses stood in the doorway smiling.

"I'm Ken," he offered as he reached out a small, pale hand for me to shake, "you must be Daryl." He said cordially, like a kindly long lost uncle as a smile slowly pushed across his time-worn face.

"Um. Yes," I stammered, momentarily taken aback by his appearance. "Paul sent me for a test. I mean, to get some pictures," I said. "He told me that you are the best," I lied unconvincingly.

"Oh, really? Paul said that? Well, I do try my best, you know. Paul is very sweet, isn't he?"

"Yes, I answered, not accustomed to hearing men referred to as being *sweet*.

His face looked as if it were shaped by hand using warm, clear wax, the lines and creases amplified by a greasy combination of perspiration and moisturizer. His snow-white hair was long over his forehead and as greasy as his face. He looked pale and unhealthy, with features that appeared to be melting towards the floor. I half expected to see pale, waxy flesh drip from his face and onto the tile floor. He was dressed in a rumpled white cotton dress shirt and a plain pair of khakis with no belt. His shoes were generic black lace-ups with black socks, the same kind that my Chem professor used to wear. He smiled at me with a static grin that was hard to read, plastered onto his face like a bumper sticker. I looked around for an assistant or makeup artist but saw no one.

"Let me look at you," Ken said as he walked closer and stared up at my face as if he were studying an archeological find. He looked me up and down as if he were appraising the value of a draft horse on a Kentucky farm, all with the same set smile on his sweating face.

"Hmmm, I see what Paul means," he said as he placed his left hand over his mouth. "First, we need to get you some makeup and do something with that hair."

Again, I stared around the open room at the front of the brownstone to look for a makeup artist. I soon realized that there was no one but Ken and me. Ken walked over to a dark wooden table and picked up an antique silver tray with a few containers and makeup brushes on it.

"Here, sit in this chair," he instructed, "The light is quite good right now," he said while strolling towards the same area.

I sat down without speaking as I tried to work out what the deal was.

"You can take off your jacket and backpack and put them over there if you want," Ken said, as he motioned theatrically towards a small upholstered chair that sat alone, away from the furniture that seemed to be arranged for socializing around his ornate marble fireplace. The apartment was so quiet that I could hear Ken take the caps off the makeup bottles and set them onto the silver tray.

I was a little confused about the makeup, I wasn't sure why I needed it, but I was new at this and Ken was the professional. He began by dipping a triangular foam sponge into a large glass container filled with beige foundation. He started around my mouth and worked up to my eyes and forehead, seeming to cover my whole face with liquid foundation. There was no mirror for me to watch what he was doing. He then started pushing something around my eyelids that felt like a dull pencil.

"Do I need that?" I asked, unable to restrain myself from asking if I really needed eyeliner.

"Oh yes, yes, yes," he responded with pursed lips as he continued to apply the mascara, like a mother hen clucking at her chicks, "Trust me, it really helps bring attention to your be-a-utiful eyes, darling."

I was becoming more and more uncomfortable, and I was beginning to sweat. I started to wonder what the hell I was going to do with the pictures Ken was going to take with the eyeliner and the makeup. If Paul had not told me that Ken was the influence behind the famous Bruce Weber, I would have made up my mind that Ken was a major league pervert who enjoyed his *sessions* with young men without the interference of assistants or hair and makeup people. I didn't get the impression that he was so broke that he couldn't afford to hire them for the shooting.

I silently made up my mind to get through this shooting and hope for the best. Who knows, maybe I had him all wrong.

After applying the makeup, Ken asked me to pick out a pair of pants from a wicker laundry basket that was sitting on the floor near the couch. It was a jumble of green, khaki, denim and white pants and shorts. I picked out a pair of green army pants and asked Ken where I should change.

"Oh," he replied slowly as if it was a very strange question to ask, "there's a powder room near the front door." He looked away and made a dismissive motion in the direction of the powder room with his right hand as he walked back towards the couch.

I walked into a small powder room with black and gold wallpaper and a wall sconce that looked like a miniature crystal chandelier. There was an antique mirror with faded gold leaf around its oval frame over the white pedestal sink. I closed the door and took off my Levi's, shoes, and socks. I pulled the pants over my legs and started to button them up the front and realized that there was only one button at the bottom of the fly, three buttons were missing leaving the fly almost completely open. I quietly put my jeans back on and went back to the laundry basket to find another pair of pants with more buttons. I went through them one by one and discovered that they all had most of the buttons missing, except for a zippered pair that had no zipper at all. The first pair I chose had the most buttons of any of the pants, so I went back into the bathroom and did up the pants as best I could, leaving my Hanes on underneath to cover what the pants did not. I walked into the living room and waited for Ken. He appeared from an area that looked like the kitchen and looked at me with a wolfish half-grin.

"These pants don't have any buttons, Ken," I stated flatly.

"Oh?" he said, with a look of mock surprise as his eyes widened behind the thick lenses of his glasses, "I think they're okay, can you take off your underwear? I think it will ruin the lines of the pants and I think it will show in the pictures..." he said, as he looked intently at the white BVD's that showed above the one button.

"I think I'm okay, Ken. I'll make sure the underwear doesn't show," as I did my best to cover my white underwear by hiking up the green shorts.

He sighed dramatically, visibly disappointed as he shook his head slowly back and forth. He seemed to be a man who was not accustomed to being told *no*, even if it was done in a nice way.

"Why don't you have a seat?" he asked while turning to face the makeshift studio in his living room as he made a sweeping motion with his right hand. I walked over and sat on a plush antique couch piled high with plush pillows. I sat on the couch and Ken arranged himself behind his Nikon camera on a short tripod, loaded a box on the back, and took a picture by pushing down on the plunger he held in his right hand. The light behind the fabric diffuser flashed with a popping sound. Ken pulled a Polaroid out from the box at the back of the camera and immediately began shaking it in the air, holding it between the thumb and forefinger of his right hand by the corner. He did this for half a minute and then peeled the plastic film from the front of the Polaroid. He tilted his head to the right while looking at the picture and raised his shoulders slightly before he handed the Polaroid to me. I looked down at a picture of someone I didn't recognize. There was thick black eyeliner around my eyes, and the concealer had completely erased the dark circles from under my eyes. The Polaroid was black and white. Although the pants were unbuttoned at the top, they looked almost normal and didn't show anything. The boy in the picture looked like a theatrical character; not the person I was accustomed to seeing in the mirror. For the first time, I noticed that my jaw looked like a cartoon super-hero jaw with my bottom teeth set at just a hair short of an *under-bite*. Maybe Ron had been right about my jaw; it might be a liability after all. I began to wonder if I were making a mistake and had misjudged my ability to fit in with the classic, chiseled faces of the models who were on the billboards, commercials, and magazines all around. I tried to relax....

8

BREAKING FREE

When I had been at the grocery store in Missouri taking the campers shopping for our weekly groceries last summer, I had seen a GQ magazine. I was intrigued by how much the model on the cover looked like me. I opened up the magazine and saw several pictures within the editorial section as well as a few pages of this same model for Calvin Klein. His face was rounder than mine, but he had the same jutting jaw and broad shoulders as I. It was the first time that I had believed that I could actually be a model and make some money to go to a college better than Monmouth.

I left Monmouth College on my nineteenth birthday to go to New York by way of Indianapolis. The only reason I matriculated at Monmouth in the first place was to get away from my family and have a safe place to live and three meals a day. At seventeen, I went on a partial aid-based scholarship thanks to my ACT scores, but my mediocre grades kept me from getting any real money from them. I made up the rest of the tuition with loans that seemed easy to get. I knew I would leave Monmouth from the first time I saw the rust stained swimming pool, the tiny campus, and the small town with a movie theater that aired only one movie per week.

I came back my sophomore year for one reason only; to set things straight with a Theta Chi football player named Jim White. He was angry with me for dating Jeanne. In his simple mind, he was next in line to date Jeanne after her boyfriend, a star football-player named Mike who graduated in 1980.

Jim was a large-framed fullback with no neck who did everything he could to make my life miserable; banging on Jeanne's windows at two in the morning, following me with his frat brothers at night on campus and calling me *pussy* and *faggot* as he dropped a shoulder into my chest and pushed by me on the narrow sidewalk that curved from building to building across the patchy grass. I wanted to beat the shit out of him or at least grab him by his polyester shirt collar and set things straight, but he was never alone; he always had at least two other football players with him.

I spent all of my free time when I came back to Monmouth my sophomore year training to kick Jim's ass. I did hundreds of push-ups, sit-ups, jumped rope for an hour at a time and hit a heavy bag that I rigged up in my room so many times that I punched a hole in it. I bought a clear plastic mouth guard from the tiny local sports store on Main Street and kept it in my right pocket of whatever pants I was wearing at all times to protect my teeth from a punch in the mouth. I knew that I was leaving Monmouth to become a model in New York City and I didn't want to get my teeth knocked out in a fight before I even made it to the city. I decided to sign up for the big intramural wrestling tournament in mid-November as part of my training. I made it to the finals at 162 pounds and beat a hulking wrestler from Theta Chi who seemed to weigh at least fifteen pounds more than me. He started out the match by laughing at me and slapping me hard in the face with his right hand. I noticed the look of shock on the faces of his loud and obnoxious Theta Chi brothers as I beat their *ringer* with a score of eleven to one.

The only point he got was when I used a *cross-face* and ended up choking him with my right arm, which caused the heavy-set ref from ATO, another football player fraternity, to give a point to Cole for using the illegal move. I won the tournament, and everyone was in shock in the old gym that smelled of sweaty socks and mildew. Everyone in my fraternity started to call me *Chi-killer*. I was so exhausted by the final match that I sat in the shower for over an hour and then puked in the toilet before going to bed at eight that night with a headache that seemed like it would push my skull apart from the inside out.

A week later I followed Jim out of a party at my fraternity into the narrow hallway near the old soda machine that was filled with cans of cheap Black Label beer. I walked up close to him and blocked him from leaving out the front door. He looked at me with a mixture of fear and confusion as I calmly asked him to step outside so that we could settle things once and for all. I was nervous, and my stomach was tight as a drum as I felt sick inside, but on the surface, I was as cool and smooth as mountain spring water.

Jim stammered out, "I don't have a problem with you man," as he took two tentative steps back until his shoulders bumped against the soda machine.

I took one step forward and asked, "You don't? Really?

Then why the fuck have you been following me and pushing into me when you have your *girlfriends* with you, and calling me *faggot* and *pussy*? Sounds to me like you have a problem with me, wouldn't you say?"

His expression suddenly changed to all fear as he started to apologize profusely while calling me *dude* and *buddy* as he pleaded with his hands out in a *mea-culpa* gesture. I started to smile and even let out a short laugh. I was completely shocked at his reaction. His appearance had led me to believe that he was a real badass who would fight me in a second if given a chance, but instead he was almost begging me to forget the whole thing and be buddies. I shook my head from side to side as I worked out how to end things; I was tempted to punch him in the face, but instead settled on something simpler with no blood involved,

"Just stay away from me, got it?"

"Yeah, that's cool, I can do that," he blurted out with a passive expression that signified his defeat more than if I had punched him.

I turned and walked out the front door, then let the moment sink in as the cold dry air of the November night cooled my face and bare arms. The stars were sharp and bright overhead and seemed to twinkle happily from above. Everything was now settled, I could leave Monmouth without any loose ends. I was not leaving because I was afraid; I was leaving because I wanted to get the fuck out of this dead-end school. I was leaving on my terms, alone.

I walked into Dean Conner's office the next day and told her that I was leaving Monmouth to go to New York, I left out the part about the modeling. She suggested a *leave of absence* in case I wanted to return to school next year. I pretended to consider her request, more for how beautiful she was, than because I had any thought of ever returning to Monmouth.

9

SHOOTING FOR PLEASURE

"Are you ready?" Ken asked with a hint of sarcasm mixed with good humor.

"Yes, should I look at the camera?" I asked ignorantly.

"Oh yes, *please* young prince, could you tilt your head down and then look up with your eyes?"

Does he know Marcus and Ron or what? I thought to myself. Can I really take all of my pictures with my head tilted down and looking up with my eyes?

I tilted my chin slightly down and looked up at the camera, putting my hands on my sides to keep myself from sliding off the pile of pillows on the couch.

"That looks good, now just *relax* and really look into the camera lens."

I felt anything but relaxed. I pretended that I was comfortable and not throwing up inside.

"That's good Daryl...very good," he said in a hushed tone as he began to perspire from his waxen face. He continued to push the handheld plunger with his thumb, taking picture after picture, each one the same as the last while quietly humming a tune to himself.

After he finished two rolls of film, he abruptly stopped.

"I think we have some good pictures for your portfolio," he said while looking out the window as he wiped the sweat from his brow with a white towel.

"Okay, are we finished?" I asked while slumping barechested on the couch.

"Oh *yes*, we're *finished*," he said with a cheery sarcasm as he looked away again, indicating that he was bored with the conversation. "You *must* tell Paul that I said hello, won't you? I'll send the negatives to Paul and print up a few of my personal favorites for your book. Okay?"

I knew Ken was gay, and although I was comfortable working with him, this knowledge tempered my trust of his motivations. I had a teacher named Mr. Tillman in the sixth grade that was gay. He lived five houses down from me and had a roommate named Klaus. When I was younger, my brother and I would skate past his house by way of the frozen creek that ran through his backyard. Mr. Tillman would come out into the backyard and yell down at us in the creek below to *get the hell off his property*. We laughed at the way he pronounced his words when he yelled and skated away trying to figure out if we would skate back by his house on the way home or take off our skates and walk around on the street. We told my mom, and she smiled slightly and said that Mr. Tillman lived with a *friend* and laughed to herself when she said the word *friend*. Mr. Tillman turned out to be my sixth grade Special Op teacher at Paddock Elementary School. He was tall with a large nose and hair that looked as if it was made of kinky light brown and gray wire. He dressed in tweed jackets and patterned shirts with wide ties that had a big triangular knot around his neck. When he wasn't wearing a tie, he would wear an open shirt with a silky ascot around his neck. He was profoundly unattractive but carried himself like a handsome, wealthy aristocrat. He had a way of moving his arms and legs that made me think of a marionette as if a string needed to be pulled a certain way before he could move. All of the boys decided he was gay, though we thought being gay was how you acted, not that he had sex with his roommate Klaus. We based our opinion on his voice and the fact that his hands were often at right angles to his wrists. And although he yelled at Stokes and me when we skated by his house when we were younger, he never seemed to lose his temper in the classroom. He was American but had an accent that made him sound like a wealthy English aristocrat from the nineteenth century. He wasn't interested in actually teaching us anything, and like Mr. Englehart, he assumed we were all geniuses that already knew more than anyone else in the school, with the possible exception of himself. His mornings consisted of reading the Wall Street Journal while the class did whatever the hell we wanted, as long as we didn't disturb him. Late in the morning, he would lecture about some random subject that he had on his mind and sometimes encourage us to read or write *something*.

Early in the year a few of the really smart and devious boys in the class realized that Mr. Tillman loved talking about the intricacies of the stock market more than anything. They decided to have one boy ask Mr. Tillman about the stock market every day, and while he was teaching that boy his love and passion of stocks, the rest of the class would shamelessly goof off. The arrangement was that we would draw straws and the one with the shortest straw got stuck with Mr. Tillman for most of the day, listening with feigned interest as he babbled on about the stock market, the economy and the importance of the treasury department. The trick was to pay enough attention to be able to answer Mr. Tillman if he asked a question of us to determine if we were listening to his lecture. It was the last thing in the world that I wanted to do. I was afraid that Mr. Tillman would see through me right away since I was a terrible liar and this was *definitely* a lie. As it turned out, I only drew the short straw once. I listened to Mr. Tillman with multiple head nods and a few fake questions for clarification as I looked around the room occasionally to see what the other boys were up to. Mr. Tillman seemed annoyed early on that I didn't understand why the stock market was important and why the prices rose and fell. I felt stupid and clueless but was somehow able to occupy Mr. Tillman for two and a half hours. The other guys looked at me like I was an amateur and shook their heads slowly from side to side with their eyes towards the ground when Mr. Tillman ended my private lecture two hours before the end of the day. Mr. Tillman asked all of the students to take out their social studies books and turn to page 133.

Ken Haak was a lot like Mr. Tillman, even down to his sophisticated, erudite way of talking; as if he needed to polish up the English language with a few well-placed fake inflections. His longish-white hair was even damper and greasier than when we first met two hours ago. His shirt was more rumpled and his waxen face was covered with a thin layer of sweat. I was okay with the fact that Ken was as gay as Mr. Tillman, but this knowledge did cause me to question his motivations in taking pictures of me in buttonless shorts from a crotch eyed view. I saw a stack of polaroids on the table outside the bathroom of guys with no shirts and some almost completely nude. Although they were not *pornographic,* they *definitely* showed more than I would have been comfortable with. None of the guys looked comfortable, they all had expressions that told me they would rather be anywhere else than having nude pictures taken in Ken's studio. A few years later Ken published a coffee table book that featured many of the guys that I saw on the table at his studio. Some of the photos were really embarrassing. I was happy that I did not let Ken take pictures that would be featured in his book. I felt lucky that I got out of his studio with some run of the mill "hot model without his shirt on the couch" pictures.

I knew that to talk with Ken directly about my discomfort would mean a quick end to the shoot, and a quick end to my career as a model, so I pretended I was asking Mr. Tillman questions about the stock market, and we had a pleasant and meaningless conversation while standing near the front door. Ken casually mentioned that he wanted to work with me again, but I knew that this was the last time I would work with Mr. Haak. He was too old to waste his time on someone who was not interested in *playing the game.* There were too many other models that were hungry for the chance to work with Ken in crotch-less shorts and *semi's* for him to waste his time on me.

Those were the young men that Ken was interested in. He was no longer shooting for money or fame; at this point in his life, he was shooting strictly for pleasure.

10

JUST PRETEND

It was sunny and cold out on the side street lined with brownstones that crossed the massively wide Park Avenue. I did not wear a watch but thought it was around one o'clock. I turned right onto Park Avenue making my way past the grim faces of the pedestrians leaning forward and walking with a determined look of purpose as if they were fighting a stiff headwind.

I made my way back to the glistening lobby of the new building that the agency was in and signed in quickly at the curved desk. The elevator was quiet and empty as I took a ride up to the eighth floor. I exited the elevator into the lobby of Legends and walked past the receptionist and around the glass wall. There was a lot of activity, and every model I saw seemed more suited for life in front of the camera than me. I received silent stares and one "hey" from another model as I searched for the one face I knew. Paul was sitting at a modest desk on the other side of the clear acrylic half wall that held the cards for all the models of the agency. I waved to him, but he was talking to another model and didn't notice me. I walked to his side of the wall and turned to look at the cards of the models that seemed so sophisticated and professional. Doubt again pushed at me from behind my eyes. I did not look like these guys at all. Was this really a good idea? I heard Paul call my name and turned towards his desk as he rose to greet me with a ready smile.

"How did it go with Ken?" he asked with a wide smile that seemed to indicate that he knew *exactly* how it had gone with Ken.

I pulled the three by four inch Polaroid from my jacket pocket and handed it to him. "It was good," I said with as much enthusiasm as I could muster.

"That's good. Ken called and said that he liked you but he didn't know if you were entirely relaxed while he was shooting."

No shit, I thought to myself. "Really?" I questioned dumbly, with a feigned look of surprise as I tilted my head to one side, not knowing what else to say.

"That's okay," said Paul through another wide grin, "I really don't see you doing that type of work anyway. There is something very different about you and your look, you're not going to be right for every photographer, but there are a few that will take a chance on you, and that may lead to some good modeling jobs.

"I'm not sure if these pictures will help your book, but Ken is a good place to start. We need to get you some pictures that look like you and look better than what you have now. Can you go out to meet another photographer today? She's downtown in SoHo."

"Okay," I said with some hesitation, I was trying to take in all that he had said about me and the shooting I just had with Ken. The fact that the next photographer was female seemed like a good thing to me.

"Her name is Jade Albert. She's doing a shoot today for a catalog. Jade said that you could come by and take some pictures with the girl who is shooting for the catalog. You can get something to eat and head down to her studio at four; she said she has clothes for you to wear and a makeup artist should still be on set when you get there. Here's the information." He handed me a post-it note with an address, and the name Jade Albert scribbled below.

"Thanks, Paul. Is there anything that I should know or do?"

"Nah, you'll do fine. Jade is very cool and *very* good. You should get some pictures that we can use. Come back in the morning; the agency will be closed by the time you finish shooting tonight."

"Sounds great Paul," I offered with feigned confidence, "see you in the morning."

He offered a thumbs up as he turned back towards his desk, picked up his phone from the receiver and pushed one of the flashing clear buttons with a light behind it. I turned away and noticed most of the models that had ignored me when I walked in were now staring at me as if I posed some sort of threat to them. I nodded and mumbled *hi* several times as I made my way to the elevator through the crowd of models. Not one of them seemed to want to shake my hand, so I opened the heavy glass door, walked out, and pushed the *down* button on the elevator. It was as quiet and empty as it was on the ride up.

The late-day winter sun offered light without warmth, and the wind pushed at me steadily as I walked towards Park

Avenue. I had a return ticket to Westport, Connecticut and four quarters for phone calls in my pocket.

I had thought I would be returning to Connecticut by now and had not brought any money for food. I hadn't been paid for my work at Table Works in Westport on the Post Road and had just paid the rent for March to Sofie, leaving me completely tapped. I knew I could walk the twenty-eight blocks to Jade's studio, but I wasn't looking forward to the walk back to Grand Central. I started down Park with my head down in a quick New Yorker walk, trying my best to ignore the smells of the steaming hot-dogs and roasting chestnuts that seemed to be on every street corner. I was hungrier than I thought.

After a slow, cold hour of walking, I arrived at Fourth Street and found the studio. I searched in the shop windows for a clock to find out what time it was. I finally asked a young man with *dreads* pushing a rack of clothes down the wide, cracked sidewalk what time it was. He walked by me and yelled out "three-thirty," without slowing down.

Good, I'd made it with some time to spare. I walked to a dirty building with trash bags piled high on the curb. There was a row of dirty white buttons to the right of a black steel door and I found the one that read J. Albert. I pushed the button and a voice shouted back within seconds from the small circular speaker, "Who is it?" The loudness of the voice startled me, and I started to explain who I was without pushing the small white button next to the speaker. "Push the button!" the man's voice shouted. I found the button quickly and pushed while talking into the speaker. He buzzed the door before I finished and I scrambled to pull the door open before the buzzing stopped. Inside the door, I faced a set of narrow concrete and steel steps with a pipe railing. I walked up the stairs looking for any clues to determine where the studio was. The first floor had two steel doors with no names, only numbers. On the second floor was a door that had a small piece of paper taped on it with scotch tape that read J. Albert. I knocked on the door and waited, looking up and to the side at nothing. The door was yanked open by a slim man with long, greasy hair, loose t-shirt, and jeans with holes in the knees. He turned and walked away as I entered the darkened room, closing the door quietly behind me with my right hand. The room was completely dark except for the bright lights of the shoot that was going on towards the back of the studio. I stood just inside the door, unsure of where to go and simply watched the lights flash every few seconds and listened to the strobes whine as they got ready for the next shot.

A girl was sitting on a white, square plywood box. She had one knee up, and her body was sideways towards the camera with both hands clasped around her raised knee, her other leg was stretched out onto the floor in front of her. She had her head turned toward the camera and moved slightly each time the lights recharged. She had full lips and large eyes with thick, dark lashes. Her hair was cut short to the back of her neck and was filled with large curls that were a mix of blond and light brown. She was wearing fitted white Capris with espadrilles and a loose-fitting white and blue striped cotton sweater. She seemed to have no extra weight on her body, her breasts were small, and she wasn't wearing a bra.

The woman behind the camera was an older version of the model in front of the camera, only fuller in the hips and dressed all in black. I could not see her face clearly, but I could tell she was an attractive woman. I stood and watched without talking for almost thirty minutes before a young woman with a clipboard in her right hand and a pen around her neck came up to me.

"Did Paul send you?" she asked, looking up from her clipboard.

"Yes." I said, "Is this a good time? It looks like you're very busy."

"Not really," she replied while she looked away. "You can sit with Cheryl, and Jade will take a few rolls of you. Come over here," she said, motioning with her left hand. We walked over to a rack filled with clothes. "This should fit you," she said as she handed me a white and blue cotton sweater with buttons up the front. "Don't worry about your pants; Jade will be shooting you and Cheryl from the waist up. Go over to Glenn and have him do something with your hair and put on some makeup."

I took the sweater in my hand and walked over to a chair with a softly lit mirror behind it where a man stood with a comb and scissors in one hand. He had a row of hair clips clipped on the loose v-neck of his black t-shirt. He was slim and tall, and his hair was bleached white and cut short on the sides and back.

Although he was as tall as I, he looked to be twenty or thirty pounds lighter.

"You must be Glenn," I said quietly. "I'm Daryl, nice to meet you."

"Um-hmm," he answered while motioning with the hand holding the scissors and comb towards the seat in front of him.

"What do you want me to do with *him*?" he asked the

young woman with the clipboard as he stood with his comb and scissors in one hand and his other hand on his hip.

"Just get that hair out of his face and do something about his skin. Jade only has time to shoot one or two rolls with him and Cheryl. It's only a test...."

Glenn put the scissors and the comb down and put his hand under my chin and lifted as he looked down at me, shaking his head from side to side without speaking. "What *did* you do to your hair?" he blurted out with a look of disdain. "It looks *soooo* damaged," he said, without waiting for an answer. He put his hand into my hair. "Do you use any conditioner?" he asked, knowing the answer to his question before I replied.

"No," I replied guiltily. "Should I?"

"Of course you should! Oh my God, you're kidding, *right*?" he exclaimed in an exasperated voice. "What do you wash your hair with?"

"I usually use Prell shampoo or sometimes a bar of soap." I knew this was the wrong answer before it came out of my mouth.

"Soap?!" he almost shouted, "Are you fucking kidding me? I am going to put some *product* in your hair and comb it off your face. You really need to take care of your hair, and it is *waaaay* too long, by the way." He stated with a mix of irritation and disbelief.

I could tell that Glenn did not want me to answer, so I sat quietly facing the mirror while he went to work. He squeezed some clear looking gel onto his hand and then rubbed his hands together before working the gel into my hair starting at the sides and repeating the process on the top of my head until all of my hair looked wet and shiny. He picked up a plastic brush with widely spaced bristles and began brushing my hair straight back. He made little clucking sounds while he worked and his tight-lipped expression betrayed how he felt about me and my damaged hair. After a minute of brushing, Glenn messed my hair with his hands and then pushed my hair back with his fingers, tugging at it lightly to get the thick waves to lie flatter and look natural at the same time. He stood in front of me and held my face in both hands looking disapprovingly at my hair. He stopped the clucking sounds and turned back to the table with the mirror to grab some foundation and a sponge. He lifted my head up with the tips of his fingers and tilted a small beige makeup bottle onto the sponge before dabbing it under my eyes and onto my face around my eyes and cheekbones. After a few lifts of my face and more disapproving looks down at me, he went to work on the areas around my mouth, repeating the same process, until, a few minutes later, he was done. He grabbed a small tube and squeezed a little of its contents onto his little finger, said, "Keep your mouth slightly open," as he carefully applied the thick liquid to my lips. "You're all set," he stated flatly as he turned back to his table and picked up a can of Coke and took a long drink.

I put down my backpack and walked over to the area where the shooting was happening. The girl with the clipboard walked up to me, held out her right hand, and said, "I'm Lisa, Jade's assistant. Jade and Cheryl are taking a break. They'll be ready to shoot in a few minutes."

"Okay. Thanks," I said with a weak smile.

The studio was very cool but comfortable. People were talking but their voices were so hushed that I could not make out what they were saying. I continued to stand with my arms slack at my sides for what seemed about ten minutes until Lisa came over and grabbed me by the sleeve saying, "Sit here," as she led me to the white plywood box on which Cheryl had been sitting. I sat down on the low white box and squinted my eyes and looked into the darkness surrounding the bright lights that shone from three sides onto the area around the box.

Cheryl walked out of the darkness and seemed to glide over to me, her feet never actually leaving the ground, with long, flowing strides. She was graceful and fluid, and I couldn't take my eyes off of her. She walked close to me, placed a long-fingered hand on my shoulder and said, "Hi, I'm Cheryl," as she smiled, showing her straight, white teeth.

"Hi," I answered shyly, "I'm Daryl."

"Nice to meet you, Daryl," she said with a mixture of warmth and amusement.

"Cheryl, sit with your front to his back. All of the pictures are going to be tight, from the waist up," Jade instructed from behind the camera.

"Okay, honey," Cheryl responded playfully to Jade.

"Daryl, that's your name, isn't it? Pretend that you and Cheryl know each other and you are just having fun together. Can you do that?" Jade asked without waiting for an answer to her question.

"Okay," I responded too quietly for Jade to hear.

"Just have fun," she said as she looked through the lens of her Nikon camera.

Cheryl wrapped her legs around my hips and her arms around my chest, pulling herself close to me from behind. I could feel her warm breath on my right ear as she snuggled her face close to mine from behind. She smelled of flowered soap and hairspray. I could feel her warm body pressed against my back.

"Are you having fun? We're supposed to be lovers. Can you do that?" she asked repeating Jade's words. "Relax; just have fun. Jade is a very good photographer; you can get some good shots from this," she whispered in my right ear slowly and sweetly, as if we had been lovers for a long time and this was the most normal of conversations.

She continued to whisper in my ear while Jade took picture after picture. Jade didn't give any more instructions but seemed almost to be speaking to herself as she worked from behind the camera. "That one looks good. Okay. Yes, that is not bad. Good, good, good. Okay, Cheryl, that's it, honey."

Cheryl continued talking to me and seemed to move after each shot. After the first ten or twelve shots, she moved her hands up and started to squeeze my chest with her long fingers, and then she squeezed my arms, all while continuing to talk to me in a low, hushed bedroom voice that only I could hear. I started to relax and forget about everything but Cheryl, smiling and laughing as I let her voice take me away from the studio and my life, floating away in my mind as I felt only pleasure course through my body. I felt safe and warm and loved as we sat on the hard plywood box in the middle of Jade's studio. Even though I knew that she was only pretending to like me, it still felt real. I seemed to be hovering in a place between fantasy and reality, the only thing grounding me was the understanding that none of this was real, like a dream in which my eyes were wide open; an intoxicating fantasy that felt infinitely better and more real than any reality I had ever experienced.

I had grown up in a home that taught me not to trust

anything or anyone. Anything that was good or exciting or pleasurable was either a lie or very temporary, leaving me lower than where I had started. To feel anything in my family was to feel pain and misery, there was no happiness and very little hope. I grew up learning to expect nothing from my family or from life, so I eventually learned to never experience disappointment; only a low-grade sadness tempered with a strong dose of indifference. This colored everything I experienced from a very young age.

Whatever I loved in my family would be taken away from me, teaching me that to love anything or anyone would result in loss. I changed myself from an overly emotional and caring child into a careful and distant adult. If no one knew what I cared about, then they wouldn't try to take it away from me. Self-esteem and happiness were the two things that my family was most interested in destroying. I was ten years old when I realized that was the way life worked for me. My young mind understood that not only did my family not want me to be happy, but that they also wanted me to feel as bad about myself as they felt about themselves. From Mom and Dad on down, it was the unspoken rule: The Janney family was held together by their collective misery. I had memory after memory to remind me what it meant to be hopeless and unhappy, forcing me to understand how impossible it was to reach the foolish, mythical land of happiness. It was a philosophy and way of life that I thought was typical of all families when I was young. It was not until I left home at seventeen that I realized how far from typical my family really was.

The flashes of the camera stopped suddenly, and the main lights of the studio were turned on, jarring me back to reality. Cheryl patted my shoulder and offered; "Good job, kid. I think you took some good pictures."

"Thank you Cheryl, and thanks for taking the pictures with me," I said earnestly with an expression meant to let her know that I did not want our time together to end just yet.

"No problem kid. I'm sure we'll see each other again," she said as smiled with a look of understanding.

"I would like that," I said like a little kid that has a crush on his teacher, knowing instinctively that this would be the last time I ever saw Cheryl.

Lisa walked over to me and pulled a small Polaroid from her clipboard and said, "This is for you," as she handed me a picture of Cheryl and me almost cheek to cheek looking at the camera in the bright lights.

"Thank you," I offered as I stared at the image in front of me.

I noticed that my eyes were a color blue that I had never seen before; a deep water blue from the ocean. I always thought my eyes were more of a green than blue, but the Polaroid showed Cheryl and me with very similar blue eyes. I noticed that her eyes were bloodshot at the corners and her makeup was on heavy around her mouth and forehead, trying to cover the rough acned skin beneath. I was surprised that I looked fairly decent in the Polaroid, good and like myself. I carefully tucked the picture into my day planner and then wedged the planner into my overstuffed backpack.

I quietly got changed in the corner of the studio and folded the sweater neatly and and placed it on the chair in the makeup area. I said, "Thank you," to the air behind me. After waiting a few moments for a response, I said,

"Goodbye," to no one, and left the studio the same way I came in; unnoticed.

11

THE DARKNESS OF SLEEP

Night had fallen hard and cold onto the dirty, litter-strewn street and the wind pushed a white Styrofoam cup across to the blackened curb, wedging it in the open space at the side of a rusty and torn sewer grate. The streetlight was dim and flickering off and on. A wall of garbage closed off the sidewalk from the street, some of the black plastic bags ripped open with their contents vomited onto the filthy sidewalk. A large rat with a hairless tail and matted hair on his back hustled down the street while staying close to the garbage bags. He reminded me of the commuters I saw at Grand Central, rushing into and out of the trains with tight lips and stiff, swinging arms in the dim light of early morning and the heavy dark of night, scurrying to catch the next train home; then back to the city to run all day on their squeaking exercise wheels until night fell, and they could do it all over again. I followed the same streets back to the agency and then to Grand Central. My hunger did a good job of blocking out most of the cold and any thoughts of the day. I tried hard not to scurry as I worked my way north to Grand Central.

The ride back to Connecticut on Metro-North was quiet. I had to work hard to keep myself from falling asleep to avoid missing my stop in Westport. I started to read *Catcher in the Rye* but found myself daydreaming and dozing as I thought about Holden Caulfield alone in a seedy New York hotel arguing with a hooker. Stowing the book, I decided to watch the towns go by, thinking about what life would be like if I lived in each of them. It was a game that I had played with myself when I was a paperboy. In the winter, I would go collecting for the newspaper after dinner in the dark of night. I liked the bitter cold of winter with the clear night sky showing the bright lights of the stars and moon. I would spend my time walking from house to house looking at the lights of each house and trying to determine by the warmth of the lights whether that house held a happy family within its walls or a family like mine; if the children were hugged after hearing a bedtime story, or if they were left to get themselves to sleep in uneasy silence or while hearing their mom and dad scream at each over everything from money to divorce while the child wrapped their pillow around their ears and rolled from side to side until the voices faded away and the child slipped into the darkness of sleep. The scenery started out grim and sad as the train rolled slowly through Harlem and the buildings with their missing windows and boarded up storefronts, giving way to the decent looking high-rise apartments that were, in reality, worse than the buildings in Harlem. The *projects* seemed impossible to escape and infected with crime not from outsiders but from those that lived within each building.

Soon the lights became brighter and the streets cleaner; houses stood neatly in rows, each a copied version of the house before with a different porch and paint job. The cars in the parking lots were newer and more expensive, and the people were much better dressed. Almost one hour exactly from the time the train inched out of Grand Central the brakes screeched to a halt as the conductor announced loudly with a *crackling* voice, *Westport—everybody out for Westport.* I lifted my backpack onto my shoulder and waited for the sliding glass and metal doors to open while staring at a well-dressed businessman on my right and an equally well-dressed girl who appeared to be a student on my left. They stared straight ahead, refusing for even a moment to acknowledge that I existed in the same space as them.

The doors opened jerkily, and we all walked into the cold night air at the same time, the group turned left to make their way to the tunnel that crossed to the south side of the tracks. I stood near the railing on the right side of the platform and waited for the people exiting the train to shove and shuffle past me. They reminded me of cattle fighting to be first in line at the stockyard to be hung upside down by a meat hook, hit in the head with a sledgehammer before having their throats cut to allow the excess blood to drain from their bodies. After they had all passed and filed down the stairs to the tunnel, I began walking slowly through the tunnel with garbage on the sides that smelled of stale beer, cigarette butts, and urine.

I did not bother calling Barb for a ride home; she was at least twenty minutes away and little Sean and Jessica would be fast asleep by now. I started to walk away from the station towards Riverside Avenue; I tried to hitchhike after getting about a half mile from the station, but the drivers of the BMWs and Mercedes didn't even acknowledge my existence, so I went back to walking. I couldn't really blame them.

I had learned in the three months of walking in Westport that *nobody* walked in Westport. I felt the eyes of disdain drilling holes in my back as I walked home most nights, eyes averted as if I was invisible from the front. I won't lie, it bothered me, and I often thought how everyone walks in New York City. Laziness as proof of wealth was the gold standard in Westport, and I was walking to my closet of a room that cost 180 bucks per month and had no money in my pocket. To say that I didn't belong in Westport would be a gigantic understatement. I was way out of my element, and couldn't begin to understand the unchangeable difference between myself and the Westporters who whipped by me in clean cars with impeccable outfits. It seemed the good citizens of Westport would always help me out by reminding me that I would forever be an outsider.

The traffic lightened as I turned right onto Riverside Road. The street was dark except for the occasional lamp post set near the road to light the way to the houses bordering the Saugatuck River. There was no sidewalk, so I stayed close to the half-thawed piles of dirt-covered snow that had become hard as river ice. The cars gave me no space on my left as they accelerated smooth and fast towards downtown Westport. I wanted to turn around and flip them off and yell fuck you but realized that might not be the best idea, so I just kept walking with my eyes on the uneven roadside in front of me.

A long and cold thirty minutes later, I was walking up the front yard of 82 Riverside around to the backyard that was fenced in by a broken-down stockade fence with a crooked four-foot space to walk through to the back porch. Gap-toothed Bobby had nine partial frames and bodies of rusted-out cars in the backyard, a fact that must have made the house to the north very unhappy. He was a short, bald, Scientologist who wore clothes and glasses that seemed to have been pulled from the 1960's. He loved to talk to almost anybody. I was lucky enough to hear part of his life story while eating a bowl of cereal late one night at the cracked Formica table that sat alone in our crappy kitchen.

He told me that he was from Ohio and that he was an inventor. I never saw him leave the house and for some reason, Sofie seemed to like him. Sofie told me that his wife Judy had told her that she and Bobby were going back to Ohio to live with his family because Bobby didn't have a job and they were running out of money. Judy and Bobby had the large bedroom on the second floor near the bathroom. Judy was a stunning beauty with smooth skin, blue-gray eyes, and an hourglass figure. Sofie told me that their marriage was arranged for them by an Elder in the Church of Scientology about a year ago. Judy was pregnant and had started wearing Bobby's shirts as maternity clothes the last few weeks. I could not figure their marriage out. I saw a look of doubt and confusion etched across Judy's face as she seemed to be working out in her head what she was doing with Bobby and what she would do in the future, leading me to believe that I was not the only one confused by their odd pairing.

I walked under the solitary yellow light bulb shining bare and alone and opened the unlocked back door, then turned to open the refrigerator, and took a long drink from my carton of Tropicana orange juice. After using the bathroom, I walked slowly and quietly up the narrow, steep back stairway, worked the combination on my locked door and walked into a room lit only by the street lamp shining from across the street. I fumbled under the lampshade for the knob to turn on the one light. My room was cold from the air that crept down from the attic stairway. I took off my jeans and pulled on cheap red sweats and an old white sweatshirt, set my alarm for six, got into bed, and then reached up to turn out the light. Before I could begin to think my second thought, I was fast asleep and dreaming about things that had nothing to do with me or the day I had just had.

I arrived at Grand Central early on Tuesday morning and went directly to the small coffee shop that I had noticed last week with the $1.25 breakfast special; eggs, bacon, toast, and hash browns. I was very hungry and wanted to eat before meeting Paul at the agency. I ordered the special with the eggs over easy and rye toast with butter and a glass of ice water with a slice of lemon. I sat down at the counter and gave my order to a gaunt, dark-haired man with gray and white checkered pants, white shirt, and a white apron stained brown all down the front.

I started to eat my greasy, runny, eggs as soon as he placed my plate on the table, then the bacon. I mopped up the runny yolk with the thick pieces of rye toast. I finished with the hashed browned potatoes that were crisp on the outside, and moist on the inside. I cleaned my plate and drank down my glass of water in one long drink. After paying at the small worn counter and leaving a seventy-five cent tip, I walked out the door and turned towards Park Avenue.

The sun was shining brightly above the tall sentinel-like

buildings, and I looked up to see the white sunlight cut through the shadows high above the sidewalk, but I could not see the sun. I walked quickly on the wide walkway with a slight smile on my face. I was looking forward to see what was on the schedule for today at the agency. A feeling of well-being and hope rose up in me as I tried to imagine life as a working model in New York City and abroad. I watched the faces of the people flowing towards me on the sidewalk and saw grim expressions with sad eyes and tight lips. I laughed to myself and walked into the lobby and onto the elevator that carried me to the 8th floor.

It was 9:05 and the agency was packed with models. Some were leaning close to the bookers who had phones cradled on their necks and chins; writing on large white calendars, as they talked to the models surrounding their desks while on the phone. A few of the bookers jumped up from their desks to scan the racks of modeling cards and pick out the cards of the models whom they thought were right for the job, putting the callers on hold and quickly dropping the phone receivers on their desk. The models looked anxious, and the bookers looked frazzled by the flurry of activity; motioning to the group of models to keep the noise down. Paul was busy talking to two models who were asking him questions; he was shaking his head from side to side while holding a phone between his shoulder and neck. The two models walked away from Paul with their heads down and sat on the floor on the other side of the half wall speaking to each other so intently that their heads were almost touching. Paul noticed me and signaled for me to come over to his desk with his free hand.

"Wow," I said looking around, "Things are really busy this morning."

Paul nodded sagely without responding. I wondered why he would take on another model when there were so many models already with his agency.

"How did it go with Jade?" Paul asked without looking up from his paperwork, "Did she give you any pictures?"

"No, but I think it went well," I responded. "I really like her. She was nice, and she seems like a good photographer."

"Well, don't like her too much, she mostly shoots women, so you'll probably never work with her again. We need to get you some pictures fast; the head booker from an Italian agency is coming here tomorrow to meet with all the models in the agency. I have a feeling you may be what he is looking for...if we can get some pictures that show you in a better light than what you have in your book."

I nodded enthusiastically while surveying the competition, silently wondering how I would ever get any work with so many models working for an obscure agency that I had never even heard of. Maybe modeling was just a numbers game. Get as many models as you can to join your agency, then hope and pray that some of them get work and ignore the ones that don't get jobs. I began to think that getting an agent was not a very impressive accomplishment as the doubt crept slowly into my head.

"You need to go to this address downtown. The photographer's name is Clark Noonan. He's a very good photographer and he has the wardrobe at his studio from a shoot that he just completed on Friday. You need to take some good pictures with him; we're really running out of time here, Daryl. After you are done you need to bring all of the rolls back to the agency; tell him that Paul told you to take all of the film. We'll develop the film into slides and then return the negatives to him. There isn't time to make a new book for you; we'll have to just show the slides to Calvin and hope for the best."

I took the piece of paper from Paul's hand as he turned back to his desk and said, "Thanks, Paul," as I carefully made my way back to the elevator through the sea of models. I could feel the cold looks from behind as I walked past.

Clark's loft studio was spacious and well furnished. The ceilings were high with exposed steel beams set into red brick walls. It was old but looked very clean with large, new windows installed on the street side of the loft. The old freight elevator with the black painted accordion gate and a single row of solid brass buttons opened directly into the loft. I was met by a small girl with tight black jeans and black and white Keds high tops. She wore a loose men's v-neck t-shirt and a chunk of a watch that threatened to fall to the floor dangled from her slim wrist. She had a serious face with cheeks lightly spotted with freckles. Her brown eyes were large and intelligent. Long, straight, brown hair hung down to the middle of her back, corralled by a simple white scrunchy. I immediately knew that she had the sort of body that a man couldn't easily forget if he were lucky enough to see it.

"Are you Daryl?" she asked as she stood in front of me with her arms crossed.

"Yes," I replied, shaking off the thoughts running through my head.

"I'm Claire," she stated flatly with a tone that let me know she was all business. She extended her right hand for me to shake, "Come with me, we need to get your hair done and then get you some clothes."

I followed her to a table in the front corner of the studio with chairs set up facing the large industrial windows that looked out onto the street below. She motioned for me to sit down and looked at my hair.

"Your hair is too long, but we don't have time to cut it today. I'll try to do what I can to make it look a little more current," she said as she reached for a spray bottle.

I nodded in agreement without speaking and sat facing the large windows in front of me. If I was not aware that my hair sucked a few days ago, I was certainly aware of it by now. Somehow I knew that my hair *sucking* was only the beginning of the flaws that would be pointed out to me in the days and months to come.

Within ten minutes she had pulled the hair off of my face with a thick gel that hardened until my hair was fused into the style she wanted. She spent the next five minutes applying some foundation to my cheeks and around my mouth with the same style sponge that Ken and Glenn had used on Monday. She lifted my face gently with her hands and looked at me as if she were studying a bruised cantaloupe at the grocery store.

"Okay, good," she said. "Go over and see Brian, Clark's assistant. Good luck," she continued as she turned and walked over to sit down on a large couch.

"Thanks," I replied awkwardly as I stiffly stood up.

Brian gave me a sideways glance and motioned for me to follow him over to the back corner of the loft with the low hanging industrial lights. He was short with thick black hair, cut short at the back and sides and swept across his forehead like a dark triangle. He was dressed almost the same as Claire except for the addition of an arm full of dark bracelets that seemed to be made out of some kind of hard leather. He pulled a sweater, pants, and loafers with cotton socks from the rack and floor and he handed them to me quickly; "These should fit," he said as he turned away." You can change here and then go over to where the lights and camera are," he said over his shoulder as I strained to catch his words while he walked away.

I took a quick look around the studio and determined that everyone was pre-occupied and that I was all but invisible. I quickly changed into the clothes, folded my jeans and sweater, and placed them on my socks and boots. My white socks were dirty, so I made sure to roll them up and push them into my beat-up hiking boots. The sweater was made of thick cotton the color of the deep sea and the pants were made of plush brown corduroy. They fit perfectly, and silently I wondered why. I pulled on the socks and shoes and walked over to the area where the lights and cameras were set up, feeling foolish and awkward in my new wardrobe. A tall man with clothes that looked very similar to what I was wearing walked up to me and introduced himself with a firm handshake; "I'm Clark," he said with a warm smile. "Paul said you need some good pictures fast. I usually charge for tests, but I think I can use some pictures from today in my portfolio, so I won't charge you."

That's good, I thought to myself, because unless the pictures cost me less than twenty bucks the shooting would be over before we got started.

"Thank you," I replied with genuine gratitude.

"Why don't we start with some pictures over by the couch," he directed with another wide smile and a theatrical sweep of his right hand.

I walked over and sat down on the couch. He started to shoot film almost immediately, and the pop of the large lights flashing seemed to happen much quicker than the lights at Jade's studio. Before I knew it, we had finished a roll of film. His assistant changed the body of the camera quickly and then removed the roll of film and placed it in a labeled clear plastic bag before re-loading the body of the camera with a fresh roll of film. Clark finished the rolls quickly, holding down the button that made the camera sound like the automatic cameras in the Nikon commercials on television.

He gave little direction, except to nod his head slightly when he liked something. I was not thinking consciously of changing my position; instead, I tried only to imagine how a good picture might look. There were no mirrors to see how I looked, so I just sat there and looked to the side, into the camera, or over the camera. I had no idea what I was doing and felt stupid and slouchy on the soft leather couch. I got the impression that Clark owed Paul a favor, and that he would rather be doing anything besides taking my picture. After five changes of the camera body, Clark said loudly, "That was good Daryl, I think I may have a job coming up that you would be perfect for."

"Really?" I questioned with too much surprise in my voice.

"Yes. It doesn't shoot until next month, but I would like to use you for it. It's a German catalog job. I get to choose the model; there's no art director on this job."

"Great," I said, with enthusiasm tempered with the *it's too good to be true* thoughts that immediately spoiled the feel-good moment. Something about the way he said it made me think it was possible, but not probable. I had a long history of being lied to and let down by people; this didn't feel much different.

"You can take the film back to Paul and have it developed. Tell Paul that I want the negatives after you're done making prints or slides from them. Okay?"

Clark handed me five rolls of thirty-five-millimeter film sealed inside a sandwich size Ziploc bag. I carefully placed it in the front pocket of my backpack and turned to shake his hand.

"Thank you, Clark. I appreciate the pictures. I look forward to working with you," I offered with more hope than I felt.

"You're welcome," he said while he continued to shake my hand. "Good luck," he said as the elevator door opened up and I walked in. I caught a glimpse of everyone getting back to work as I turned to face the open door and push the button marked 1.

12

CALVIN'S CHOICE

Paul had the slides developed and told me to come back at 11:30 on Wednesday. I jog-walked back to Grand Central in time to catch the twelve fifty-three express to New Haven. I made it to Table Works at 3:30 and worked until 8:00 with Wendy and Kristan.

Wendy was the owner's daughter and despite her youthful face was almost thirty years old and poised to take over the business from her porcine father who was not as healthy and energetic as he once was. Her mom was a classic beauty, all smiles, nice jewelry and tailored outfits. She seemed to hate working at the store, wanting only to gift wrap items purchased at the store and gossip with Kristan. Mr. Borgens seemed only to be waiting until it was time to go home to eat and watch some TV. He was tired and slow moving and seemed to increase in girth every few weeks.

I first met Wendy at the Post Road Diner in Westport on a Wednesday night after church while getting breakfast with Lou. I overheard two women talking about needing help at the store, and I leaned towards them across the narrow aisle and said that I was looking for a job without even knowing what the job was. Wendy turned towards me and told me where the store was and asked me to come by the next afternoon. I did, and she and Mr. Borgens agreed to hire me. He was jolly and had a warm smile and a thick head of hair. He had a body that was carrying a lot of fat and very little muscle, he seemed incredibly weak for his large size, even down to his weak, fat-fingered handshake. Mr. Borgens put me to work in the back room, down the carpeted stairs behind the cash register, cutting up cardboard boxes and unloading dishes and cups to be displayed on the showroom floor. Mr. Borgens' son, Chip, was in charge of all the ordering and receiving of merchandise for the store. On most nights Mr. Borgens left the store at 6:45, leaving Wendy, Kristan, and me alone to run the store. I got up the nerve to ask Wendy for an advance on the money owed from last week and the hours I had worked today. I had asked Mrs. Borgens a few weeks ago for an advance, and she had said flatly; "We don't do that."

I was more than a little desperate and needed money for the train and food. The words felt strange in my mouth as I asked as nicely as I could for the advance. Wendy explained quietly as we stood alone behind the counter that she could not write any checks until Friday morning at the earliest, to which I quietly replied, "Okay."

She then turned towards the stairs behind the counter and walked downstairs. She returned a few minutes later with a brown leather purse and pulled out a trim, fashionable wallet. Then she pulled out five 20 dollar bills.

"This is a loan until you get caught up. I won't take it out of this week's paycheck. Is this enough?" she asked as she handed me the crisp bills, a worried smile coming over her freckled face.

"Yes, Wendy. Thank you! I'll pay you back as soon as I can," I spouted with too much enthusiasm, unsure if Wendy or any of the Borgens could understand how much of my life was spent trying to survive; wondering where my next meal would come from almost every day; relying on the generosity of others to make up for what I lacked.

I have to tell you; it didn't feel good. I went downstairs to get a box filled with earthen mugs from Peru, labeled them with price tags and brought them up to the showroom and stacked them carefully on an unfinished wooden table near the other pottery mugs. A song came on the radio about a woman who had traveled the world and been to *paradise*. I thought of all the places I could go if I were a model, allowing myself to daydream as the song played on and on.

The chorus was prophetic, warning not to be fooled by paradise with the chorus: *I have been to paradise but I've never been to me*. The singer was talking about missing out on a normal life with a family and a husband in exchange for her pursuit of *paradise*. I didn't care about going to *me*, I only wanted a little slice of *paradise* where money was easy and tomorrow's food was not all that I thought about with a slow burning panic flashing over my heart each and every day, knowing the thin line separated me from the filthy homeless men and women I saw shuffling down the streets pushing shopping carts filled with black garbage bags crammed full with all their worldly possessions. Selfishly, I dreamed of how my life would change if I became a top model. I smiled to myself indulgently at the thought.

Wednesday morning I woke to the jarring buzz of my clock radio at 7:30. I rubbed my face with my hands and went downstairs to the kitchen. Bobby and Kathy were having coffee and tea and they smiled with a look that told me I was intruding on their morning *alone* time. I turned the corner and went into the tiny bathroom, took a quick shower, brushed my teeth, and shaved with a used single bladed disposable *Bic* razor, using some bar soap for shaving cream. I washed my hair with the same soap and rinsed off under the hot, weak shower stream, breathing deeply and enjoying the heat as I allowed the water to hit my back and neck and then stream down my lean body. I finished by washing my front and below before reluctantly turning the water off. I reached for the frayed blue towel that hung on the back of the door and dried off my face and hair. I held the towel to my nose and smelled the damp BO smell that wasn't from me. I silently made a note to keep my towel in my room, wondering who would want to use my smelly towel. I looked into the small mirror with the bare bulb above it and wondered if the face I saw in front of me was a face that could be paid for simply having a photograph taken and printed in a magazine. A pair of cold green eyes stared back with a look of steely resolve. I silently prayed to be the man whom I saw in the mirror.

I caught the commuter bus to Saugatuck Station from the side of Riverside Avenue. I still had some singles left from Tuesday and peeled one off and stuck it in the Plexiglas box with the slot on top to the right of the driver, then sat down in an open seat towards the front and looked out at the sun and the river to my left. I exited the bus at the train station and waited in line to buy a round-trip ticket from the fat man with the fast moving fingers who sat behind the glass ticket window. I slid the money to him, and he slid two tickets through the small opening at the bottom of the window. He announced without looking up at me that the train would arrive at 9:22. I looked up at the analog clock high on the dirty wall of the station and saw that I had time to get a juice at Tommy's across the street.

I stood on the cold platform waiting for the train to arrive from New Haven. A few smokers flanked me on the platform while the remaining Metro-North passengers sat in the cramped, stuffy station waiting for the train to arrive. Beautiful women with warm fur coats and practiced smiles and suited businessmen reading the Wall Street Journal did their best to ignore the existence of all that sat around them. I felt an icy wind push through the legs of my jeans and cut into the side of my face as I looked to the north for the light of the oncoming train. Within minutes the train stopped on the tracks near the concrete platform. I slowly entered the train when the sliding doors opened as the conductor announced the train schedule over the scratchy, tinny intercom. There were no empty seats on the car I entered, so I walked towards the back of the train, pulling hard on the heavy doors between the cars and walking outside and then back inside the next car. No one looked up as I walked down the aisles with my hands at my sides and my backpack securely strapped on my shoulders. I settled into a seat facing forward as the train jerked and swayed around one of the many curves on the track from Westport to Grand Central. Looking out the window, I tried to imagine that I was anyone but myself.

I was jarred to reality as the light of day disappeared, and the lights of the car seemed to grow brighter as we entered the dark tunnels leading to the labyrinth of platforms and train tracks that surrounded Grand Central. The doors opened and the faces with suits filed out onto the platform while I sat and waited until the car was mostly empty, picked up my backpack and walked down the empty aisle and out the door. I ate the same breakfast at the same dive as I had the previous day and enjoyed it just as much. I walked out and down Park Avenue with my jacket zipped up against the cold arriving at the golden lobby with a red face and ears.

After waiting in the lobby for about five minutes to allow the blood to drain from my ears and face, I took the elevator up to Legends on the eighth floor. I opened the glass doors into the waiting area and gave a weak wave to the disinterested receptionist who looked at me with a slight eye-roll and a gentle shake of her head from side to side as she looked back down at her work. I looked away from her and walked around the glass block wall into the booker's area where I was met with the low hum of dozens of male voices talking excitedly simultaneously. There were between sixty and seventy models packed into the back area, some sitting on desks and others sitting on the floor with their backs against the Plexiglas half wall that held the black and white cards of dozens of male models. I looked slack-jawed at the collection of models who all seemed more polished and deserving of work than I as I squeezed through the crowd of bodies, settling into a spot in the back corner of the agency near the water cooler. I carefully took my backpack off my shoulders and placed it on the floor between my legs. I noticed that all of the models had slick light-gray books with the name *Legends* printed on the front in black letters, so I kept my cheap oversized photo album portfolio zipped inside my backpack, as I silently prayed that no one would ask to see it. The bookers looked up from their desks with annoyance as they tried to talk on their phones in the midst of the noise. I was amazed that all of these models worked for the same agency. A few of them looked over at me while I stood in a corner. I made an attempt to wave, but they had already turned their heads away and continued loudly with their intense conversations reminding me of the popular kids in high school; the ones who acted as if it were a cardinal sin to even acknowledge someone who was not in their group. It didn't bother me, and I kind of agreed with their visual summation of my status in the group of models. They instinctively seemed to know that I had no business moving into their territory and that I was not in their league. Well, *fuck them*, I thought as I stared straight ahead. Suddenly, Paul came out of a darkened room in the center of the agency and looked around. He waved to me and then motioned with his hand for me to come over as his face flashed a bright smile of recognition.

"Daryl!" he called over the loud buzz of voices. "You're here. Good, good, come over here. I want you to meet Calvin."

"Hey, Paul," I replied with a smile. "Am I late?" I questioned in a loud voice as the room fell silent and all eyes turned towards me.

"No, no, you're fine come on in," he said, waving me over again with his right hand while smiling a big welcoming smile.

I excused myself through the dense crowd of models. They didn't move out of my way and looked at me as if I smelled bad as I made my way over to Paul. I now had everyone's full attention, which made me feel even more uncomfortable than being ignored; actually much more uncomfortable. Being ignored was something that I could deal with; being noticed was a different story.

I walked into the darkened room and saw an elegant black man sitting on the plush black leather couch. He had his long legs crossed at the knee. Uncrossing his legs, he rose effortlessly and extended a pink-palmed hand as he smiled with a warmth and sincerity that I hadn't seen before, "I am Calvin, nice to meet you," he said with a rolling Caribbean accent.

"Nice to meet you Calvin," I said as I reached out to meet his hand with mine. His fingers were long and delicate, and I felt that if I squeezed too hard they would break like breadsticks. He was almost as tall as I but weighed about thirty pounds less. His face was shiny, and his white-toothed smile seemed to never leave his face, especially when he was talking.

Without thinking, I asked quickly, "Where are you from?"

"Why, I am from Milano, of course," he said graciously.

"Is your accent Italian?" I asked foolishly. I could hear Paul try to stifle his laughter.

"No, bello, I am originally from Trinidad," acting as if my question wasn't stupid.

Paul interrupted us and offered; "Calvin was a very big model in the seventies. He was the first black man on the cover of GQ magazine."

"Really?" I spat out with too much shock in my voice. Again Paul chuckled and Calvin joined in with a laugh that was full of mirth and devoid of sarcasm.

"So bello, Paul tells me you have a *very* bad book," Calvin said with a warm smile as he changed the subject back to business.

"Yes, I don't think the pictures are very good, but I took some tests this week that are much better," I said in a voice that couldn't hide that I was slightly embarrassed by the truth of Calvin's comments.

"Good, good," he said quietly as he walked towards me to look more closely at my face.

"I think Fabrizio will like him very much," he said to Paul. "Can you look to the side?" he asked. As I turned my head, he looked even closer and said, "Bello, bello."

"I told you," Paul said to Calvin while smiling and nodding his head. Calvin continued to stare at my face from an uncomfortably close distance.

I had figured out quickly that Calvin must be gay by his voice, his actions, and the way he dressed, but I did not feel uncomfortable when I talked to him; he seemed to be a genuinely nice guy that just happened to like men more than women.

Paul dimmed the lights and motioned for me to sit down on the couch between him and Calvin. I slumped my backpack on the floor and looked at the white screen as Paul cued up a picture on the projector of me that Jade Albert had taken.

"Not bad," Calvin said without much enthusiasm; "but it does not really look like him," he countered to Paul with his lilting Caribbean accent, sounding like a cross between Jamaican and English.

Paul continued to go through the slides one by one from Jade and some black and white slides from Ken Haak, but Calvin refrained from commenting and stared straight ahead with his long index finger pressed against his lips as if deep in thought. I tried to watch the screen and Calvin's face at the same time, attempting to divine his thoughts through intensive observation. A random slide that Lou had taken at the Westport YMCA of me doing a handstand seemed to catch his eye, and the next picture of me doing a transition jump for a floor exercise routine caused him to rise out of his seat a bit and say, "Bello, it looks like he is flying!"

Paul stopped the slideshow on that picture as Calvin turned to me and said, "I cannot take your book to Beatrice in Milano, she will never want to bring you to Italy. I want to only take the picture of you flying."

"Of course," Paul blurted out with an animated face. "Of course, perfect, fine."

"I know Fabrizio will want to use you for his work," Calvin said as much to himself as to me or Paul "Do you know Fabrizio's work?" Calvin asked as he turned towards me with another one of his warm smiles.

I silently shook my head no, burning with embarrassment inside that I had no idea who Fabrizio even was.

"Do you want to come to Milano, bello?" Calvin questioned as he continued to look at me.

I looked over at Paul who was now standing as I searched for some clue as to how I should answer his questions. He nodded his head up and down with a wild look in his eyes as he mouthed the words *yes, yes*, over and over.

"Yes, Calvin," I responded evenly, not knowing when or how I would ever be able to afford to go to Milan.

"Good, good," he said with a smile that took over his whole face, "I guess there are other boys that want to see me before I go. It has been a pleasure, bellooo," he said cheerfully and sincerely as he extended his hand for me to shake one last time.

I met his hand with mine and responded, "Nice to meet you, Calvin." I smiled back at his infectious enthusiasm as the excitement of what just happened spread from my mind to my body. I had considered the possibility of going to Italy someday to model. I was not sure that I was going, but something inside of me told me that what had just happened was going to change everything. I walked out of the room with a smile that seemed like it was going to break my face. The talk in the room seemed to quiet quickly, like turning down the volume on a stereo as I walked into the crowded booker's area. I backed out of the darkened room and made my way slowly to the elevators. I felt a hand on my right shoulder as I tried to make my way through the models waiting to meet Calvin, I turned slowly and saw Paul with a big smile on his face. He motioned for me to come into his office behind the glass wall and told me to shut the door.

"That went great!" he whispered loudly, trying to control his excitement as he sat down behind his desk.

"You're going to Italy!" he blurted out with his hands extended, palms up.

"Really?" I asked with my heart pushing at my ribs as I sat down in the chair.

"Yeah! That was great, he *really* liked you; I mean *really* liked you! He wanted me to tell you right away."

"How many people are going to Italy?" I asked, trying to process the new information that I was hearing from Paul.

"From this agency, you mean? Just one. You," he answered quickly.

"Are you kidding!? How is that possible? There's still a room full of models that he hasn't seen yet."

"I know, I know," Paul said. "Many of them have seen Calvin before and the others are just not right for the market right now. They're here to meet Calvin because they know he is in town; they're all hoping for the break that *you* just got. You're different, and right now *different* is what they want in Italy."

My head was buzzing so loudly that I had a hard time concentrating on what Paul was saying. I understood that I was going to Italy, but there had to be some catch to it; no one would just send me to Italy and pay for the flight. It sounded too good to be true. Slowly the words started to get through the buzzing in my head, and I could hear again.

"You are going to Italy next Friday!"

What? I thought as dozens of images and ideas raced through my head as I considered the possibility of leaving the country to work in Italy for two months. I wasn't ready; it was too soon, and most of all I was scared of the unknown and of flying all the way to Italy only to return a complete failure.

"That's really soon Paul," I stated flatly. "Do you think I'm ready?"

"Yeah, don't worry. Calvin will watch out for you," he said as if his *prized pig* had just won the blue ribbon at the local fair. Paul had the enthusiasm of a gambler who had bet on the long shot at the race track and won. I was turned down by everyone, including his bitchy receptionist with the long nails, but Paul had given me a chance. Calvin didn't seem to be full of shit, and he didn't seem like a man who liked to waste his time.

"Do you have any money saved up," Paul asked as a serious expression washed over his face.

I shifted uncomfortably in my seat as I thought how best to answer his question. I had no money at all, but I thought that being completely honest about this might be a mistake. "I have some money," I said vaguely.

"Do you have two thousand dollars?" he asked with the same serious expression. "Calvin's agency will pay for your flight to Milan, but you need to cover your living expenses until you get work. The minimum that we recommend you take with you is around two thousand dollars."

I resisted the urge to laugh out loud. It might as well have been two million dollars. Paul had no idea that I was living day to day and really had no way to make any significant amount of money in such a short time.

"I don't have that kind of money, Paul," I said quietly, with a feeling that this might be a deal breaker for the whole trip.

"That's okay," he said as he rubbed his face with the palm of his hand. "Do you have anyone that you can borrow money from; friends or family?"

"I don't think so. My mom has already told me to go back to school, and all of my friends in Connecticut have even less money than I do."

"Well," he said with a long pause as he exhaled loudly; "try to borrow some money from your family and your friends. I may be able to get you one or two modeling jobs that will help you get the money together. Don't worry about it; we'll figure this out," he said unconvincingly. "Come to the agency in the morning, and we'll come up with a plan."

"Okay, Paul," I said with as much enthusiasm as I

could muster. I left out the part that I could barely afford train fare to and from the city and that I spent most of my day dreaming about the food I couldn't afford to buy.

The conversation about money brought me down to a low-grade sadness with grays and blacks taking the place of color. I left the agency quietly and made it all the way back to Connecticut and into my room without speaking to anyone, the voices in my head getting progressively louder as the night fell like a velvet curtain from the sky, extinguishing the light with its thick, dark folds.

13

MAKING IT WORK

The next day was a blur; I don't remember if it was overcast or sunny, rainy or clear. I made my way to the agency and met with Paul in the open area where the bookers made their calls to book jobs. It was depressingly quiet with only two heavy-set female bookers slumped over their desks with their telephone receivers cradled between their solid shoulders and chins. Paul sat at his small *booker desk* wearing the same clothes that he had worn the day before. His hair looked unwashed, and he needed a shave. He seemed distracted and agitated. He motioned for me to come and sit with him.

He leaned towards me and whispered; "I have a modeling job that pays five hundred dollars, cash. It's not through the agency. "There will be some nudity," he said with a forced casualness. I immediately wondered what magazine would have nudity. Paul answered that question before I could ask; "*It's* for a gay men's magazine, an ad for condoms." I told Paul that I couldn't do a job like that. Paul sighed loudly and put his head into his hands to illustrate his disappointment in my decision.

A model wearing a tight shirt and too tight jeans overheard the offer Paul made to me. He blurted out, "She-it, I'll do that job for five hunner dollars!"

Paul shook his head dismissively and said, "I'll talk to you later, Kyle," as he motioned for Kyle to step away with a brushing motion of his right hand.

I shrugged my shoulders and held my hands with my palms facing up as I thought *are you freaking kidding me? My first job in a gay porn magazine? No fucking thanks. I would rather be homeless.*

Paul laughed, and said, "That's all I've got." He reminded me again that I needed to try to get some money before going to Milan.

"Did you ask your parents for money?" he asked as I got up to leave.

"Yes," I answered dully while looking out the window at the building across the street at two men in shirts and ties talking with each other while they leaned over a big conference table.

"Well?" he questioned.

"My mom said that it was a waste of time and that I should be in school," I said; knowing that what she had actually said was;

"No. We won't give you any money, period."

She was convinced that everything was a *bad* idea and she wouldn't support it, no matter how great the opportunity. I knew before I called what her answer would be. A big fat *no* with a side-order of unsolicited advice to go along with it. She went on to tell me that I was a disappointment and that Stokes was doing very well at Principia

College, and that if I didn't go back to college now, that I would *never* finish. I knew she was right. I knew my younger brothers looked up to me and that they would be tempted to drop out of school like I did, but I still wanted to take the chance. I saw no other way to get the money I needed to go to a good school, an east coast school. I really didn't know what the hell I was doing, but I didn't want to give up and believe the general consensus that I was a *delusional ass* thinking that I have what it takes to be a model.

"Keep on trying," he said as he turned back to his phone and shuffled some papers on his desk intently.

"I'm not even sure that they will let you get on the flight if you don't have at least a thousand dollars," he added casually, without looking up from his desk. "You leave next Friday on a charter flight with three other models from different agencies, Zoli, Ford, and Elite. Do your best to get the money together before then. You can call me next Tuesday to get all the information. Oh, and you need to get a passport as well."

My head was spinning with all the things that needed to be done before next Friday. I had no idea how to tell Barb that I was leaving and I needed to find out what to do with all the crap that I had at 82 Riverside that I couldn't take with me to Italy. I thought back to a conversation I had with a dark-haired model at Zoli about the need to go to Europe if you wanted to have a good book and be successful in the states. I secretly hoped that I would be the one model who *didn't* need to go to Europe, would be discovered in New York City, and have a lucrative career before returning to school at Yale or Harvard after buying myself a Porsche 911 SC Turbo with my earnings. I didn't think I would ever go to Italy and was really not interested in going, either. I thought of it as being forced to live in a foreign country without friends or family, cut off from the states, and two months was a *very* long time to me.

I called Barb when I got home and told her the news. She cried softly and said, "This is it; you're not going to stay with me; we're over!" with the pain in her voice pulsating from the receiver into my brain. I hadn't thought that I would be gone so long that it was a sure thing that our relationship would end; that we would both move on. In an instant, I changed from a boy who thought he had something into a man who knew he had nothing.

I started to sink into the familiar state of sadness without boundaries, an empty pit of despair and self-loathing as I thought more and more about how little I had on all levels. I went to church, but felt no more spiritual than when I was eleven years old. I had a job, but no money or transportation. I had a girlfriend with two kids and a wealthy father whom I had never met, and she was convinced that as soon as I stepped onto the plane to Milan that we were finished as a couple, maybe even as friends. I felt even lower hanging on the metal cover of the phone booth as I tried to shield the receiver from the rush of the late night winter wind. I remember mumbling I love you as I fell deeper and deeper into the well of self-pity that had opened up beneath me. I had masterfully turned a *once in a lifetime* opportunity into a time that was even darker than the days when I had no opportunity at all. I shook my head from side to side as I tried to clear the dark thoughts from my head. We exchanged goodbyes, and I walked back into the cold wind, my chapped hands jammed into my coat pockets and my shoulders hunched to keep out the icy fingers of winter. The night mirrored my soul perfectly.

Sofie and Lilly were friends. They were both high-end caterers. When I told Sofie that I needed money to travel to Italy, she graciously told me that I could work three parties in the kitchen washing dishes and that she would pay me twenty dollars an hour in cash. Each job started at nine in the morning and would end at about midnight.

Lilly had two more jobs on Monday and Tuesday night, from three until midnight. Lilly was from France and had never gotten her driver's license in the states, so she agreed to pay me twenty-five dollars per hour if I would drive the van with the food. I volunteered to run the commercial grade Hobart dishwasher all night for a wedding at a castle in New Canaan with three hundred people. I had stripped off my white dress shirt and tie and worked in my white t-shirt after the first course dishes came back onto the long stainless steel table to the right of the Hobart. At the end of the night, I had to load the van and take out all of the trash to a dumpster down the driveway from the castle. It was bitter cold outside, and the sweat froze on the hair at the back of my neck. The kitchen was warm and steamy, and I began to sneeze after the second garbage trip to the end of the long driveway. Sofie paid me cash for the weddings and I knew that she was paying me more than she paid the professional waiters who came in from New York City. They referred to themselves as *catering whores* and were as funny as they were professional. They had smart-assed comments about every guest each time they returned to the kitchen to refill their hors d'oeuvres trays. I smiled to myself as I heard their barbed comments, keeping my eyes focused on the constant stream of dishes that piled up without a break on the right side of the Hobart.

Sofie kept an eye on me and seemed to be surprised

that I had volunteered to do the worst job in the kitchen and not choose to serve the champagne and puff pastries on trays all night. I never told her that I could not face the wealthy wedding guests and serve them. I would rather do *anything* than weave my way through the sea of trust fund babies and beautiful women looking for a millionaire to fill their closets with designer clothes. I was rough around the edges and embarrassed by my lack of class and my mediocre education. In their minds I was invisible.

Lilly's parties were much easier than Sofie's. They were both art exhibits; one in New Canaan, the other in Darien. The setting was more intimate and Lilly was only handling the food, not the cleanup and flatware rental. Since the only available jobs were waiter and bartender, I reluctantly put on a black vest and black pants and served hors-d'oeuvres on a tray. The waiters, whom Lilly referred to as *her gays*, noticed that I completely sucked at serving and took pity on me. A tall, thin waiter with blond hair spiked straight up pulled me aside and gave me a few pointers on how to hold the tray, when to talk, and when to keep my mouth shut. I spent most of the night working on balancing my tray and the *keeping my mouth shut* part. It was an awkward experience, but the night went by quickly and everyone seemed happy when the last guest left for the night. I did some cleanup with Lilly and her assistant, then drove her back to Westport.

Lilly paid me in cash, the same as Sofie. I had one more job that I did on Sunday to get some extra money for the trip to Italy. I was tired and feeling run down, but I needed to get all the money that I could before next Friday. Sofie seemed to be more interested in my traveling to Italy than anyone else. She continued her tight-lipped expression as if she needed to work to keep her lips pulled tight across her straight white teeth. My mom and dad both thought that my news about traveling to Italy was a joke, a scam; as if I couldn't possibly have been chosen over anyone else to work in Italy. In my mom's mind, it was either a mistake or a scam; a way to get money from me by conning me into believing I had the chance to become a model. My parents were strange that way. I could always count on them to put me down, especially when I had some good news to tell them.

It had gotten so bad in high school that I tried to keep all news from them, both good and bad. The truth was that I didn't have that many good things to tell them in high school, anyway. In my mind, the comments from Mom and Dad about going to Italy seemed justifiable, and fifty percent of my mind thought that they were probably right; it probably was a joke. A joke on me.

14

THE LAST NIGHT

The hours and days disappeared until soon it was the night before my flight to Milan. It was cold and clear; the stars pricked white holes in the dark fabric of night. I wanted to go to sleep early and then see Barbara and her kids on Wednesday before I left at eleven that night.

The rotary phone rang a loud bell ring against the quiet of the night. I raced down the back stairs to answer it.

"Hello?" I answered on the second ring.

The line was quiet. I listened without breathing.

"Barb, Barb? ...is that you?" I asked with desperation pinching my throat, changing the way the words sounded to me.

I heard soft crying, but still no answer.

"Hi," she offered weakly, trying to hide her crying so that I couldn't hear it over the phone.

"Are you okay?" I questioned as images of what could be wrong flashed through my mind.

"I'm okay," she answered quietly "It's Mike." There was a long pause. "He came here tonight."

"He did?" I cried out, unable to control my anger or my voice.

"Yeah, I'm okay now, but he threatened me with a gun and tried to force me to have sex with him. I told him the children were asleep and that I would scream. He yelled at me for about ten minutes, called me a lot of names, took the keys to my car, and then left. I think he was high."

"Stay there; I will come and get you. I think I can borrow Sofie's car."

For some reason, Sofie didn't want me to borrow her car but said that she would drive when I explained the situation to her. She grabbed her keys and glasses after I woke her from a dead sleep and followed me out to her old, white Honda. Surprisingly, Sofie didn't ask me any questions about Barbara; she kept her eyes straight ahead and drove faster than the speed limit. She had a look of determination in her eyes as she leaned close to the windshield that was smeared with salt and mud from the road.

It wasn't clear to me if she was driving to get Barbara and her two children to help out, or if she was only doing it to help me. She was a hard read. I got the feeling that she saw something in me that she liked; that, and the fact that she was slightly crazy, too. We took 95 to exit 23 and then drove back to Barbara's house that was near the McDonalds on the Post Road, tucked away among tiny one bedroom houses with dented storm doors and no garages, leaving their cars parked bumper-to-bumper along the street tight to the concrete curb.

Barbara was dressed and at the front door with Jessica bundled up in a warm blanket. Sean was still sleeping as

I walked in quietly, lifted him over the edge of the crib, and covered him with a wool blanket that was folded on the small dresser that sat near the door. He looked up at me still half asleep and smiled; then his eyelids fell soft and heavy until they were closed again as he breathed slowly and steadily, back asleep. Barbara's face was white as chalk and her lips were drained of color, as she whispered,

"He could come back any minute, his friends live across the street, and they'll call him when they see us leaving together."

"It's okay Barb, we have time, and he doesn't even know where I live."

Barbara offered a weak, courageous smile as we both hunched over to protect the children from the cold and moved quickly and silently to the car that sat close to the curb with the engine and lights turned off. We bent down into her car and I arranged Sean gently in Barbara's arms in the back seat. She bowed her head towards Sofie and quietly whispered, "Thank you," while Sofie stared straight ahead with her lips set and her eyes wide open.

I sat in the passenger seat and turned back to check on Barbara, she had strapped Sean in and was holding Jessica in her arms.

"We can go," I said quietly to Sofie as she pulled away from the curb, turning on her lights after we got a few hundred feet away from Barbara's house.

We eased onto the Post Road and headed to the turnaround to get onto 95 and back to exit seventeen on the southbound side. I was sleepy and wanted to doze off for the fifteen-minute ride back to Westport, but I forced myself to stay awake. Suddenly the inside of Sofie's car lit up with someone flashing their brights from behind. I turned around and saw a car racing up from behind us, it stopped less than three feet from the back bumper and then swerved hard to the right and came up on the passenger side by driving on the shoulder. I looked over and saw a man with long hair and a dark, sparse mustache who was gesturing and screaming something at me through the closed window of his car. He rolled down his window and yelled,

"Pull over the fucking car you pussy!"

I looked at him and then back at Sofie, she was staring straight ahead and had a *death grip* on the steering wheel. Barbara said from the back of the car with a fear that changed the tone of her voice,

"That's Mike. Just ignore him."

I did my best to ignore his insults and kept looking straight ahead, kept breathing, and waited for this moment to pass. Suddenly he started swerving his car close to Sofie's as if he intended to hit our car. I rolled down the window as he screamed out with desperation and rage,

"Pull over you pussy. I will fucking kill you!" he screamed.

I looked closely at him with his slender forearms and his slim-fingered hands gripping the wheel so hard that his knuckles had turned white, his eyes looking crazy and loosely focused on me and Sofie's car.

"Pull over," I said quietly to Sofie, as the anger overflowed from my fast beating heart into my arms and chest. I was almost beyond control as the anger swept over me like a flash fire over a dried field.

"No," she said without taking her eyes off the road; refusing to look at me or Mike.

"Sofie, we need to do this, he will follow us all the way back to our house."

"No," she said again with more force this time, "this is my car."

She was frightened but determined. Mike continued to scream at me, and I started to yell back with a mocking tone in my voice, which only got him angrier causing him to approach that state that comes at the end of anger when all a person can do is scream and cry out of frustration. Mike was close to that point, and I knew that he was finished even before he really got started. We ended up losing him at the tollbooth between exits eighteen and seventeen. He didn't have the thirty-five cents to get through the tollbooth. I never saw Mike again.

Barbara, Sean, Jessica, and I all stayed in my *closet* of a room. I spent most of the night standing in the open space of the floor shifting from foot to foot, rocking Sean in my arms as he fell into short, fitful moments of sleep. I was sitting on the edge of the bed still holding Sean when the sunlight shone into the parking lot of the Catholic school across the street, while Jessica slept peacefully on my bed next to Barbara. I took a mental picture of the softly lit scene, knowing that it would never be like this again.

15

ACROSS THE POND

I arrived at the JFK airport three hours before my flight left for Milan. I had two laundry bags that I bought in the Bowery for a dollar each from a street vendor with sad, watery eyes. One of the bags was purple, the other red with white drawstrings to pull the top closed. My blue LL Bean backpack was stuffed with books, clothes, and a shaving kit. I dragged a cheap plastic suit bag as I lifted the heavy laundry bags up to the counter. All of my clothes were from a second-hand store in Palatine or the Goodwill in Westport. I should have left half of the crap in my bags at home or thrown it in the garbage, but I had this weird feeling that I might need a stupid heavy wool double-breasted suit that didn't actually fit. I guess I'm some kind of low-grade hoarder.

I lifted my bags onto the space on the side of the ticket counter and pulled out my ticket from the front pocket of my backpack. A middle-aged woman with hair dyed from gray to brown at the counter told me that the bags could not be *guaranteed* because they were not actually luggage and she asked me to tie a tag with my address on each bag. Then she kicked them onto the conveyor belt behind her with her foot.

I walked away from the ticket counter, down the long hallway, through the security checkpoint to gate twenty-three. I was wearing a pair of too-tight jeans with two cycling award patches above the right knee to hold the pants together, an acrylic white winter sweater with blue snowflakes, and a green baseball jacket from the army navy store. I had cheap white sneakers and carried a blue handkerchief in my back pocket to blow my nose every ten minutes or so. I knew I looked like a kid, a loser, but I also knew that I had no choice; nothing else that I owned would look any better. I checked my black wallet with my traveler's checks and counted: $450.00 in traveler's checks and twenty dollars in cash; more than a little short of the two thousand dollars that Paul had recommended. I watched the business travelers look at me out of the corners of their eyes; pretending not to watch me as they stared. They seemed to be trying to figure out what I was doing on an international flight. I was wondering the same thing.

I knew there were other models on the plane, so I scanned the faces of the passengers in the waiting area to see if I could pick them out of the crowd. I located one guy that looked like a model. His dark brown hair was cut short on the sides and back and was long in the front. He was wearing jeans and a loose sweater with a knit cotton scarf looped and tied loosely around his neck; more for style than for warmth. He had a long face, near perfect white teeth and nice luggage that matched. I wanted to ask him if he was going to Italy but decided to stay put with my luggage and book and wait for the plane to board instead.

I was caught off guard by the load boarding announcement. I had fallen asleep in the waiting area and was jolted awake by someone's luggage bumping into my leg. I was disoriented and stumbled over to the gate and fumbled for my boarding pass. The nozzles that blew fresh air were on high as I located my aisle seat in the middle of the plane. A large, sweat-covered man took ownership of our mutual armrest with his beefy forearm. I looked at his arm and then stuffed my bag beneath the seat. He stared at me as I sat down and moved his sweaty arm back and forth on the armrest, making sure that I knew the armrest belonged to him. I met his *pig-like* gaze and shook my head from side to side slightly, making sure that he got the message that I had noticed and was not impressed. I silently cursed my bad fortune in sitting next to Jabba the Hutt and not Princess Leia. I closed my eyes and tried to do my best imitation of sleep; I fell asleep before the plane took off from the runway.

I was jarred awake by the violent up and down motion of the plane. Jabba had turned as white as typing paper and was gripping the armrest with his fat hands so hard that his fingers had turned white and red. I quickly looked around at the mostly panicked faces and saw that each stewardess had strapped herself into her *jump seat* with the four-point racecar harnesses that were attached to their seats. They stared stoically ahead, their backs ram-rod straight. The plane was jumping really hard with the turbulence slapping up and down at the wings like a child hitting an airplane mobile. I tried to think of a prayer that would help me feel better as the plane continued to jolt me into temporary weightlessness and then back down hard onto my seat, wanting to convince God to let our plane make it to the airport.

My fear left me as quickly as it had started after I resigned myself to the fact that there was nothing that I could do to stop us from crashing into the dark water of the sea. If it were going to happen, it would. For some reason, I found it reassuring that I had no control. I started to relax, closed my eyes, and fell asleep again, waking every ten minutes or so. The violent gusts pushed us around the sky for over an hour, as the storm tried to rip the wings off the plane. It was a nightmare that I was determined to sleep through.

Then suddenly, everything was calm, and the airplane was quiet, except for the steady thrush of the jet engines and the shooshing sound of the fresh air nozzles on full blast. I glanced over at Jabba who was covered with a cold, clammy sweat that covered every inch of his sickly-pale, gray face. He had demurely placed both of his arms onto his lap as he looked at me sheepishly. Jabba seemed genuinely changed and offered a weak smile towards me as a silent *mea-culpa* for hogging the armrest earlier in the flight. I simply nodded my head and sleepily turned my back towards the aisle. I had a dry mouth, and drool was running down the corner of my mouth from my sleep. I had missed the meal and had to take a leak, badly. I got up stiffly as my right leg cracked loud enough that an old man with no hair looked up at me with a weirdly familiar smile. I shook off his stare and made my way to the bathroom at the back of the plane. Everything seemed to be going better than I had expected, we were all alive, and I now had full use of our mutual armrest.

I relieved myself as the airplane shifted below my feet

and flushed the miniature steel toilet. I turned to wash my hands in the warm trickle of water from the mini-sink in front of the shiny mirror and glanced at my reflection in the dim light and was taken aback by how my face looked, my green eyes seemed to almost glow in the half-light of the tiny bathroom and my face looked like it was sculpted from dark stone instead of flesh. I shook my head quickly from side to side as if to wake myself up from my dreamlike fixation on my own face. As I unlocked the bathroom door, I noticed a dark-haired woman waiting in the narrow aisle for the bathroom. When I looked up at her, I found she was staring at my eyes with a strange half-smile. I tilted my head to the right, puzzled, and walked back to my seat. I attempted to ignore her stares for the rest of the flight.

Our 747 wobbled in for a three bump landing as the passengers let out a collective sigh of relief when the captain reversed the jet engines and angled the flaps as high as they would go to slow the behemoth down as fast as possible. When the plane stopped near the terminal, everyone jumped up in unison, as if their seats had suddenly become electrified. I got up slowly and then sat back down in my seat after letting Jabba move into the aisle to join the throng of people anxious to get the fuck off the plane. The stewardess made a crackly and inscrutable announcement about how to connect to the flight to Milan; all I understood was the word *Milano*. After the plane emptied, I asked the stewardess with the CB style microphone about the connecting flight to Milan, and she told me that the flight didn't leave for three hours and that the baggage would not be re-routed to that flight. Translation: I had to pick up my luggage myself and check it into the flight that would take me to Milan.

I couldn't understand the voices booming out on the public address system speakers in the airport as I walked towards the baggage claim, following the pictures of a stick man reaching for his luggage that rested on an angled line.

I followed the baggage claim signs down the main corridor of the airport and onto the down escalators, trying to look for clues as to what country I was in while walking. An overhead sign with large white letters on a blue background read *Brussels*. I realized we had landed in Belgium—why? No fucking clue–I guess it made sense to the person who set the flight schedule. I grabbed my two beautiful laundry bags and the plastic suit bag, which now had a tear on the bottom corner, and struggled up the concrete steps to the main level of the airport and over to the Air France counter. The laundry bags had no handles, so I carried them by wrapping the nylon drawstrings around my hands, and half lifted and dragged them up the stairs. By the time I made it to the counter, I was considering leaving one laundry bag and the suit bag behind to lighten my load; the two bags were heavy, and they cut off the circulation to my hands enough to turn them both a deep reddish-purple.

The lines were empty at the Air France ticket counters except for three men of equal height, age, and dress. I knew they were models and they looked at me with at least partial certainty that I was the fourth model. They were standing in the middle of the large area in front of the ticket counters talking and laughing. I attempted a wave at the group, and one of them walked over to me. He was about my height and had blue-black hair combed to the side, held in place by some sort of shiny gel which gave him an *old-time movie star* look. He was wearing khaki pants, topsiders without socks and a crisp white button-down shirt under a well-tailored tweed blazer.

He extended his right hand while smiling from ear to ear and said,

"Hi, my name is Rick. You must be the other model going to Milan, right?"

"Yes, yes I am," I said as politely as I could. "I'm Daryl. It's really nice to meet you," I continued as I extended my right hand and shook his hand with a firm grip that matched his.

Before we finished shaking hands, I had forgotten his name.

I checked my luggage and walked back over to the trio with my blue backpack secured over both shoulders. All three had dark hair and dark eyes, except for the model that I had seen before we left New York. His eyes were your standard issue blue. They all had real luggage and were well dressed; I stood out as a contrast to their appearance and their coordinated ensembles. I thought to myself that I would never be fashionable. In a way, I wanted to be fashionable, but it seemed both out of my reach financially and I did not have the build to pull it off. My shoulders were too square and too broad, my legs were bowed and on the short side, and I had a long body with a small waist and thick arms that tended to bunch up the sleeves of any suit I wore. I was also very uncomfortable wearing anything that would be considered *nice*, preferring jeans and a white t-shirt to anything fashionable. The wheels of doubt started to turn in my head with the chorus of *what the hell are you thinking* playing loudly within my packed skull.

I listened while nodding to each one of them as they took turns telling the group who they were and how successful they had been in the past and how successful they were going to be in the future. I did not have the same dream, and my story sucked, so I kept my mouth shut and my crappy portfolio in my backpack, knowing that I could not compete with their photos and their stories. Rick had done a shooting for GQ with Bruce Weber. It was a bunch of guys on a baseball field, laughing, getting dirty, pretending to throw the ball around with their shirts soaked with water. He showed me a portrait with ten other guys that he was in. The picture was very small, but it was taken by Bruce, so it was one of his best pictures. It was now official; I had no fucking idea of what I was getting into. I felt like I was far from home in a place where I should never have gone. I waited while the three models boarded the plane ahead of me and followed at a distance. They stowed their luggage and sat down. I slumped down into my seat and waited for the plane to take me to another country that I knew nothing about.

When the plane landed a few hours later, I looked out the small window with the thick glass to a dark sky with the faint lights of the one-story airport buildings with a lone control tower at the end illuminating the low clouds. The airport was smaller than I had expected and I searched the scene outside my tiny window for clues to how Milan would treat me for the next two months. Everything was simpler than had I thought it would be as if I had landed in a time two decades earlier than 1982. Brock tapped me on the shoulder and asked, "You coming?" while flashing his Pepsodent smile.

I looked up and answered, "Yeh, sure. Where are we going?"

"Into Milano. The agency will be open soon, and we can take a taxi there after we go through customs."

I followed the trio to an empty baggage claim area and grabbed my luggage from the squeaking conveyor belt. The bags were too heavy to sling over my shoulder, so I had to drag-lift them over to stand in the long line that wound its way to a series of glass-walled booths where the customs agents sat. Brock and Rick pretended not to notice that my luggage was actually two cheap polyester laundry bags, but Hank could not hide his contorted facial expression of contempt. I knew that as far as Hank was concerned, I had no business being in Milan, let alone attempting to become a model. I had to agree with him, his perception of me seemed to be a very safe bet.

We grabbed our bags and waded through the long customs line together. Hank told me to tell the customs official that I was in Italy on vacation and that I was a student. Up until that moment, I didn't realize that it was illegal for us to be working in Italy; I had assumed that Calvin and the agency would take care of the required paperwork. It hadn't occurred to me that I'd need to lie to get into the country. I pretended that Hank's suggestion didn't surprise me and gave him a look and a silent nod to make it clear that I understood while hoping that the customs official would not ask the questions that would require that I lie to the first person I would speak to in Italy.

The customs official took my passport and flipped it open to the first page with an efficient flair. He was a young man with dark hair, he looked up at me through the glass and then back down at the small photo in the passport with the insignia stamped in the corner. He said something in Italian to the other customs agent to his left and then slid the passport back to me through the opening in the glass and motioned with his hand for me to move along. I nodded and said, "Thank you," to the top of his head as he looked down and wrote on his little ledger with the tightly spaced lines.

I searched for Hank, Rick, and Brock in the crowd of people who had made it through customs. They were not there, and I decided to follow the group of people who were on my flight to the *ground transportation*. I walked through the turnstile and down a well-lit flight of stairs into an open area with doors that led out to the gray concrete road outside of the glass doors.

Rick sauntered over to me with a wide smile plastered on his face.

"Is this where we catch a taxi?" he asked me.

"I think so," I answered while holding back the urge to say, *no, this is where we line up for the pony rides; didn't you get a ticket?*

"Cool, great to be in Italia isn't it?"

I hadn't really thought much about it. I had just arrived in a place that I knew nothing about and had no idea where to go or what to do, and how long I was going to be here. The voices on the intercom all spoke Italian, and the people who walked by us stared and pointed while talking quickly to each other in what was either Italian or a very strange kind of Spanish.

They seemed to be making fun of us, curious about what four big Americans were doing at the airport on a Thursday morning more than anything else. I didn't see anyone over five feet six inches tall and felt taller than I had felt when in the United States. There didn't seem to be many Americans at the airport.

Brock looked up from his book and gave me a surveying glance. We were the closest in age; he told us that he was 22. I couldn't help but think that he looked much younger than I did. I had always been told that I looked older than my older brother Stokes, and I had been able to get into bars at the small Midwestern town of Monmouth without being carded when I was seventeen.

There was a sharpness to my face and a hardness in my eyes that seemed to come from age and experience. I had been told that there was nothing *cute* about the way I looked and that I wasn't exactly handsome either. When I asked a senior in my fraternity why people that I had never met at the small college did not like me, he said it had something to do with the set of my jaw. He told me that my jaw said *fuck you, go ahead and hit me*. I knew what he meant and got a sick feeling in my stomach when he said this. Having seen pictures of myself from the side, I knew that my jaw was set so far forward that I barely avoided the underbite that always seemed to make a person look stupid and stubborn. Early in life, I had figured out that looking tough causes you to get more shit than looking like a wimp, as if everyone is offended by your face and wants to make a point of proving that they are not intimidated by you. I had tried being low profile for a few weeks to avoid getting shit from the guys at Theta Chi, but had no success. When I had told my roommate, Mark, about my plan to be low profile he had laughed out loud saying;

"You can *never* be low profile!" He continued loudly, "Everyone notices you no matter what you do."

"Can't I just fly under the radar and be left alone?" I asked, knowing that he was right and finally understanding that I would never be normal, average, or invisible.

"Are you freaking kidding me?! Most guys would kill to have what you have. Sorry, my friend, you're going to have to put up with this jealousy shit for the rest of your life. Unless you get a new face, that is."

"Why don't you have a problem with me, Mark?" I asked.

"Because I'm a loser and I get to be part of something because I'm your roommate. Do you think Sig Ep would have pledged me if I weren't your roommate? I know they weren't going to pledge me until you talked to Vince. They want you because you will bring the girls to the keg parties, and Theta Chi hates you for the same reason. You've gotta take the good with the bad, my friend."

For a 6' 3" windbag who was pulling a solid D average, Mark could be a pretty smart SOB sometimes. I knew he had a point, but I wished that it were different. If you added up my sharp face, my broad shoulders, and my compulsive habit of slicing people up verbally like a butcher slices meat, then you had a recipe for a guy that people love to hate. If anyone were able to get through those three things, they might find out that I am not as bad as I seem. At nineteen, I had come to realize that I was never going to win any popularity contests, ever.

I lugged my purple and red laundry bags and plastic suit bag outside to the taxi stand. It was warm and humid outside, so I took off my army surplus baseball jacket and tried to stuff it into my already full LL Bean backpack. Brock did the same, but Rick and Hank kept their tailored sport coats on. Brock was wearing a light blue, v-neck t-shirt, the style that I wouldn't be caught dead in. He had strong arms and a long swimmer's build. He looked to be about my weight but seemed to be more solid in the chest and legs.

His hair was dark, on the long side, and combed back away from his face. His skin was smooth, and his eyes were sky blue. I could not imagine getting any modeling jobs if Brock were my competition.

Brock, Rick, and I climbed into the back of the taxi while Hank got into the front. He gave the address of the modeling agency to the driver. He looked in his rear view mirror at us sitting in the back seat. The dark-haired, bearded, taxi driver flipped a lever on his meter and pulled away from the curb directly into fast-moving traffic. I rolled my window down and tried to enjoy the scenery.

Within twenty minutes we pulled in front of a three-story brownstone with a restaurant at the street level.

Hank paid the driver, and we walked through the open glass doors to the small cage that was the elevator. After a quick ride to the second floor, we entered the wide open room that was the agency.

A small woman with a tan face and dark hair quickly got up from her desk and greeted us enthusiastically; "Ciao, Ciao bello, welcome! Come in, come in," she said while gesturing for us to come forward with both hands.

"I am Kristina, and over here is Pepea," she said, indicating an even smaller woman with a blunt pixie cut and small black-rimmed glasses who waved from her desk while continuing to talk on the phone without looking up.

Kristina had a very strong accent and a bright smile. "I will be your booker," she announced enthusiastically, "Welcome to Milano!"

"Thank you," I said while looking for a place to put my luggage that wouldn't be in the way.

"You want to go to your pensione? Yes, I am sure that you do. You would like to unpack and make a shower, no? Si, si. I will get a taxi to take you to your pensione right away."

That sounded good to me, I was tired, my teeth felt like they were covered with moldy sandpaper, and I wanted to lie down and take a nap. I hadn't slept very much on the two flights from New York and had not slept at all the night before I left. I was far beyond tired.

Rick and I were soon met at the curb by a taxi that took us to our pensione. Looking out the window, I saw old-fashioned trolley cars rolling by on tracks with power wires running above in all directions. People stood inside, holding onto bars at eye level to keep from falling down. The trolleys looked like train cars without engines, boxes on wheels with glass doors and windows and colorful, painted tops that reminded me of the circus train cars that I had seen in children's books. They seemed to go too fast and to change direction too quickly. I silently wondered if they ever jumped the tracks that seemed to crisscross everywhere on the busy streets. Drifting off to sleep while thinking of the trolley cars I woke to Rick's shaking me and saying,

"Dude. Dude. Wake up...dude."

I stumbled out of the taxi and dragged my bags out of the trunk. Rick looked wide awake and happy. How did he do it? Hadn't he just taken the same, never-ending flight that I had? I was so tired that I didn't even want to think about it anymore.

"This is the place. I wonder if Mama Leoni lives here," he said, more as a lame joke than as a question.

"Uh-huh," I answered as I tried to blink myself awake.

We walked up two flights of narrow stairs and knocked on the door with the number twelve on it. Rick knocked with a rap-a-tap-tap pattern and looked over at me with a smile and said, "This is cool, isn't it?"

I had no idea where Rick was coming from and couldn't understand his over-the-top positive mental attitude. He didn't seem to be on drugs, so it must have come naturally. Man, were Rick and I nothing alike!

A round woman with an old-fashioned dress, wire-rimmed glasses, and steel gray hair held tight in a bun opened the door and said, "Come, come," as she turned to walk down a narrow hallway that was on the other side of the door.

Rick looked over at me again with a big smile as we walked through the door. The woman opened a door on the left side of the hallway and said, "This you room," as she nodded her head gravely up and down.

Rick said, "Thank you, this is great," and tried to shake her hand, but she gave him a look that seemed to indicate that she had no idea what he had just said. I pushed past Rick and stuck my bags in a corner by the big windows, took my smelly sneakers and socks off, and flopped face down on the bed. The covers were cotton, and they smelled fresh and washed. Pat must have come into the room and closed the door behind him.

"Do you want to take a walk and look around?" he asked, with way too much enthusiasm.

"No," I said, my voice muffled by the soft down pillow.

Whatever else Rick might have said, I didn't hear. I fell asleep almost instantly.

For the next twenty hours, I drifted in and out of sleep. Each time I opened my eyes to the still bright light of the old-fashioned ceiling fixture, I would observe a different scene.

The first time I awoke in a fog and saw Rick sitting at the corner desk with his legs crossed at the knee and leaning over a book that looked like the Bible. He was wearing only his blue dress socks and briefs, looking intently at the words he was silently reading. I rolled towards the outside wall, turning away from the light, and fell into a dreamless sleep while clutching at the soft pillow.

After what seemed like many hours of sleep, I awoke again to see Rick looking into the mirror on the wall and applying pink blobs of something on his face with what looked to be a Q-tip with a clear plastic handle.

"What are you doing?" I asked, without much real interest.

"Zapping my spots, dude."

"What spots?" I asked, straining to see his face in the dim light.

"My zits man. Gotta zap 'em."

"Okay. Got it," I mumbled before rolling over to my side to go back to sleep. I wondered why I felt like crap and did not have any desire to move or speak or even open my eyes. Sleep came over me quickly like a dark, thick blanket, smothering the light and life out of my mind, leaving behind only silence.

The last time I awoke, I felt much better, and hungry. Rick was on the hard tiled floor in the middle of the room doing push-ups in his underwear. I sat up on the bed and dully watched him crank out some loose backed push-ups with a forceful explosion of air on each trip up. I thought that he was either extremely weird or very confident. Either way, I couldn't see myself doing push-ups in my underwear in a hotel room in front of a guy that I had just met.

"How many reps are you doing?" I said, pretending that I cared; regretting the question before the words were out of my mouth.

"Five...sets...of...fifty," he breathlessly replied between pushups.

"Oh," I said stupidly without interest. I was even less interested than I thought was possible.

He stopped doing push-ups and turned towards the mirror to check himself out. He must have felt he looked pretty damn good, because he stayed in front of the mirror for about five minutes, checking himself out from all angles. He probably would have spent another five minutes looking at his ass if he had eyes in the back of his head.

He finally had enough of his reflection and turned towards me and asked, "What do you do for those forearms, my man?" while pointing at my arms.

"Nothing. Why?" I asked, completely confused by his question.

"Well, you look like Spartacus, that's all. Kirk Douglas had some forearms, kinda like you," he said while admiring his own biceps, alternating flexing first the right one and then the left. I was waiting for him to kiss his biceps, but he stopped and pulled a too-tight white t-shirt over his head.

I had never heard anything about my forearms. I turned my hand's palms facing up and looked at my forearms. I guessed they didn't look too bad.

"Can we turn off the lights?" I asked, "I want to sleep for a few days."

"Yeah, sure," Rick replied with a laugh. "I'm going to take a shower and then hit the sack."

"Have fun," I said as I rolled over one more time to go down and away into that quiet land of nothing.

I woke up to a room filled with harsh, dusty sunlight that filtered through and around the heavy drapes that covered the windows. There was honking and engines revving; noise from the street below. I pushed back the drapes and looked out the windows that were as big as doors to the street. I saw cars, mopeds, and pedestrians bustling just below our second story window. Pat was already dressed and had his hair combed and his backpack sitting neatly on the bed.

"What time is it?" I asked, rubbing my eyes with the backs of my hands. I felt worse than when I fell asleep the night before.

"It's seven-thirty in the morning, bro. Don't you have to go to the agency this morning?" he asked, with more cheer than I was ready to handle.

"Yeah, yeah, I am supposed to go to the agency," I said, as I tried to wipe my face awake with my right hand.

"You'd better hurry. I'm leaving in about ten minutes if you wanna share a cab."

"Okay," I replied while scrambling to unpack my shaving kit and a towel and walking out the door to the bathroom that was across the hall. Thirteen minutes later we were standing by the side of the cobblestone road, hailing a cab.

16

ITALY IN SPRING

Thirty minutes later we arrived at the agency, Kristina was waiting for me at the entrance to the open room that housed the bookers. "Bello, you need to go to this address now. Joseph is going to the same job; you go with him," she said to me with a sense of urgency, grabbing me by my arm and pushing me back towards the elevators before I could even reply.

A model who was shorter than I with black hair and a beautiful brown leather backpack motioned for me to follow him as if he were a guide on an African Safari, a stoic look of determination on his face. He walked past the elevator and taking the wide marble stairs two at a time, had gained thirty feet on me by the time we reached the street level. He turned right and took off at a quick jog as I struggled to keep up, silently hoping that whatever form of transportation we were using was no more than a block away.

At the corner, Joseph stopped and looked to the left and right and motioned that this was the spot by pointing to the ground. Within minutes a loud, clanging trolley arrived close to where Joseph was standing and came to a screeching stop as the metal brakes pressed hard against the metal train-style wheels.

"Do you have a token?" he asked without looking at me.

"No," I replied defensively, wondering how I would have known to get a token when I arrived yesterday.

"I'll loan you one, but you need to pay me back as soon as we get back to the agency."

"Sure," I replied. Thanks, *money bags* I thought to myself as I looked out one of the low windows onto the busy street.

We stood in the center aisle of the trolley between men and women a head shorter who smelled of sausage, cheese, and stale red wine mixed with a healthy dose of BO. I grabbed onto the smooth chrome bar that ran from front to back while Joseph expertly balanced himself without grabbing the bar. The ride seemed to go on forever. Looking over at Joseph who was busy calmly reading from a paperback book that he held in his right hand, I got the feeling that Joseph did not want to talk to me.

Joseph and I were the last ones off the trolley. The landscape looked like the end of the world, abandoned buildings, fields of weeds littered with huge chunks of broken concrete, rusting iron fences and beams, and trucks and cars without wheels littering the landscape.

"Are you sure we're in the right place?" I asked Joseph as I looked around.

"Yep," Joseph said confidently as he looked down the abandoned looking street, "We just need to find number 1527."

I didn't see any buildings that appeared occupied. They all looked like factory structures with few windows that were unbroken, or were not painted with graffiti. I looked for numbers to let us know how far we had to walk on the burned outstretch of broken and desolate pavement.

After walking for thirty minutes, we came upon a building that looked like an old airplane hanger with the curved roof of a Quonset hut. In the parking lot were two dozen young Americans who looked like models. Joseph walked towards the group of models and began talking to them while handing out high fives and putting his backpack on the ground. He pretended that he didn't know me.

Some of the guys were playing football with their shirts off. It looked as if they thought they were playing in the *Super Bowl*, very seriously, while in reality, no one was paying attention to them. A few of the girls and guys were trying to take advantage of the late morning sun and had taken off their shirts to catch some rays. The girls were stripped down to bikini style bras and rolled up tight denim shorts. The guys were shirtless and wore tight Jordache or Calvin Klein jeans.

I stood and watched the football game, thinking about joining in, before sitting on the concrete curb, feeling comfortably invisible for the moment; separate from the crowd, but close enough to see and hear what was going on.

A short, stocky model with a red bandana on his head and too-tight denim shorts with no shirt walked over and stopped a foot from me and stared closely at my face as if I were on exhibit at the zoo. So much for being invisible, I thought.

"What makes you think you can be a model?" He said quickly. "Forget that question. Why do you want to become a model?" he blurted out in one quick burst of speech while moving even closer as he continued his hard, inquisitive stare.

"To make some money, I guess. And to meet Brooke Shields," I offered tentatively as I stood up. I was looking down at him, silently wondering how he could be a model if I was considered too short by every Agency except one, and short-stack was at least three inches shorter than I. He had long slim arms, a barrel chest covered with sweaty hair, and what could only be described as chicken legs coming out of his hot pants.

"Oh really?" he answered, with a mock look of surprise and indignation while putting his hands on his hips and puffing out his chest. "Well, I *know* Brooke Shields," he said, as if this were truly the most interesting news in the world, "I was in her last movie...you know, Endless Love."

I had seen Endless Love with Lisa Smith less than six months ago and had even bought the soundtrack because I loved the title track with Lionel Richie and Diana Ross, but I did not remember seeing anyone that looked like short-stack in the movie.

"Really?" I asked, unable to conceal my blatant skepticism.

"Yep, that's right," he said, "I was her boyfriend's best friend in high school."

I couldn't wipe the expression of doubt off my face; my expression did more to call him a liar than if I had screamed liar at the top of my lungs. I never could let bullshit slide or pretend that I didn't know something that I damn well did know. It had been that way since early childhood; I had no ability to pretend and hide the way I really felt about something or someone. This was a character flaw that I was sure would be with me for the rest of my life.

Whenever I heard a bullshit story, an expression of *you are completely full of shit* would be etched across my sharp-boned face, especially around my eyes. Needless to say, this quality was not good for making friends.

"My name is Daryl," I offered, as I tried to force my face to adopt a look of pleasant neutrality while attempting to steer the conversation away from Captain Tight-shorts and his amazing movie credentials.

"What? You can't remember the scene at the school, by the lockers in the hallway? I was a jock. Seriously! You can't remember that part?! My name is Patrick, by the way. I'm just modeling until my next movie starts filming in May."

I sighed under my breath...clearly I had no luck in changing the topic of conversation.

I shook his hand and thought to myself; he's gotta be fucking kidding. I couldn't see him as a model or as an actor. Maybe he was thinking the same thing about me. I admit; I really didn't look anything like the other shirtless models running around and sweating while they played football in the parking lot. They looked like men acting like boys; dark hair, heavy beards, and chests covered with hair.

I was stuck between teenager and man; no chest hair, a few new whiskers on my chin and above my lip. I was beginning to think that my age might be more of a problem than I had anticipated. Maybe I should have listened to Jan or Joey from Ford.

"Nice to meet you," I said without hesitation.

"Yeah, you too," He said without looking me in the

eyes. I had clearly annoyed him with my weak memory of the supporting cast members of recent hit movies.

"How long ya been in Italy?" he asked while looking over my left shoulder at a petite blond who was wearing only a brown bra, overflowing with breasts like a root-beer float with too much vanilla ice cream, and very tight cutoff shorts that highlighted her tan, round thighs.

"This is my second day," I offered, as Patrick ignored my response and walked around me, heading straight for the blond; no doubt to ask her if she remembered his pivotal co-starring role in Endless Love.

I stood for a moment, then began to read *Catcher in the Rye* where I left off. I sat back down on the curb, hoping to become invisible again.

Within minutes a dark-haired man opened the side door of the building and stepped into the light. He was holding a white bullhorn in his right hand and called out, "Okay, every-a-body come into the studio, a-please."

The sweaty football players swaggered over to their backpacks, picked up discarded t-shirts, pulled them over their heads and rolled them down over their bodies, then ran their fingers through their hair or reached for plastic hairbrushes and quickly brushed their hair back into place. They shook their heads as if it made a difference in the final result. Most of the girls checked their makeup in oversized compact mirrors and added the finishing touches before running combs or brushes through their hair.

I shoved my book into my backpack and walked over to take my place in the line filing into the large warehouse. The inside was clean and bright. It had a large white painted floor with a white concrete curve that went up almost twenty feet towards the warehouse ceiling, looking like one side of a skateboard ramp.

The man with the bullhorn pushed a button, making a loud, annoying sound, then said in a strong Italian accent, "Listen up people. We need you to find some clothes and get dressed. The dressers are here to help you get dressed."

I followed the male models over to long racks with brightly colored shirts, pants, and sweaters. A short, wide, middle-aged woman with a grim expression on her face, waved for me to come over to her, saying, "come-a, come-a," while looking at me with a combination of annoyance and urgency. When I walked over, she immediately began taking off my shoes and then unbuttoned and pulled down my jeans. I tried to act as if this wasn't anything new to me. She grabbed at my t-shirt the way a mother grabs at her toddler's t-shirt when she is stripping him down for a bath, but when she got the t-shirt up to my chest, she stopped abruptly, unable to reach any higher. I noticed that she was struggling, so I pulled the t-shirt over my head and dropped it where she had put my jeans. I stood in front of my middle-aged dresser with only a pair of mostly white Hanes briefs.

She gave me a sideways look that I couldn't quite place, her lips pursed together and her eyes furrowed in concentration, as she tried to look at me without directly looking at me. I stood in front of her with my hands at my sides, self-conscious and unsure of what the next move was. After getting another long sideways look from her, she turned back to the rack and pulled off a pair of red jeans and a bright yellow sweatshirt. She handed me the sweatshirt with the same pursed lip expression and motioned with her right hand for me to put it on. She then held the jeans out with her hands and indicated that I was to put them on while she held them, one leg at a time. I was pretty sure I could have handled the pants on my own. The pants were tight in the butt and crotch and tapered down to a very narrow opening at the ankle. She pulled the snaps together and buttoned the waist and then zipped up my fly. I definitely could have done a better job at that part. When the pants were on she brushed downward on my hips and then butt with her stubby-fingered hands, as if she were smoothing out wrinkles in a young girl's dress. She then smiled a joyless smile before saying; "Okay. Ready. You-a go," pointing over to the white skateboard ramp with animated gestures using both hands.

While walking over to join up with the other models wearing equally bright and tight clothes, I started to count the number of models but lost my place when I reached thirty-seven. I guessed that there were at least fifty models in the warehouse, maybe sixty.

Bullhorn dude started talking to us with the horn on full blast. He introduced the director, Carlos, before giving us instructions. Carlos stood at the edge of the white painted floor next to what looked like a lifeguard's chair on wheels. At the top of the rig was a slim, gray-haired man sitting behind a very big camera with the wires coming down the back of the attached ladder. We were told to line up in rows of ten. That seemed pretty simple, but twenty of the models argued about who would be in the front line. *Bullhorn guy* stepped in and chose ten models to stand in the front row boy-girl-boy-girl, sending the remainder to fit into the other five rows. Eighty percent of the models tried, again, to get into the front row, which was the row closest to the guy with the camera. I got stuck in the middle between two girls that wouldn't even look at me. They were too busy concentrating on the task at hand to notice me. I was nervous but relieved that I was in the middle of the group, knowing that I would not be noticed in the commercial. There seemed to be no real pressure, so I relaxed and waited for them to tell us what to do.

For the next three hours we took two steps forward and then attempted to jump up with our hands in the air at the same time with big smiles on our faces. I'm pretty sure that I was smiling and laughing at the same time. The models closest to me refused to speak or smile between bullhorn guy's countdown, "three, two, one, a-jump!" he would say loud and slow.

He repeated this every thirty seconds or so. After three hours he told us that we were finished and that there was food for us on tables at the far side of the warehouse. I asked around while we were eating if there was anything else that we needed to do, and a very blonde male model with ultra-white teeth shook his head and said,

"No dude, I think we're done for today."

I nodded and smiled before turning to the buffet to make myself a sandwich. After piling pieces of tough, red meat on a big roll and adding some kind of cheese, I spooned on spicy brown mustard and closed up the sandwich, smushing it into the table with the palm of my right hand. There were tiny bottles of red wine and big, green glass bottles with screw tops filled with a carbonated drink with a flavor similar to Sprite soda. I poured some of the room temperature drink into a clear plastic cup and sat on one of the metal folding chairs that had been set up close to the windowless wall. I listened to the other models talk excitedly about the commercial while I chewed on my tough sandwich.

A group of male and female models talked about the job and then started to talk about jobs they were up for. One had a chance at a Versace campaign; another had been put on hold for a swimsuit job in Spain, someone else was *up* for a shooting in Men's Vogue, and so on. I was not sure exactly what they were talking about, but it sounded very interesting. I finished my sandwich without joining the conversation and looked for Joseph to ask how to get back to the agency.

17

GROOMED FOR SUCCESS

I followed Joseph into Beatrice. Kristina popped up from her chair and walked over to where I was standing.

"Hey, bello. They really like you, man!" she said while giving me double thumbs up when she said the word man.

"They did?" I said in disbelief, more than a little confused.

"You gonna be the main one in the commercial. Well, with another girl as well!" she continued.

"Really?" I said, almost to myself, not understanding how that was even possible. Joseph scowled and stormed out of the agency and down the stairs.

Calvin walked out of a room at the back of the agency and greeted me with his sing-song Caribbean accent, "Ciao bello! Isn't he beautiful?" he said happily as he turned to face Kristina, his face and forehead shining like a black pearl under the lights of the agency. He was dressed fashionably; wearing a pale blue sweater, cream slacks, and a white scarf that looked like a miniature tasseled, cotton blanket.

My face flushed with embarrassment.

Calvin continued, "Ohhh, don't be shy my young prince. Next week you will meet the great Fabrizio Gianni!"

"He will love you! Right, Kristina?" he asked as he turned towards her with his long-fingered hands clasped together in front of his face like a man in prayer.

"Oh yes, baby! He will-a love this boy. He is-a beautiful boy. No, not-a boy, a bea-utiful, *sexy* man."

"Oh Calvin, you did very well my sexy black man."

Calvin smiled even bigger and put his hands on my face and said, "Come, my prince, we need to fix that hair. Fabrizio will never work with you with *that* hair!" as he moved his hands from my face to my shoulders, shaking me affectionately.

He laughed from his belly while leaning his head back and showing his white teeth. Kristina walked up behind me and wrapped her surprisingly strong arms around my waist and gave me a hard squeeze.

"I want to try your name," she said randomly as she released her grip around my waist and moved around to my front.

"It's Dareee-ll, isn't it?" she questioned earnestly.

"Yes Kristina, that's it, perfect," I lied with a face-cracking smile on my face. She shifted and started to squeeze my waist from the front this time. I put my arms lightly around her shoulders, feeling her smallness firm against my front until Calvin tapped me on the shoulder and said,

"Come on! Time to go, bello!"

Kristina reluctantly released her grip and looked up at me with large brown eyes, slapped me playfully on the butt and said, "Okay, you get outta here you *sexy beast*. We gotta work to do."

She playfully clapped her hands together and smiled with her mouth and eyes, then turned away and walked back to her desk.

Calvin took me to a hair salon down the street from the agency. It sat between a shoe store and a dress shop on a narrow cobblestone street. I walked in the open door as Calvin said something in Italian to the dark-haired beauty who stood behind the small counter in front of clear glass shelves filled with bottles of hair care products.

She walked over to a long row of sinks and spoke to a young girl with short cropped hair whose ears were filled with silver earrings. She was wearing a tight black v-neck t-shirt with matching black pants. The young girl looked at me, nodded and then smoothly wrapped a brown cotton towel on the wet head of a woman in her early thirties. She dried her hands and then turned to look at me before motioning for me to follow her.

I watched her walk in front of me and took in every curve of her body, following each fluid twist of her full hips beneath the sheer fabric of her tight black pants. After I sat down in a low-slung barber's chair, she wrapped a brown plastic sheet around my neck. She reclined the chair towards the sink and then guided my head down to rest in the smooth curve at the front edge of the sink. She ran her fingers through my dry hair and then started the water from the hand-held sprayer and began to spray my hair with hot water while running her fingers through my hair and around my ears. I looked up at her, and she smiled back at me with an expression that I could not read; pleasant without flirting. She tilted her head to the left and right while looking down at my hair, then stopped the water and squeezed shampoo smelling of oranges and strawberries onto my wet head.

She slowly began to massage the hair at the back of my head and then worked her way to my ears and the front of my head. Her touch seemed to linger at the backs of my ears and the nape of my neck. Her touch felt better than any shampoo I had ever had. I wondered if this was a special shampoo treatment, just for me, or if this was the standard wash. She repeated the cycle of shampoo and massage a few times; each time felt better than the one before. I wanted the shampoo to continue for hours.

She efficiently rinsed the soap from my hair with a constant stream of warm water while running her fingers through my hair from front to back. She then dried my face and the back of my neck with a warm cotton towel finishing by rubbing my ears between her thumb and fingers, ending with a gentle pinch to each ear at the same time. I could feel my face grow hot and red as she tilted the chair up to the sitting position while looking intently at my face. She then turned and silently walked away. I looked over to the front entrance and saw Calvin looking at me with a smile that he was trying to hide with his hand. "I think she is in love with you, don't you think?" he asked as he tried to stifle a laugh.

"No, no," I said with a shake of my head and a slight frown, "I don't think so."

"They are going to make you look like a movie star!" He finished as he turned back to his chair at the brightly lit entrance to the salon.

A thin man with a body full of right angles and a face like Ichabod Crane approached me from behind and looked at my reflection in the mirror in front of me. He pawed at my hair with an expression of disgust and boredom as his skin pulled tight across his boney face. He started to cut my hair without introducing himself. He hummed a classical song to himself as he cut from one side of my head and then from the other, all while continuing to hum what sounded like Mozart. He looked down at my hair and then at my reflection in the mirror while standing behind my chair. He razored the hair around my ears and at the back of my head, leaving the front untouched.

Calvin looked over his shoulder and said, "Good, good. I think Fabrizio will like your hair much better this way." He placed his long fingers under my chin and lifted my face to get a better look. I looked into the mirror while still seated and turned my head from side to side to see over the ears. It did not look good to me; it looked unfinished, and the white skin around my ears contrasted with my face and neck. Ichabod removed my hair-covered poncho and took one last disinterested look at my hair before he turned on his heel and walked away. Calvin and I walked out onto the sun-drenched street and ambled back to the agency.

Before I got on the plane to Italy from New York, I had spent hours imagining what Milan would be like. The few models that I told about my trip told me stories about drugs and models who became stuck in Milan, without money or a place to live, and no work for months. I had not heard anything positive about going to Europe. I hadn't bothered to ask them if they had ever been to Milan or how long they stayed there, so my imagination, which tended to lean towards the glass half empty and filled with poison, dreamed up wild fantasies of being slipped drugs in my drinks and of being arrested and put into a windowless prison and forgotten about, or of being unable to handle the awkward sexual advances of gay men and older women in the fashion world.

I had figured out within two minutes of meeting Calvin in New York that he was 100% gay, but I did not feel that he was interested in me or anyone else who wasn't gay. He was my first connection with the Beatrice agency. I trusted him, even though he had never asked me to.

My ability to trust people had been a problem for me for as far back as I could remember. I had learned in the last ten years that I couldn't trust my parents and had learned more recently that I couldn't trust my older brother Stokes. I was grateful that I didn't have a loving family that supported me and wanted me to succeed at whatever I chose to do with my life.

It made it much easier for me to go away to school when I was seventeen and now to travel across the Atlantic to live in Milan and model. I knew that my family was anxiously awaiting the imminent news of my failure. On the flip side, I knew that my mom would never lose a night's sleep worrying about me while I was gone. This allowed me the freedom to live my own life, without feeling guilty that I wasn't living up to a family ideal.

I spoke to a few other models in New York, and they all said that they missed their families every day and that their parents, especially their moms, called them at least once a day. I did find myself thinking about my two youngest brothers, Jason and Andy. By now, they were six and five, and I had not lived with them since they were four and three. I felt guilty that I had left them to go away to college when I was seventeen, and I knew that I would never have a relationship with them if I spent all of my time away. The situation with my dad made it a sure bet that I would never live at home again, whether they wanted me to or not. I thought about them and dreamed of spending time with them on long visits home; taking them to places that we couldn't afford to go when I had no money. The thoughts brought a smile to my face. I really loved both of them and was proud to be their brother. For this minute, in this place at this time I did not feel like crap about myself, I felt like I had a shot at a good life, not a good chance, but a chance.

18

HOW NOT TO BE

Days ran together as I went to the agency each morning and got a list of the appointments for the day. Most of the appointments were open calls, for every model in the agency, so I would attach myself like a 180 pound remora to a group of four or five guys in the morning and follow them through the twisting narrow streets of Milan to my appointments.

I walked to most of my appointments, keeping my mouth shut and listening to the other models while trying not to fall too far behind the group. They walked and talked fast and could give a shit if I kept up with them or not. Every model was in competition with every other model; *kill or be killed* was the unspoken code, survival of the fittest. I didn't see it like that. From my perspective, the photographer either liked your look or he didn't. Having fewer models show up for the job interview wouldn't necessarily mean that I would have a better chance of getting the job. If the job called for a dark haired model with dark eyes, then they wouldn't hire me, no matter how few models showed up for the job. I could see that no one looked at things the way I did. I didn't know if this was a good thing or a bad thing.

One warm and cloudy Friday afternoon I walked to an interview in a large room without any chairs. The models all watched the client flip through the pages of each model's books. He was a tall Italian man with glasses and bald on the top of his head. He sat at a plain wooden table with pictures scattered across it and quickly thumbed through the pages of one model's book; a slick model with thick, neat black hair, white straight teeth, and a strong build.

I heard him introduce himself as Rob. He was a singer and performer from Vegas who thought of himself as the *king of all things modeling*, walking and talking as if we were all lucky just to be in his presence. He had told me earlier that he really had a way with the ladies. Rob acted as if he thought that he was the greatest thing since *Skippy smooth peanut butter* and proceeded to tell me how awesome he was and that he *knew* that he was *destined for greatness.*

The interviewer took one quick look at Rob and then proceeded to flip through the pages of his book so quickly that it was impossible for him to focus on any of the pictures. He closed the book with an inadvertent, loud smack and then pushed the book across the table to Rob and indicated with an impatient wave of his hand that he wanted to see my book next and that Rob should leave. Rob's face had become almost completely red as he blurted out to the interviewer,

"What the fuck is wrong with you, asswipe? Do you even know what you are looking at you douche?!"

Rob spat the words out through clenched teeth, and his

hands were closed into hard fists. I waited awkwardly with my portfolio in my hands and looked to the interviewer to see how he would react to what Rob had said. I was not an expert on how to get a modeling job, but I was pretty sure that Rob was going about it all wrong. He continued to rant as he walked out and ended up giving the interviewer the finger with both hands as he pushed open the door with the panic bar using his butt as he backed out of the room while glaring at the interviewer with his best hard-ass stare. I got the same treatment from the tall Italian, shrugged my shoulders, grabbed my book and walked out the door even quicker than Rob had as I stuffed my crappy book into my backpack while walking out the door. Rob stood near an iron bench with one foot on the seat and repeated his story to two models with blank expressions on their faces. I tried to hurry by without being noticed, but Rob reached out and grabbed me by the arm and pulled me to a stop. He turned abruptly towards me and pushed his book into my chest and said, "Here, dude. *You* look at this book and tell me what you think."

I reluctantly sat down on the wood and iron bench with the leaves of some kind of maple tree shading the late day sun from my head and began to carefully look through his book. I took care not to do any *flipping* of the pages. Rob stood close behind me and looked over my shoulder, pointing out some details that the interviewer had obviously missed in each and every picture on every page, saying things like, *Oh man, that was a great shot!*, and *Not too many guys have a picture like that, dude,* followed by *check out those abs. Does anyone else have abs like that? That is a legitimate eight pack my friend!*

I kept silent and nodded with faux approval as I worked

my way through his book. His book seemed to go on forever. I thought to myself that many of the pictures looked very similar. I understood Rob's point as well as the interviewer's. Hell, I would be flipping through the pages of my hundredth book of the day, too, no matter how great the pictures were. I finally made it through Rob's book, turned to him, and lied unconvincingly,

"Wow, some really great stuff in here.

I don't understand why that guy didn't spend more time on your book," I ended with some trumped up sincerity.

"Damn right! That guy was a douchebag. I wonder how the fuck you say douchebag in Italian? Fucking a-hole. Who the hell does he think he is? Just so you know, I could *totally* kick his ass…I'm a freaking black belt in karate, by the way," he said as he gave a few chops and a respectable front kick into the air.

I watched and nodded with all the neutrality of Switzerland as I looked for a chance to get away from manic Rob without causing an incident. I did not want to get in a fight with *captain eight pack* over my insensitivity to his urgent need to be validated by a nineteen-year-old who didn't know shit about modeling. I was only a mindless audience that needed only to watch the one-man play that was unfolding before me, a witness to the greatness that was Rob Callisi, lucky as hell to have a front row seat.

"Well," I said with finality, pausing to find the right words to end our conversation without getting Rob pissed off and using his black belt skills on me. I settled on a very weak and unconvincing, "Gotta go, Rob, see you later," as I thought to myself what a *freaking psycho*, while getting up from the bench. I ran to catch up to the other models.

I needed to get one of those little plastic-coated maps of the city so I could start going to appointments by myself and avoid ninety percent of the bullshit of walking with a group of models, especially if they were anything like Rob.

Rob caught up with me just after I reached the group and continued where he left off, un-phased by my quick departure. He continued to tell me about all of the people who had crapped on him, how many girls he had slept with, what a jerk his dad was and how famous he was going to be; why most of the other models were fucking losers, how he treated women.... In short; how he was going to be a big star; just as soon as he could get someone to look at his book for more than thirty seconds.

19

MARPESSA

It was late in the day when we returned to the agency. The sun was sinking behind the low brownstone building and the late afternoon light filtered playfully through the leaves of the small tree that stood in the middle of the sidewalk. Rob and the other models sprinted up the marble steps two at a time to check their schedules for Monday with Kristina and Pepea.

I lagged behind on the sidewalk and eyed the handwritten menu of a small restaurant with chairs and tables that spilled out onto the wide sidewalk. I was very hungry and would much rather eat than continue to serve as a bullshit *sounding board* for Rob. I understood tortellini: twenty-three hundred lire. I sat down at one of the tables and pointed out to the young waiter with curly dark hair and full nose and lips what I wanted on the chalkboard. I pointed to a water bottle that sat on an empty table and held up one finger and said, "Uno agua, por favor."

He bowed slightly and said, "Grazie." I put my backpack under my chair and put my foot on one of the straps.

I soon felt the presence of someone standing on the other side of the table as a shadow rested on the small round table. I looked up at a tall girl smoking a cigarette and looking at the seat on the other side of the little round table. The light of the sun seemed to be radiating from all sides of her.

"Is someone sitting here?" she asked before taking a long drag on a cigarette held between long, delicate fingers. I was frozen by her beauty and stared up at her blankly without speaking.

"Is someone sitting here or not?" she repeated with a lighter than air laugh.

"Uhhh, no, no. You can sit here," I stammered as I stood up to introduce myself, "I'm Daryl."

"Yeah," she said, "I know," with a strong Dutch accent. "I am Marpessa."

She was almost as tall as I and was wearing a puffy, shapeless mini-skirt and a tight white, men's tank top over bare skin. The shirt left little to the imagination of the size and shape of her full breasts beneath.

Her skin was the color of coffee with extra cream, and her hair seemed to go everywhere but flat on her shoulders. Her bare legs were impossibly long, and her feet and calves were wrapped in the straps of brown leather gladiator sandals. Her face was flawlessly heart-shaped. Her eyes were golden–yellow, like ripened wheat in the late day autumn sun. Her lips were full and parted to show white teeth that were perfect in their imperfection.

My stomach jumped weightlessly like a drop on an old wooden roller coaster as my heart began to beat fast and hard within my chest. My face flushed red as I sat motionless, letting my eyes take in all that was in front of me.

"You are a model with Beatrice, yes?" she asked while continuing to smoke with her head tilted back.

"Yes," I said while trying not to stare at her, fearing that she could fly away like a bird at any moment.

"Me, too," she said with a crooked smile, again showing her white teeth. "How old are you, anyway?"

She asked with genuine interest in a sing-song voice that did not seem to fit the harsh Dutch accent that formed her words.

"Nineteen," I said, puzzled by the question.

"Wow, dude. You are much younger than the other guys," she said while holding the cigarette between her lips and balancing the long red and black cylinder of ash at the end of her cigarette. "You don't look nineteen. Did Calvin choose you?"

"Yes," I answered, looking away from her and down at my hands in an attempt to slow my heart from beating through my ribs and onto the table.

"Hmm," she pondered while looking across the table at me through half-lidded eyes.

"I don't see why he chose you. I have worked with some of the guys that Calvin picked, and they are not at all like you."

My heart sank as I listened to her words. I knew without knowing that a woman like Marpessa would never be with me; at the same time, I knew that I would be fascinated and in love with her for a long, long time to come.

"I'm not sure, maybe you're right. I was beginning to think the same thing myself," I said while looking across the table and into her bright golden eyes. I silently dreamed of pulling her close to me and kissing her full lips and feeling her lithe body push into mine, blocking out all of the world, and falling down into her as she let go and fell into me; losing myself in everything that was Marpessa.

She tilted her head back casually and returned my gaze without blinking as she put her cigarette out in the small glass ashtray in the middle of the table.

The young waiter brought a large bowl of pasta to me. Marpessa ordered a glass of white wine. I silently watched as she lit up another cigarette and began to smoke, imprinting everything about her into my head as she looked at me through half-lidded eyes with a mixture of curiosity and disinterest, as only a beautiful woman can do.

A male model with blond hair and a jumble of teeth suddenly appeared at the table to the right of Marpessa.

"Hey...can I sit with you guys?" he asked enthusiastically as he pulled out a chair and sat down backward on it before Marpessa or I could answer him.

Marpessa shrugged disinterestedly as I nodded in reply without enthusiasm.

He sat backward on the chair, draping his forearms over the back.

"My name is Keith; Keitho in Italian," He said with too much energy as he smiled and showed off jumbled and stacked teeth that pushed his lips out whether his mouth was opened or closed.

"I'm Daryl and this is Marpessa," I offered; wanting him to leave, but knowing that he would not.

"Hey there," he said to Marpessa, like a used car salesman. She effortlessly ignored him.

He gave her a mock look of surprise as if he was wounded by her treatment of him, letting both of us know that it was her loss with a shrug of his shoulders.

He quickly turned his attention to me without missing a beat.

"What makes you think you can be a model, *Sport-o?*" he questioned as his puffy lips moved up and down over his jumble of teeth.

"Not sure," I answered quickly, "I just thought I would give it a shot."

"Wee-eell," he said with concern, "you need to have something that makes you unique; makes you stand out from all of the other losers. You know, the short guys with no chance of making it in this business."

I looked blankly at Keith and then over at Marpessa. She was only partially listening to the crap that came out of Keith's mouth; he didn't seem to interest her, and she was too busy with her cigarette to focus her full attention on him. Her head tilted back and her eyes closed as she took long, satisfying drags on her cigarette, and exhaled lines of thin blue smoke into the air.

Keith tried to ignore her as she beautifully ignored him while he continued to speak to me, leaning closer to me as he said,

"My speci-a-lity is my abs. I do a lot of fashion work without my shirt, you know? My abs are my *forte*," he said while patting his stomach through the opening at the back of the metal chair.

"Your *forte?*" I questioned, unable to conceal my amusement at what just came out of his mouth.

As soon as the words were out of Keith's mouth, Marpessa opened her eyes fully like a snake noticing the rat that has just been placed in the corner of her herpetarium. She rose up in her chair and hissed ever so quietly,

"Your abs? Really? Let me see those special abs,

Keith-o," she said, gesturing with her cigarette for him to lift his shirt up.

The confidence washed from his face as he stammered, "Well, I haven't really had much of a chance to work out since I came to Milano, and you know, the pasta and pastries." He trailed off, hoping that her request would be forgotten and he could resume telling us about how great he was.

"Come-on Keith-o, let's get a look at those *special abs* of yours," she said in a voice that dripped with sarcasm and enthusiasm simultaneously. Now she was interested in the conversation, and she was not going to let Keith-o spoil all of her fun.

"Okay, okay," he said reluctantly, looking almost ready to cry as he pulled up his shirt and showed us his *six-pack*.

"Oh my god, you are so full of shit!" she spat out while laughing meanly at Keith. "My new friend here has much better abs than you do. Show him," she said to me with a wicked smile while taking another long, satisfying drag on her cigarette.

I reluctantly stood up as I wondered how the *fuck* she knew whether I had good abs or not. I slowly lifted up my loose fitting t-shirt in the front and said, "Okay?" as I turned to face Marpessa.

She gave me an exaggerated nod and a truly evil half smile as her eyes opened wide as she said to Keith without looking in his direction; "Okay, Now *that's* a set of abs, Keitho." She reached across the table and touched my stomach lightly with the fingertips of her right hand. I noticed that her fingernails were cut short and had no polish on them. Electricity coursed through my body like a shock from a live wire as her fingertips lingered on my bare skin. I slowly pulled my shirt back down and sat down in my chair. I tried without success to pretend I was interested in finishing my pasta as Marpessa gave me the same cold, yet interested look that a cat gives a mouse she is playing with before ending his life.

Keith stood up quickly and knocked over his chair onto the sidewalk while giving Marpessa and me a hard stare as he walked quickly away.

20

ROCK JAW

Calvin invited me out to dinner that night with some of the other models and all of the bookers from the agency. He introduced me to Michael Harder while we were at the agency and arranged for Michael to meet me at the pensione and take me to the restaurant. I went home on the trolley and put on what I thought was a decent outfit for going out to dinner. Michael arrived at eight and said that the restaurant wasn't far, so we could walk. Michael was almost thirty and seemed to be dressed well no matter what the occasion, as if he got a sheet with tips on what to wear. He began to smoke as soon as we walked out onto the street, signaling with a nod of his head to turn left. He had a look of someone with money, like the people who lived in the Inverness Development near my high school in Illinois. They had lots of money, and their clothes all seemed to fit better than the clothes my parents wore.

They all seemed to have plenty of time; never in a rush. I guess money can do that to people—too rich to rush. Michael walked in a way that made it clear that he was not in a hurry. He leaned back and ambled down the sidewalk while taking long drags from his cigarette without stopping. As we walked, I spent my time looking around at the closed shops and posters covering the walls of small newsstands that seemed to sit desolate on every street corner. I noticed that there were full-color posters of beautiful women that were almost completely nude. I stopped in front of a really large poster of a very beautiful, very naked woman with large, upturned breasts that she seemed to be pushing up to the sky with her two hands as she tilted her head back and closed her eyes. Michael stopped and looked up without much interest as I said, "You don't see pictures like this in New York City," with a big smile and a quick shake of my head from side to side.

Michael nodded his head slightly and started walking again. I tore myself away from the poster that I was considering taking with me to show to my friends back in the states and began to wonder why Michael was completely immune to the allure of the young blond on the poster. I worked it out in my head that he must be bored of the posters after seeing so many of them in the city that it held no more interest to him, or he could just be much more mature than I was. We began to talk about the very warm weather when I spotted a very tall, very sexy woman ahead of us wearing a tight, red, sparkly dress. Her legs, hips, and shoulders were amazing and her gait was fluid and filled with sexuality. I told Michael that I was going to run ahead and get a look at this beautiful lady from the front. Michael nodded his head with a slight smile pulling at the corners of his mouth as he continued smoking his cigarette. I ran up ahead quietly on the street near the curb, trying to stay a respectable distance away from the woman; not wanting to scare her.

When I got closer, I started to walk and then passed her on her right, as if I was in a hurry to get somewhere. When I was about fifty feet ahead of her, I turned to look at the front of this beauty and saw instead a garish transvestite with fake boobs, glitter eyeshadow and pancake makeup over sallow cheeks finished with round spots of bright red rouge. Her lips were painted bright red with a very glossy lipstick. She gave me a knowing look and then gave me a wink. I was unable to conceal my shock and immediately looked down at the curb as I sprinted back to where Michael was walking with his same unhurried stride. He was laughing quietly and said with a smirk,

"How did that work out for you? Was she hot?" I shook my head from side to side and my face flushed red as I began to laugh. I'm not sure what was so different about Michael, but I knew one thing for sure; he was much cooler than I was.

The restaurant was packed with an equal mixture of beautiful young people and wealthy looking older people. The group from the agency sat at a long table that was covered with bright white butcher paper, rolled out and folded at the corners to create one giant horizontal easel for the customers to draw on. There was pasta and bread on the table, and they had saved two seats for Michael and me at the end of the table closest to the entrance. To my surprise, Marpessa was sitting at the far end of the table. She waved her cigarette in the general direction of Michael and me as a form of greeting before returning to her conversation. Michael walked casually around the table and gave everyone kisses on both cheeks, including Marpessa.

Kristina came over to me and greeted me with two kisses, and Calvin shook my hand with a mock stern look, asking why we were so late. I sat down with Kristina on my left and Michael on my right. I listened to the talk around the table as Michael began to draw on the white paper with one of the small colored crayons that sat in a small glass in the middle of the table. He skillfully drew a three dimensional five-story building as viewed from the street; the perspective was near perfect. I looked over at the picture and asked,

"What did you do before you were a model?"

"I was an architect for a few years after college," he said without looking up from his drawing.

"Wow, that's cool," I said, sounding more foolish to my own ears as the words escaped my mouth.

"Not really," he said flatly. "This is much better."

"You mean modeling?" I asked dully.

"Yep, modeling," he said quietly while looking up at me.

We started to talk about our families, and he told me there were nine kids in his family.

Before I could ask about any details of his brothers and sisters, he began to draw a simple, cartoon of each of the nine kids in his family. Above each picture, he would write their name. The boys had on cartoon pants and short hair; the girls had triangle dresses and long, straight or curly hair. They were all lined up in a row with big smiles when he was finished.

The restaurant was loud and filled with smoke as we ate course after course of delicious Italian food. I couldn't understand what was being said, but I could tell that everyone was having a good time and that I was a part of things, even if I didn't understand what they were saying. I excused myself to no one and got up from the table to go to the bathroom. The bathroom was stylish and clean. An attractive woman walked out of one of the stalls tucking her blouse into her skirt as I walked over to a urinal shaped like a giant porcelain tic-tac that had been hollowed out. I did a double-take, thinking that I had gone into the wrong bathroom, but after seeing the reflection of two other guys in the mirror, I realized that the bathrooms in Italy must be unisex. What a country, I thought to myself.

When we left at about eleven thirty, I was tired and full and almost happy. I went back to the pensione and went to sleep on top of the sheets.

The next few days were spent showing clients my weak book at go-sees. I was completely out of money and asked Calvin if I could get an advance from the commercial we shot on my first day. He calculated how much money I would keep after all of the deductions and I was left with about 220 dollars. I was completely confused by the tariffs, agency fees, bribes and other inexplicable deductions. I told Calvin that I really didn't have any money left, even if he gave me the money from the commercial. He told me that I could move to a cheaper pensione filled with other models. It cost only ten thousand lire per night instead of the twenty-two thousand lire I was now paying. I thanked him and asked if I could move on Saturday. He said yes, so I packed up my laundry bags and took a cab over to the pensione at 8:00 on Saturday morning.

After a quick taxi ride across the city, I got out and looked up at the large stone building with wide stone steps going up to doors that opened into the lobby. The stocky taxi driver smiled a gap-toothed smile and nodded as I gave him a tip that I thought was correct before pulling my bags from the trunk.

Two young girls with tight men's v-neck t-shirts and loose shorts ran down the stairs while looking at each other and laughing. I watched them walk down the street as I lugged my bags up the steps, sweating like a marathon runner by the time I reached the top of the stairs. I dragged the bags behind me on the smooth marble floor of the lobby over to a long wooden counter that was as wide as most bars. I let my bags slump to the floor and stood in front of an area with a large open book and a very old looking telephone that sat on the counter. Behind the counter was a large cabinet filled with small wooden cubbies that held pieces of paper and envelopes sitting diagonally. A severe looking woman with a peasant's build and thick brown and gray hair suddenly appeared from a doorway covered with beads that formed a curtain. She held out a thick hand, palm up and said in a thick accent, "pass-a-port please."

I bent down to retrieve my passport from my backpack. She took a look at the picture and then back to me and then said firmly,

"This is room key, you-a passport stays here. Second floor. Room two-two. No, go on the first floor."

She turned on her heel back towards a metal cabinet hanging on the wall, opened it with a key that appeared out of nowhere and set my passport carefully on the top shelf, locking the door and removing the small key in one motion. She then turned away from me and walked back through the beaded curtain without looking back.

I turned towards the lobby and took in the layout. The floor was white and gray marble, and the décor looked very old but well preserved. There were mirrors on the walls set within ornate golden frames; some hung close together. There were two fancy brass ashtray stands, one at the entrance and one at the bottom of the marble staircase. Plush cushioned red velvet chairs with golden legs and frames set neatly against the wall wherever they would fit. Two old men were sitting on the chairs while smoking small, hand-rolled cigarettes as they read the newspaper. A small old man with thick glasses, gray stubble, and white hair that grew only on the sides of his head placed the paper on his lap and looked over at me as if to decide if I was visiting or a new resident. He nodded slightly as if to welcome me and then turned his eyes back to his paper.

I thought about how cheap the room was in comparison to my first pensione, and I couldn't understand the price difference. I liked the open space, and it seemed much easier to come and go without the buzzing in and greeting the family members who lived downstairs as they smoked and watched American television shows on their small TV with the rabbit ears down the hall from my room.

I dragged my bags up the marble steps and then lifted them onto my right shoulder.

I passed through the wide hallway of the first floor and saw only a small man in his forties looking at the floor and heading quickly towards the staircase. He scurried down the stairs as I made the turn to go up the stairs to the second floor. Two young American men walked down the steps, smiled at me and said, "Hey," as they walked down into the lobby. They were clean cut and wearing loose cargo styled shorts and tight tank tops with flip-flops.

Room twenty-two was at the top of the stairs. The door was open, and I walked in. The room was dimly lit by a single light fixture on the ceiling. A low slung bed sat awkwardly in a corner of the room, leaving a wide open space where another bed must have sat near the window. The window had thick square bars running vertically with heavy shutters that were partially opened to the outside. I pushed the shutters further open and looked out to a courtyard with a stone patio and clotheslines running across with everything from shirts to bras hanging from plastic clothes pins that held them tight to the taut, white ropes. A staircase with a black iron rail went diagonally by my window.

There was no glass in the window opening. I wanted to take a shower but didn't know where to go. I unpacked one of my bags and placed my clothes in an old armoire with peeling, wooden veneer doors. I located my almost-white towel and shaving kit and walked out the door, locking the door with the thick key with a blue plastic tag engraved with the number *twenty-two*.

As I started down the wide hallway, scanning the doorways for a sign indicating that a bathroom was behind it, I saw a young man who looked about twenty-three years old look out of his doorway as I passed by. He came out into the hallway.

"Hey, whaddaya doing?" he asked in a thick Boston accent with a smirk of a smile.

"Looking for a place to take a shower," I answered while turning to face him.

"Well, it's not on this floor, my friend. There's a one-room shower on the third floor and a toilet at the end of the hall on the third floor. There are also two showers and toilets on the first floor, but we don't use the first floor, not allowed. My name's Tommy. You a model?" he asked in a very thick Boston accent as he extended his right hand.

I shifted my towel and shaving kit to my left hand and extended my right hand. He squeezed my hand hard, as if to make a point, and flashed a smile that gave me a good look at his really unfortunate set of teeth, spaced wide and yellowish-gray from years of smoking.

His hair was brown and thick, cut short around the ears and at the back with a long shock of hair slashing across his forehead. He had not shaven for a few days and wore white, cotton stretch wristbands with red stripes. His forearms were covered with thick, curly hair and he appeared to be very strong.

"Yes," I offered. "This will be my third week here. My name is Daryl."

"You just got here then," he said with a dismissive shake of his head. "I been here for two and a half months, bro."

Tommy reached into the side pocket of his army pants and pulled out a pack of unfiltered Camels, shook the box with a flair so that a few cigarettes came partially out of the pack. "Want one?" he asked with a less agitated expression.

"Um, no. I don't smoke. Thanks though," I answered while shaking my head slowly from side to side to emphasize my words.

He looked up at me skeptically before pulling a cigarette out of the pack with his teeth and lighting it with a fancy flick of his old-fashioned, shiny Zippo lighter. He flicked the lid closed before placing it in his front pocket and shoving the pack of cigarettes back into the side pocket of his pants. I silently wondered if the cigarette would fit in the gap between his two front teeth.

He held the cigarette backward between his forefinger and thumb as if he were in a war movie and smoked it with a pinched and serious expression pulled across his face; as if it were his job. His face did not relax when he smoked like Michaels and Marpessa's. I wanted to get to the third floor to shower, but I knew that Tommy was not finished talking.

"I been here almost three months without much work, but next Monday, I got a job that is gonna be my big break," he said in between hard drags on his cigarette. "I'm doing a shoot for Ital-yan Vogue," he said, "with Gianni. You heard-a Fabrizio Gianni?" He questioned with a doubtful expression on his face as if he were interrogating me for a crime that I needed to confess to.

"Calvin mentioned his name," I offered.

"Well, Fabrizio is the real shit. He is the best in Milan; very cool guy. He is straight, and he likes to work with straight guys," he said as he continued to suck the smoke out of his cigarette before adding, "Yeah, I know Calvin. Is he the one who brought you to Milano?"

"Yes, he came to my agency in New York a few weeks ago."

"Yeah," he said with a furrowed brow, "just what we need, more fucking models in fucking Milano!" he spat out. "I know Calvin too. He brought me here from Boston, and not much has happened. Did he tell you that you may not get *any* work? I bet you five *dawlers* he didn't tell you that, eh? That you can run outta money and get your ass stuck here in Milano? There are plenty-a guys at the park that thought they would make it here; now they're begging other Americans for money and stealing food, sleeping on the floor and trying to figure out a way to get back to the states. There are a lot of American models in Milano and not too many jobs. Did they fucking tell you that Mr. Daryl from New York? I didn't think so." He smiled mechanically after his little speech as a way to add some humor to his negative rant.

I was thinking that Tommy didn't really want an answer to any of his questions or a comment on his statements, so I kept my mouth shut and waited for the speech to continue.

Suddenly a true smile pushed onto his face as he said with a glint of happiness in his eyes; "But everything is gaaw-na change Monday. I'll be working with Gianni for Ital-yan Vogue. Hey," he said with excitement, "you can tell people that you met me—you know—when I'm famous. How's that sound buddy?" he questioned as he took another long drag on his cigarette.

I still didn't think he wanted an answer. I nodded sagely with a tight-lipped smile to indicate I understood. Yep, I definitely understood.

I took a long, hot shower in the open room with the terra-cotta tiles on the floor and halfway up the walls. I dried myself off, took a quick look in the mirror, put on some sweats and a t-shirt and returned to my room. The stone walls and floor of my room were cool to the touch, and I felt very tired all of a sudden. I lay down on the small bed and began to read. The book was soon on my chest, and I was fast asleep, dreaming about Connecticut and the people from 82 Riverside Avenue.

I awoke to the loud ring of a heavy phone that sat on a small table near the bed. Still foggy from sleep, I picked up the receiver, "Hello?"

"Ciao, bello. This is Calvin. I am downstairs in the lobby."

"You are?" I asked.

"Yes, bello! Come down; I need to talk to you."

"Okay," I said.

Calvin was standing near the entrance to the pensione. He was smoking a small, dark cigarette that didn't make much smoke. When I got closer, I could smell the spicy smoke from his cigarette.

"What's that?" I asked Calvin while pointing at his cigarette.

"A clove cigarette. It is not bad for you; it is all natural."

"Isn't tobacco natural, too?" I asked.

"Yes, yes bello, but it is not the same thing," he said curtly, indicating that he was bored with the topic.

"Anyway, bello, I have some news about Monday. You are going to do a job with Fabrizio for Italian Vogue!" he said excitedly.

"Okay," I said without much enthusiasm. I knew that I should be very excited, but I didn't feel very excited for some reason.

"Aren't you happy?" he asked while taking another drag on his mini-cigarette.

"Oh yeah, Calvin, very happy," I lied, trying to think back to a time before I lost happiness. I couldn't remember back that far.

I remember being sad as far back as nursery school, getting hit in the eye with a curved two-by-four by a bully, waiting in the office at the desk by the window, large chunks of ice held together by a wet towel pressed against the cut below my right eye, blood staining the white towel. The bone-deep cut stung and my cheekbone seemed to throb each time my heart pumped more blood through my veins. All I could think about was not getting blood on my shirt and pants. My face hurt good, and the ice burned with a dry coldness. In a strange way, I found myself liking the pain as if it were a friend. The pain made me feel. I liked the warmth of the slow flowing blood and the fire in the twin gashes that were just below my eye. Mrs. Ridley told me in her fairy voice that I needed to get stitches right away.

I knew without asking that Mom would never take me to a doctor to get stitches, no matter how bad the cut. From that point on I knew that I could count on pain and disappointment to be a big part of my life. Happiness became a fairy tale, a unicorn that did not exist; it was something I decided to stop chasing when I was ten years old, leaving me to live cold and alone within my mind. I watched the world from a place that was mine alone, a place unreachable by those who thought they knew me.

Calvin took me to dinner at a small restaurant to celebrate the Vogue job on Monday. I think that he was happier about the job than I was. He gave me general instructions about what to do on Monday and told me a few stories about what it was like when he was a model in the seventies. He had faith in me and it seemed very important to him that I succeed. I caught onto the concept quickly enough. Calvin chose me and Beatrice spent money to get me to Italy, hoping to make money from my working. If I was not a success, then Calvin was not a success. My failure would most likely reflect badly on him. I knew that he was sincere and honest and that he definitely wanted me to succeed. He asked about my family as he continued to tell me about his experiences in the seventies. I looked at his shiny face and spare shoulders as he spoke and thought that he seemed too small and frail to be a model. Maybe things were different back then.

"Have you met any of the models at your pensione?"

"Uhm, yes," I answered while chewing on a juicy piece of thick, rare steak. I swallowed and drank a big gulp of the carbonated water and continued,

"A guy named Tommy."

"Tommy?" Calvin interrupted. "Oh yes, little Tommy, he is working with you on Monday!"

Great, I thought to myself. If Tommy thinks he will be fucking famous from his Vogue job on Monday, what's he going to think when we are working on the same job? I think Mr. Boston is more than likely to blow a gasket and give me a speech about the new models taking the jobs of those that have paid their dues and other shit like that. Tommy may have been in Milan longer than I, but he definitely didn't get it. I tried to keep things in perspective as I continued to savor my delicious steak.

"Is Tommy a successful model?" I asked while looking up from my plate.

"Well, he does get some work," Calvin answered hesitantly, "Why do you ask, bello?"

"I dunno. Does he do a lot of fashion work?" I asked, sticking with the topic.

"Some. Fabrizio really likes his look, although he is not completely in love with Tommy as a model."

"Is Fabrizio any good?" I asked while studying Calvin's face as he thought of an answer.

"Oh, yes," he responded with an earnest look, "He is one of the best; very good and very different in his approach to taking pictures. You will see on Monday."

Night had fallen while we ate. Calvin walked with me back to the pensione. I got the feeling that Calvin didn't have anything better to do than hang out with a wannabe model that had not yet accomplished anything. I thought about Calvin's being gay, and felt sad for him, though I didn't understand why.

I never heard Calvin say anything about being gay, like Hank and Jack, two gay men who lived at 82 Riverside Avenue, did. They were very open about their homosexuality, hugging and kissing each other in the kitchen. Or like the other gay men that I had met since I had arrived in New York, the ones that tried to get a feel for how I felt about homosexuality, by talking loudly about guys' asses or about giving hummers, all the time watching me to see how I reacted. Calvin wasn't like that, but I still felt sad when I thought about his being gay; it seemed to be a lonely life to lead.

Sunday morning was bright and hopeless as the sadness washed over me as I struggled to open my eyes to the sunny assault of the morning. I dressed quickly and got out of my room, walking through the lobby and onto the sidewalk, then started to walk in no particular direction, staring at the buildings around the pensione to remember my way back. All of the buildings were low to the ground, and the pensione rose high above the others and could be seen from some distance. I walked with my hands in my pockets, looking down at my worn sneakers as I walked without purpose. All of the shops were closed and the streets were deserted. Two dark haired men walked side by side together and stopped to look at me from a distance. One of them gave the *Heil Hitler* salute to me and clicked his heels together as they both laughed and looked at each other. I ignored them and continued to walk with the sadness pushing at my chest and from behind my eyes, not letting up.

Thoughts twisted around in my head as I tried to picture Barbara and Sean and Jessica in my mind, knowing that they missed me and hating myself for not calling for almost two weeks. Barbara was a care-worn twenty-three, looking much older than I did. She wore clothes that a woman in her mid-thirties would wear. I knew that we would never last and silently cursed my mind for playing the bad movies of my life over and over again, in black and white and color, waking dreams that would not leave me alone, no matter where I was and no matter whom I was with. It never seemed to change.

The day ran out flatly as I wandered the abandoned streets. It was getting dark when I returned to the pensione. There was a long line of middle-aged men that led up to the front door of the Pensione Lima. They were all short Italian men with hairy arms and thinning hair, shifting anxiously from foot to foot as they waited with their arms at their sides in a single file line. I stopped at the bottom steps and stared openly at the line of men and tried to understand what they were waiting for. All of the men looked away from me as I stared at them. After a few minutes, I gave up and walked into the lobby. Tommy and an attractive blond sat together on one of the gilded gold chairs; she sat on Tommy's lap with her long arms wrapped around his neck. She did not appear to be American. Tommy yelled out "Ciao," with his *Southie* accent and the girl on his lap just giggled and snuggled into his lap more as she tightened her grip around his neck.

"Ciao," I replied awkwardly.

"Whatcha doing tonight?" he asked after he took a long drag of his cigarette.

"Nothing," I answered honestly, glad to be talking instead of stuck inside of my kaleidoscopic brain.

"Wanna come to dinner with us?"

"Sure," I answered, "When?"

"I think some of the other guys are leaving in about five minutes. Meet us in the lobby."

"Yeah, fine. I don't have much money though. Is it expensive?"

"No, we're going to the back of Solferino's. The food is really cheap there."

Good, I thought as I reminded myself of how little money I had.

"Hey, Tommy?" I asked quietly as I moved closer, "Why are all those guys lined up outside?" as I nodded towards the entrance to the pensione.

"Yer kidding me, right?" he said with that same smirk of a smile. "Those guys are here to see the hot mamas on the first floor."

"Hot mamas? *What* hot mamas?" I asked as I looked around the lobby.

"*Those* hot mamas," Tommy said as he pointed to two very large women walking down the wide staircase in absurdly ill-fitting high heel shoes. I stared at the women with thick wrists, and coarse hair died a sickly shade of blonde wearing thick patterned curtains shaped into dresses.

Their blemished skin was covered with thick, greasy foundation makeup that made the eruptions on their skin look more noticeable in the bright overhead lights of the lobby. They were almost completely shapeless in their roundness, a classic egg shape. They walked as if they were on the red carpet at a Hollywood premiere, heads held high, big smiles and shoulders back, walking with a side-to-side strut that was just this side of unbelievable.

"What the fuck is going on?" I whispered, starting to put the pieces of the gross puzzle together in my head.

"Prostitutes, bro, pros-ti-tutes. Those fat-asses are loaded! It's fucking legal here, and they can finish a guy in about five minutes," he spat out with a crazy fit of laughter as he doubled over, unable to control himself.

I was unsure if I believed Tommy or not. "I'll see you down in the lobby in about ten minutes," I said, trying hard to erase the mental picture that formed in my head as Tommy told me about the prostitutes and the johns. Now I knew why this freaking place was so cheap.

I went to dinner with Tommy and his female companion, and three other male models. A small English photographer with a big head and slim arms joined us as we crossed the street in front of the pensione. He called me *rock jaw* and told the others that I looked like the *village idiot* from the side and that he didn't think that I would ever be a model. I decided that he was too small to punch directly in the face and chose to endure his stupid comments instead. I smiled weakly at no one as we chose our food from a long buffet at the back of the restaurant. The others didn't laugh at Shorty, the photographer's, jokes about my jaw. He soon shut up, which allowed him to keep his teeth in his head, at least for the rest of the night. Two of the models were in rough shape financially. They told their hard-luck stories with fear clouding their eyes in the dim light. Their words were filled with hope, but their eyes betrayed their words as they looked defeated and scared. Neither of them had worked in two months, and they were surviving on money sent from home. I listened intently to their stories as I ate my chicken marsala and drank an icy cold bottle of Kronenbourg. The chicken was very good, and the beer was clean and smooth. I listened silently and offered no words of support, feeling that I might be telling the same story in six weeks to anyone who would listen. I walked back to the Lima and into my room. As the smothering *white noise* that I knew was not actually there filled my head and the sadness returned, I fell asleep under a thin cotton blanket with the light on, dreaming in color of places and people that existed only in my mind.

21

LUOMO VOGUE

I thought about Marpessa from the time I awoke on Monday until I arrived at the studio in the commercial lot for my shooting with Fabrizio. Barbara was fading in my mind as Marpessa consumed my thoughts with wild fantasies of travel, topless beaches and long, hot nights together without end. I loathed the feelings that flowed through all parts of me, knowing that Marpessa and I would never be together. My wall of insecurity was more of a prison than a protecting fortress. I shook the thoughts from my head as I searched for the studio down the long, wide hallway. At the end of the hallway, there were two open doors that led into a big clean studio with lights set up in front of a large white screen with white wooden boxes on the floor. A tall Italian man with curly hair was kneeling by a large battery and pushing a button that started a whirring sound that ended with a flash of all of the lights together. He repeated this several times and checked the light meter that hung around his neck. He stood up and extended his right hand,

"I Carmine," he said.

"I'm Daryl," I offered as I extended my hand to shake.

"Ciao," he said, as he pumped my hand up and down, smiling broadly and showing me his crooked white teeth.

"Ciao," I said.

He had a friendly, open face with large, thick glasses perched atop a Roman nose. He was taller than me and wore the typical jeans, sneakers, t-shirt ensemble that I had seen on most young men his age since arriving in Italy.

He led me to an area where Tommy and two other male models were sitting on metal folding chairs.

Tommy gave me a hard look, and I could feel the ice as he said, "Hey," without offering his hand to shake.

A square-jawed model with a sun-weathered face stood up and walked towards me.

"I'm Kane," he said as he extended a strong hand. "This your first time working with Magic, I mean Fabrizio?"

"Yes," I answered while thinking that I had seen him in the Ralph Lauren ads back in the States.

"Good to meet you, Daryl. Where are you from? I can't quite place the accent."

"I'm from Illinois, near Chicago," I offered, pleased that he had taken an interest. Kane seemed to be the type of guy that everyone liked, even if they didn't want to.

"Not much surfing in Illi-noise," he said with a warm laugh.

"No, not that I know of."

"Hey listen. Fabrizio is a good guy. I mean really good. He must be good to make my ugly face look good," he said as he laughed loudly and slapped me on the back.

Kane's rough face was offset with sky blue eyes and straight white teeth. Sun damaged skin had caused wrinkles to appear around his mouth and eyes years before their time.

"This food is for us. Do you want something?" he asked as he motioned with his hand to a table in the corner.

I looked over at a small round table with a basket filled with croissants and fruit danishes. A few empty plastic cups sat in front of a pitcher of ice water and a pitcher of orange juice.

"Do we have time?" I asked hesitantly.

"Oh hell yes! Fabrizio is getting the clothes together and some props with the Vogue art director. We have at least another thirty minutes."

I quickly wolfed down a Danish and drank two glasses of orange juice without putting down the cup.

"Have you ever worked with Fabrizio before?" I asked as I threw the plastic cup away, still chewing my food.

"Fabrizio is the *only* photographer I've worked with in Italy. This guy shoots every day here. I should have enough tear sheets to go back to New York by the end of May, maybe June."

"That sounds great. Do you know what we are doing today?" I asked, excited that someone knew what the hell was going on.

"Some *Chariots of Fire* thing. You know, that movie with all the skinny guys from England who went to the Olympics about a hundred years ago. The one thing you need to know about Magic is that he doesn't want you to *act* like a model; he just wants regular people. No fake smiles, cheesy poses or heavy makeup; he hates all of that crap. I think you'll do fine; you don't seem full of shit to me. This modeling stuff is quite a ride, isn't it? I'm gonna ride this wave until it comes crashing into shore. Not sure how long that will be, but I'm gonna enjoy the hell out of it in the meantime. Don't worry; you'll like *Magic*. Is this your first job in Milan?" he asked as he grabbed a cheese Danish, bit off half of it, and started chewing.

"Pretty much. Except for some commercial with fifty other models the day after I got here, I haven't really done any *real* print work, just some tests in New York."

The door with the panic bar suddenly opened, and a large bearded man walked into the studio and said, "Boys, boys. Good morning, good morning! Let's get you dressed. Come over here, *andiamo*."

"That's Fabrizio." Kane whispered as we walked across the studio to meet him.

"Hello Kane, my California surfer. Have you been causing more trouble since last week?" Fabrizio asked with a big smile crossing his full face.

"Nope, unfortunately, no trouble at all, Magic. I'll try harder next time," Kane replied with a genuine laugh as he slapped Fabrizio on the back.

"Tommy from Boston, why the frown my friend? Didn't you get laid last week, huh?" Fabrizio said with a slight Italian accent as he grabbed Tommy's shoulder and shook him back and forth and then slapped him on the back playfully.

"No Fabrizio, I wanted to be prepared for the shooting today," Tommy said nervously with a punkish smile and squinty eyes.

"Oh. Well, then you *should* have gotten laid," Fabrizio said with a hearty laugh as he looked at Kane and me, then back to Tommy, who was not smiling but managed to squeeze out a half-assed smirk to let Fabrizio know that he was in on the joke.

Fabrizio looked like a bear in human's clothes. He had a warm smile with straight teeth and a full beard and a mustache and was dressed in a crisp blue button down shirt, khaki slacks, and fine Italian brown leather loafers. He wore a stainless steel Rolex diving watch, and his sleeves were rolled halfway up his forearms. He had the confident look of a man who answered only to himself. "Okay, guys. Let's take some pictures," Fabrizio boomed out in perfect English, clapping his hands together like a football coach on the sidelines.

A small female dresser helped me into a tweed jacket, shirt and tie with wool knickers and brown dress shoes. I walked toward the lights, and Fabrizio held out his right hand and said, "I am Fabrizio, and you must be Daryl."

He said it graciously, with a slight bow as he shook my hand. "You are in the first shot with my ugly friend Kane. Try not to make him look too bad," he said with laughter in his eyes.

Kane and I were wearing similar outfits. A young woman with brown hair and scissors dangling from a string around her neck stood in front of me and looked at the clothes I was wearing and then at Kane. She pointed towards the middle of the floor in front of the screen and handed me an old suitcase with leather straps and brass buckles on the sides. "Stand there," she said in a soft, sweet voice.

Kane and I stood side by side as Fabrizio said from behind the camera, with a full belly laugh, "Kane, he could be your son. That's it! A father and son going to the *O-lympics*!"

"Hey Fabrizio; maybe your son. I'm only twenty-five

years old, my friend," Kane shot back at Fabrizio with a laugh.

"It is a good thing that I like you, Mr. Sicner, or you would be working at a hot dog stand in Santa Monica for twelve dollars per day!" Fabrizio said as he looked through the camera at Kane and me.

I looked over at Tommy who was standing next to a tall, thin model with a boyish prep-school haircut. Tommy was watching Kane and me like a hawk while the new face focused his attention on a small compact mirror that he held in his left hand as he dabbed with a makeup sponge at a spot over his lip, working hard to conceal a very noticeable zit with a white-head ready to pop.

The camera and flash went off suddenly and I turned quickly, thinking I had missed something. "That was just a Polaroid to check the light; don't worry Mr. Daryl from Chicago, we have not started yet."

I was impressed that he remembered my name so quickly and knew that I was from Chicago.

"You are both going to the Olympics, okay? Hey, please start the music, will you? Think how honored you would feel if you were representing the United States in the Olympics," Fabrizio instructed as the classical score from Chariots of Fire filled the studio.

I stood with a suitcase in my hand and looked into the black lens of the camera as he started to take pictures. Kane was behind me and slightly to my right. The batteries whirred as the lights popped over and over. After twenty minutes Fabrizio stopped taking pictures and said, "That was good. I think we got it."

I was amazed at how easy it was, just stand and have my picture taken. I could get used to this very quickly.

Fabrizio did a shot with Tommy in shorts and a tank-top and then had all four of us sit, stand and kneel around a steamer trunk in front of the white screen. I was standing and didn't move or smile.

I could see the slim model with the prep school haircut sitting on an old wooden box with his right elbow on his right knee and his hand in front of his face in a loose fist as if deep in thought.

"Hey, my friend. Yes you," Fabrizio said, as he walked towards us from behind the camera, "What is your name?"

"Christian," the slim model replied with an arrogant, smug expression.

"Chris-tian," Fabrizio sighed, "What are you doing with your hand in front of your face," he asked with a furrowed brow.

"Oh," he said quickly. "Is that not good?" he asked, while pulling his hand away from his face and placing it on his lap.

"No my friend. I want you to look natural. This is not a German catalog shooting," Fabrizio said, as he stepped back behind the camera.

"Okay guys, think about what an honor it would be to represent the United States in the Olympics."

After a few shots, Fabrizio stopped suddenly and said, "Hey, Christian, what are you doing with your hand?" this time with more irritation in his voice.

"Nothing," he lied, as he continued to attempt to conceal his zit with his loosely closed right hand.

"Listen, Christian, that thing is natural and it will not show up in the pictures. Now please stop putting your hand in front of your face, okay? That's natural, don't cover it up," Fabrizio said, as Christian nodded solemnly as if he were being punished.

Christian waited five shots before covering his zit again with his hand, tilting his head slightly down and looking up with his eyes, hoping to obscure the zit and look fashionable at the same time.

Suddenly Fabrizio said; "Okay, I think we got the shot. Thank you, gentlemen," without enthusiasm as he turned away from the camera.

A few minutes later a young man came into the studio and whispered something to Christian and then Christian turned to him and replied loudly; "What? What do you mean I'm done with the shooting? I'm supposed to be getting a lot of tears from this job you little shit. I look better than anyone else here. Do you even understand what I am saying? Fuck this. This is total bullshit! I'm out of here. I don't know what the fuck is wrong with you guys," he complained as he packed up his brown leather backpack with sheep skin covered shoulder straps and threw it over his shoulder.

The young man speaking to Christian nodded solemnly and apologized quietly, signed Christian's voucher, turned and walked out of the door. Christian searched our faces for some support and someone to protest to, but only Kane and I remained. Kane looked over at me, shrugged his shoulders and said quietly to me, "See what I mean about Fabrizio, dude? Only likes real people, not bullshit."

I nodded my head while trying to hold back the laughter that pushed at my ribs and the smile that pushed at my face from behind my cheeks. We finished off the day with eight more pictures and Kane and I rode the trolley back in the late afternoon sun. We arrived back at the Pensione

Lima as the sun was burning its way through the distant horizon. We laughed at everything and nothing at the same time, posing with our hands in front of our lips and looking up at a make-believe camera. Kane didn't seem affected by the business; he just seemed to be along for the ride.

22

NIGHTMARES AND DAYDREAMS

There was a message at the front desk of the hotel from Calvin, I was to call him at home. Calvin sent me back to Vogue studios in the morning for another shooting that started at nine. I had some tea with milk and sugar when I arrived and slumped into a metal folding chair with my legs stretched out in front of me, crossed at the ankle. I waited for the tea to cool and drank it down in a few minutes, looking around for the photographer, assistant or the other models. Michael Harder ambled in through the studio door with a long sleeved dress shirt with the sleeves rolled up and loose, khaki cargo shorts, a lit cigarette dangling from his lips. He waved casually and smiled with the cigarette still between his lips and said quietly, "Hey, what's going on," without appearing to move his mouth. He shook my hand weakly and got himself some coffee and then sat down near me. He had a genuine smile on his face and seemed completely relaxed.

"What are we shooting today?" I asked, trying to start up a conversation.

"Winter clothes, I think," Michael said while blowing smoke at the ceiling to keep from blowing it in my face.

"Oh," I replied, not sure how to keep the conversation alive.

Michael picked up the conversation and said, "Is this your first job in Milano?"

"No. I did a shooting yesterday with Fabrizio Gianni. Do you know him?" I asked, trying not to sound like I was impressed with myself.

"Yeah, he's a good guy," he said with a half smile as he put the cigarette out in a glass ashtray.

"He likes working with straight guys. Kind of his thing," Michael reflected.

"Yeah," I replied, "Kane said the same thing," I answered, wondering if I should just keep my mouth shut about the whole *gay-straight* thing, still unsure of where Michael stood on the subject.

"Have you ever worked with Fabrizio?" I asked, feeling stupid as soon as the words came out of my mouth.

"No. I don't think I'm his type; could be wrong though."

This time I *did* keep my mouth shut.

A tall, slim Italian man with sad eyes behind round glasses came in and introduced himself. "I Georgio Lari," he said to Michael and me, "I am photographer." He had a very strong Italian accent and I got the impression that he did not speak English very well. Two other models followed him in, Cyril from France and Marcello from Chile.

Soon we were dressed in thick wool sweaters and wool pants. We all wore Timberland boots over heavy wool socks. I started to sweat even before I put my wool jacket and Sherpa hat on. Michael and I were told to sit on an angled piece of plywood covered with black felt. As soon as I sat down on the angled board, I began to slide down to the floor. I tried to hold myself up with the rubber heel of my right boot, but there was not enough friction to keep my butt from sliding. Soon I was dripping in sweat and my face was hot and red. I asked Michael how he was able to stay on the background.

He answered, "You're doing fine," without ever taking his eyes off the camera. I couldn't tell if he seriously thought I was doing fine or if he just wanted me to shut the hell up. Georgio, the photographer, didn't talk to us, he just kept clicking away as I slid inch-by-inch down the sloping background. Marcello had some *go to* expressions that were fun to watch when I wasn't shooting; a different pose for each picture. Chin up, chin down, smile, serious, happy. His hair was carrot orange-red and his face had more freckles than skin. He made notes when Michael and I were back on the backdrop, intensely looking around and turning his notepad sideways to make sketches.

During lunch, I asked him what he was doing and he told me that he was going to be a photographer and he was making diagrams of the lighting and camera position. I decided that he was either delusional or very industrious. He was very serious and very boring. I found myself wanting to go to sleep a few times during the shooting, and I had to bite my tongue hard to keep myself from dozing off.

Michael and Cyril were almost as serious as Marcello. I couldn't wait to get the hell out of the shooting. I got my voucher signed by the same young assistant who told Christian that he was fired on Monday. He smiled politely without speaking and turned on his heel and walked out the door. I slipped out the side door exit without saying goodbye and walked into the late afternoon sun and down the outside metal stairs, hoping that I would remember how to get back to the agency, but not really caring if I got lost in the process.

I was tired and very hungry. I couldn't stop thinking about Marpessa as I walked in the direction of the trolley stop that Kane and I had taken on Monday.

I arrived in forty-five minutes at the Lima, walked past the front desk of the pensione and took the stairs two at a time to the second floor. The porcine prostitutes gave me the creeps. I couldn't imagine anyone paying to do it, least of all with them. I was fighting the urge to think about what exactly they accomplished in five minutes behind the small locked door. I could think of only *one thing*, and that didn't seem worth it to me.

Don't get me wrong, I thought about girls most of the time, but these women were not girls; they were big men with bad wigs, thick wrists, and ankles. They had hair where there should have been only smooth skin.

Marpessa was the complete package; except for the fact that she didn't like me, she was perfect. It always seemed to work out that way. Women always seemed to want what they can't have, and then they ignore what they could have at any time. I knew that if I ignored Marpessa, she would soon want me as much as I wanted her, but I wasn't that good of an actor. I could never pretend that she didn't matter to me, my face and eyes would give away the truth too quickly.

The old dreams came back at night; going bald, getting fat, losing my front teeth, while talking with Sofie on the top of a hill under a tree. An overwhelming dread filled me in my dream when I realized that I couldn't escape, that I was stuck forever with Sofie, a woman who was my mother in this dream, sitting under an apple tree, holding me like a baby. The dream just kept going. I couldn't forget what had happened in the dreams; it was stored in my fucked up head. I knew that I would remember everything when I woke up, and that the dream would stay with me and continue if I went back to sleep, like a never-ending movie running in my mind.

Most of my dreams were violent and morbid; filled with dark skies and hopeless stories, with tragic, brutal endings. I was always at the center of each dream, close to death, but surviving the deadly actions of others. In one dream my older brother shot me five times while we were talking. He was laughing while the paramedics loaded me into the ambulance and I remember telling him that it was going to be okay and that I forgave him. I didn't die in that dream but was fully recovered before the ambulance reached the hospital where I asked the paramedics to let me out, and they did. I found myself on a strange street, alone with cars zooming by me while I stood on an empty sidewalk. Others would die in my dreams, but I always survived.

The dreams were so common that they did not cause fear in me, only an unending-sadness and a bone-wearying fatigue that stayed with me all through the day, a waking dream with the sadness of night smothering any joy of day.

Sadness had long ago replaced the fear that came to me from my dreams. When I was young, I spent long, slow passing hours wishing to be anyone but myself. The fear and sadness would keep me up all night as a child, pacing on the worn orange carpet in the second-floor hallway of our small colonial house in Palatine, Illinois. I would look at the cheap brass colored doorknob with the worn finish on my parents' door thousands of times, wanting to turn the knob and walk into their bedroom to talk to them and tell them of my dreams, that I couldn't sleep, that I was afraid of everything and nothing at the same time, but I never did. I held years' worth of questions, fears, and worries in my head. I was more afraid of my dad and mom than I was of the thoughts that tortured me in the day and in the night.

Some nights I would walk the hall until early morning when I needed to wrap and deliver the newspapers. I was looking for something that could not be found, unable to feel my hands or feet, obsessed with objects that were either *too smooth* or *too sharp*, wanting to warn people of the dangers of the cool smoothness or the sharp rockiness of the objects that filled our house. Night whispered things to me that I would not repeat to anyone. I was alone in a house filled with four brothers, one sister and Mom and Dad... there was no escape from the coldness that did not come from the icy wind of winter but from the darkness of my soul. Winter, spring, summer, and fall, these dark thoughts filled my head; especially in the summer.

I started going on appointments alone that week, preferring to get lost than to spend my days walking with a group of models that talked loudly and constantly, trying to draw attention to themselves while walking the streets of Milan. I knew that my actions led them to believe that I thought I was better than they were, but I only wanted to be alone without being lumped together with this group. Maybe I did think that I was better than they were, or maybe just different. The days were sunny and very warm, I would wear shorts and any short sleeved shirt that I could find. I would walk to the appointments that were closer than two miles and take the tram to the others. I developed a strong dislike for the trams. They were loud, hot, crowded and cost money. I would have to squeeze between people who were a head shorter than I and have to bend down to look out of the windows to watch for my stop.

I preferred to walk. I was often the last model to show up for the appointments. Most photographers and art directors flipped through my book without looking at me, closed my book politely, and pushed it back across the table while saying *grazie*, as they motioned for the next model to come forward.

At the end of each day, I would go back to the agency and sit and talk to Kristina while she took calls and gathered together comp cards of models who were being booked for jobs. She always smiled at me and seemed genuinely happy. It felt good to be in the same room with Kristina. She would say random nice things to me out of nowhere or describe one of the female models for no apparent reason. I never said much; only watched and listened. When male models came into the agency to get their appointments for the next day or to complain about having no work, I would watch and listen. The smile would fade from Kristina's face as she told a model that she had no work for him as she shook her head slowly from side to side. Most of the models would leave pissed off without saying thank you, or goodbye, to Kristina. I could see that she was accustomed to being treated badly. Kristina knew every model in the agency as well as their stats; she had a mind for things like that. Her bright smile and pretty face hid the fact that she was actually very smart. We would sit alone together at the end of the day in the empty agency with the doors open at the front and back as the warm breeze worked its way through the room, rustling the papers. One such evening, I leaned back in a very comfortable office chair and asked Kristina,

"What do you know about Marpessa?"

"Ohhh," she replied with a glint in her eye. "You like this one, don't you?"

"Well, kind of," I replied as I blushed.

"Oh come on bello, you like her, no?" she asked with a glint in her dark eyes and an interest that I had not anticipated.

"Okay, I do like her," I replied with a wide smile.

"Oh, honey. She is sooo beautiful, but no good for you, bello."

"Why not?" I asked as the smile faded away from my face, more than a little confused.

"You are a nice guy Dar-iill, but this girl, she will eat you up. Like a shark. You know?"

I was unsure of what to say, so I stared back at Kristina with a blank look on my face. Although I didn't fully understand what Kristina had said about Marpessa I knew that she was right. Marpessa was not right for me.

23

FAT BROTHERS

Friday was quiet with only five appointments, all close to the agency. They all felt like a waste of time, no one talked to me, and no one looked at me, which seemed a sure sign that they were not interested in hiring me for a job. I did not have any jobs for almost two weeks, and the money from the commercial and the Vogue shooting was almost gone. I silently hoped that next week would bring something better.

I rolled into the pensione lobby at 5:30 and wanted only to eat and sit for the rest of the night. My knees and hips ached, and I shook my head as I thought of how young I was. I had felt this pain all through high school and would wake up each morning and not be able to bend my right knee at all. I never saw a doctor and felt that this was just the way it was; pain all through the day and night. I decided to keep it to myself and make friends with the pain. Although I was only nineteen, my whole body ached like that of an old man, especially in the morning. Kane was coming down the stairs while I went up.

"Hey man," he said as he flashed a warm smile.

"Hey," I replied with a half smile.

"You wanna get something to eat?" he asked with a bigger smile that pushed at the wrinkles around his eyes.

"Sure," I answered without hesitation. Kane was one of those guys that people wanted to be around. Although we had little in common, he still seemed to enjoy hanging out with me; not feeling the need to prove himself by putting me down like most of the models I had met in New York and Milan. He seemed to think that modeling was a joke that paid him money to do nothing. I got the feeling that Kane would feel the same about himself if he worked at Burger King or was on the cover of GQ.

"Do I have time to drop my stuff in my room and get changed?" I asked.

"Yeah, whatever, just come to my room when you're ready and we'll go."

"Okay," I replied.

Tommy was in the hallway smoking a cigarette when I walked to Kane's room at the end of the hall.

"You guys getting something to eat?" he asked.

"Yep," I said as Kane came out of his room wearing the west coast uniform: flip-flops, Op shirt, and shorts.

"There is this great place across the tracks. You want me to show you where it is?" Tommy continued without any encouragement from Kane or me.

Kane and I looked at each other, shrugged our shoulders with our palms up, turned to Tommy and said, "Sure," with minimal enthusiasm.

Tommy was high octane, never relaxed, always on edge. The more I got to know him, the less I liked him. He was self-centered and had an inflated view of himself as a model. I was no expert, but I had a hard time imagining Tommy's face ever landing on the cover of GQ.

"Cool," he replied as he rubbed his lit cigarette on the sole of his shoe before flicking it onto the floor.

The night was starting to cool when we left the Lima, and the clients had already started to line up on the sidewalk in front. Kane looked over at the men as we walked by and said, "Fun night tonight, hey guys?"

They all looked at their hands and did not return Kane's stare.

I shook my head at Kane's comment and laughed into the back of my hand, pretending to cough and trying not to burst into that uncontrollable laughter that can't be stopped. The stocky men looked up and glared at Kane and me. Kane laughed with his whole body and clapped his hands together a few times as if he were having the time of his life. I knew that it was rude, but I thought it was funny, too. The men were waiting for the two fat prostitutes with their hands pushed deep into their pockets as they stood on the wide sidewalk, nervously shifting their weight from one foot to the other, studying the ground under their feet with great interest. They were all waiting patiently in line for their five minutes behind a closed door with a woman that I wouldn't touch if she paid me. It was something that I had never seen in the United States, and I judged what I saw with my narrow, bigoted, American view; as if I were any better than they were in some way.

We arrived at a small restaurant with *Fat Brothers* painted on the front window. The restaurant sat alone between two factories with large brick smokestacks that puffed gray-white smoke into the cloudy early evening sky. We walked in through the open doors. Tommy said,

"Heyyyyy," to a man wearing a white t-shirt and a stained white apron around his waist. He was around twenty years old and wore black boots without laces and Levis jeans. He was almost the same height as Tommy, and his hair was greasy and combed back in a duck's ass style. He had strong arms and his fat stomach pushed at the front of his shirt.

He stopped wiping off the tables with a wet rag and turned to Tommy and said, "Heyyyy," giving him the thumbs up sign with both hands.

Tommy turned to us and introduced us, "Hey Michael, this is Daryl and Kane. They're from the United States."

Michael gave us another double thumbs up and a very long, "Heyyyy," while moving his thumbs back and forth in the air like the Fonz.

Another man dressed the same as Michael came out from the swinging doors that led to the kitchen and stood in front of us while wiping his hands on his apron.

"This is Tony," Tommy said. Tony was much thinner than Michael.

He reached out his right hand and said, "Nice to meet you."

"You speak English," I blurted out a little too loudly.

"Yes, a leeetle bit," Tony replied as he smiled proudly, showing his large white teeth.

"Where are you from?" he asked me.

"From Illinois, near Chicago," I replied.

"Ohhh. Al Capone, gangster, you know, yes?"

I didn't know if he was asking if I knew Al Capone, or if I knew of him, either way, he was very excited that I was from Chicago.

"You know the Fonz?" Tony asked as he leaned back and did his best *Arthur Fonzerelli* impersonation.

"Uh, yes, I know the Fonz," thinking that he may have thought that I was friends with Arthur Fonzerelli by proximity, being from the same country as the Fonz.

I gave the double thumbs up and said, "Heyyyyy," in reply to Michael and Tony. They both laughed, and Tony invited us to sit anywhere we wanted as if we were his best customers as well as old friends.

Tommy was smiling as he said, "Aren't these guys fucking great? I fucking love this place; wait until you try their food, it's awesome!"

I was glad that we came to Fat Brothers.

The portions were huge and cheap. They brought a bowl of spaghetti carbonara that I could hardly finish. They had Coke with ice, and their desserts were fantastic. I had three chocolate covered balls filled with ice cream called *profiteroles*. I'm sure that I butchered the pronunciation, but Tony knew what I meant. We ate and joked and didn't want to leave when we were finished. Tommy was really cool, and I began to think that I may have been wrong to judge him so harshly. We walked back to the Pensione Lima while Tommy enjoyed one of his unfiltered Marlboros. When I pointed out a beautiful, half-naked woman on a large poster, we all stopped to look. Tommy said, "Fucking hot," as he flicked his ashes onto the sidewalk.

The pensione sat alone on a wide street devoid of the trees set into the wide concrete sidewalks that were planted throughout the city, a beige concrete desert without the busy restaurants and small shops that colored the rest of Milan. It was three blocks to the nearest tram stop and only one restaurant bothered to open its doors in the morning; a place where old men with defeated eyes would stand at the counter to drink their tiny cups of espresso, black and filled with impossible amounts of sugar; sweating awake to face a day without hope in their threadbare black and gray peasant's clothes.

I didn't miss the clang of the trolleys in the morning or the laughter of the uniformed children walking together on the wide sidewalks to school or the severe Carabinieri blowing their shrill whistles at the fast moving cars that beeped their way through the crowded intersections in the living parts of the city.

24

BLIND FORTUNE

I continued flying solo to the appointments that I was given in the morning by phone from the Agency. I was getting better at deciphering the cryptic laminated map that I kept in my back pocket. Each appointment was open-ended with no specific time to arrive, only a half day window of time to hand my book to a disinterested stranger. There was no pressure and no one to tell me what to do and how to look. I was on my own, and I enjoyed the nothingness of my job for those short weeks. I knew that this life would not last and knew without knowing that these blank days of spring would change for me as the heat of summer began to bake the sidewalks and buildings. Until I entered the living parts of the city, I was alone and almost invisible, free to breathe in the solitude without guilt as I began to forget the people who had been a part of my life only three weeks ago in a faraway place that faded from memory, leaving me to wonder if I had ever lived anywhere but here.

Kristina greeted me with a smile and a strong hug at

the end of each day. We would sit together in the cool shade of the softly lit agency and talk about the day or the girls that she worked with during the day. She was never too busy to talk to me, and I felt whole and happy in those moments at the end of each day. There was warmth without heat between Kristina and me; an older sister who thought nothing of squeezing her younger brother around the waist and talking about any subject that came into her beautiful head.

On a quiet, warm and sunny Wednesday afternoon I found Calvin and Kristina gesturing and talking frantically to a silent and slumped Tommy in the agency. I walked over and waved a silent hello to everybody and stood at a distance, waiting for them to finish with Tommy so that I could talk with Kristina.

"Tommy, you *cannot* take pictures with Fabrizio with those eyes," Calvin whispered intently as he took a close look at Tommy's eyes.

I looked at Tommy's eyes and saw the reddest eyes I had ever seen. There was no white, only red with yellow crust at the corner of his right eye. His face was a mask of pain and frustration; his hands were clenched into fists in his lap.

Kristina shook her head slowly back and forth with her arms crossed in front of her small hard breasts while hunching up her shoulders as if she were cold.

"Tommy, Tommy," she repeated softly with the worried eyes of a mother waiting at the side of the road for her child to return home late from school.

"We need to call Fabrizio and tell him," Calvin said to Kristina as he wiped his sweating face with the palms of his hands.

"But Calvin," Kristina protested, "This is a very big job. Maybe we can get some medicine for Tommy and he will get better before the job starts tomorrow."

"What did you do?" Calvin asked as he suddenly turned to face Tommy.

"Nothing!" Tommy lied defiantly as he continued to look at the floor, trying to hide his eyes from Calvin.

I was not a doctor, but I knew that Tommy had a bad, bad case of conjunctivitis, most likely from smoking, drinking, sleeping with dirty girls, and staying out in the nasty, dark clubs that pumped out loud music throughout the night as people danced on the floor and groped each other in the dark corners, hoping to find someone to spend the night with. I rarely saw him at the Pensione Lima at night, and he always looked bleary and puffy in the morning when I passed him in the hallway. I was no saint, but I rarely drank, and I never smoked. I was more than a little afraid of the clubs that seemed to be a place where nothing good ever seemed to happen. I didn't want to go looking for trouble; it always seemed to find me eventually, anyway.

"Darrilll!" Kristina said suddenly as if answering a question as she clapped her hands together loudly.

"Yes!" Calvin said with an equal amount of enthusiasm, "We can send Daryl with Tommy to Rome."

"No, no, no," Tommy said with an exaggerated shake of his head, "I'm not losing my ticket to the big time because of this *shrub*. I'm going to Rome to work with Fabrizio, and I don't need this *loser* tagging along."

"Listen, Tommy," Calvin said in a buttery-smooth voice; "Daryl is only coming with you in case you are not able to do the job. You can ride together on the train. If your eyes are better, then Daryl will come back to Milan in the morning."

"Fabrizio wants *me* to do the job!" Tommy countered angrily like a child having a fit while turning to point at me, "Not *this* guy."

Calvin picked up the phone from the desk and started to dial with a long index finger. He waited as the phone rang on the other end,

"Hello, Fabrizio?" Calvin said, "We have a problem. Tommy's eyes are a little red. We are sending another model with him just in case," he waited and listened before replying.

"Yes, yes. That is the one. From Chicago. He did the shooting with you for Vogue. Okay then. Ciao, Fabrizio."

Calvin settled the receiver onto the European style phone and turned to face Tommy and me with his hands clasped in front of his mouth, as if in prayer.

"Do you know how to get to the train station, Tommy?" Calvin asked.

"Yeah, yeah," Tommy replied impatiently, "This is *total* bullshit," he spat out as he grabbed his backpack and rushed out of the agency.

Calvin ignored his comment and said to me, "You need to follow Tommy to the train station. You need to take the express train to Rome. Fabrizio or his assistant Carmine will meet you at the train station in Rome. Do you understand?"

"Yes," I answered, "Can I have some money for the train?"

"Don't you have any money?"

"Not really."

"Okay," he replied reluctantly, "here is one hundred thousand lire. We will take it off of your account."

"Of course, Calvin. Thank you," I said as I turned and ran down the marble steps to the street.

Tommy was walking towards the corner where the tram stops and I jogged to catch up with him.

"Tommy, wait up," I said as he began to jog to keep ahead of me.

He flipped me the bird without looking back.

We arrived at a large stone building with enormous statues with soot-stained faces on either side of a large entrance with a roof held up by gigantic fluted columns that seemed to be carved from a single piece of stone. The statue faces puked out a greenish water from their open mouths into a pool filled with cigarette butts and paper wrappers floating around the surface of the dirty water.

Tommy stood in line for the tickets, and I walked up to him and said, "Calvin wants us to take the express train to Rome."

"Fuck Calvin," Tommy said in response.

"Hey Tommy, can we just cut the crap?" I asked. I was beginning to get tired of his *everybody is picking on me* bullshit.

"What the fuck does that mean?" he answered, turning around to face me.

"Let's just get to Rome and see what happens. I'm sure Fabrizio will find a way to make this work for you."

Tommy stared silently ahead.

The train was an open windowed passenger train with filthy floors and grimy windows. The air smelled of unwashed bodies, stale bread, and spilled wine. The people on the train did not look like the nicely dressed men and women I had noticed walking hurriedly in the train station; they looked like farmers and laborers with gnarled fingers and stooped backs. Tommy searched the sleeping berths for an open bed, but they were all taken. He settled into a seat at the end of the car and began to smoke as he stared blankly out the window. I stood in the narrow aisle near the pull-down seats and tried to keep from blocking the steady stream of passengers that walked through the car as the train slowly jerked itself into motion.

The train sat very low to the ground, more like a car than a train. I looked out the dust-covered windows as the scenery changed from tan and red brick buildings with small windows to open fields with randomly placed dirt roads. All of the men and woman that walked by or sat were built low to the ground with stubby-fingered hands that looked as if they had never played the piano well. I watched two old men dressed in layers of dusty clothes worn thin at the elbows and cuffs and a very old woman in a shapeless gray dress with an apron that sat upon her full lap. They were talking and gesturing to each other, flashing easy smiles with discolored and missing teeth whenever they spoke.

They laughed easily and seemed to touch each other on the knee or shoulder for emphasis when they spoke. They passed around a green glass bottle wrapped in colorful string with a flat-topped cork that one of the men held in his hand while taking long slugs from the bottle. One of the men with a full face furrowed with rows of deep wrinkles from years of sun motioned for me to come closer. I silently walked towards the small group, and he smiled and began to speak to me in Italian. I shook my head to indicate that I did not understand and he said as his small eyes brightened, "Ahhh. Americano, no?"

I nodded my head, and he offered me the bottle of wine. I held my hand up and said,

"No grazie," with a smile meant to show that I was not trying to offend.

He smiled broadly and said something quickly to the others that I did not understand and gave me a salute with his right hand as he held the bottle in his left.

"Botilia," he said to me while pointing at the bottle, "vino," he said slowly as he swirled the wine around in the bottle.

I nodded and smiled back and said slowly with as much accent as I could manage "Botilia. Vino."

They all clapped their hands together and said, "Bravo, bravo!"

I looked around to see where Tommy was and saw him squatting down with his back pressed against the side of the train. He held a cigarette between his right thumb and index finger and had his other arm pressed against the wall to keep him from falling over as the train bucked and swayed down the tracks. He stopped smoking and dropped his lit cigarette on the floor before standing up to grind it into the grooved rubber mat.

"Hey," he said to me as I walked towards him. His skin looked pale and sickly in the bright light of the train. There were scars that came from acne on his cheeks and down his neck that I hadn't noticed during our shoot last week. His eyes looked very red, and the infection had turned his right eyelid puffy; looking like a black eye that happened to be red.

"How's my eyes look?" he said with a desperate, pleading look plastered on his face.

I looked closely to see what I could easily have seen from ten feet away and answered with a serious expression to accompany my serious words.

"Not bad," I lied, "have you put any medicine on them?"

"No," he said defensively, "Just some Visine."

I knew it would take days for his eyes to clear, maybe even weeks. He gave me a tight-lipped smile as he tried to hide from me what could not be hidden. He looked at his feet.

The train stopped every few minutes and never seemed to get up to speed, as it slowed down to stop before it had time to accelerate to full speed. I realized after a long two hours of this that we had gotten on the wrong train; this train was definitely not an express. After three hours of people loading on with boxes tied up with twine and live chickens held upside down by their legs, I resigned myself to the fact that the trip would probably take all night. I started to look for a place to sit down. I left Tommy alone to wallow and began to walk from car to car in search of an open space. There was not a single seat on the train. I returned and found Tommy pacing up and down the aisle nervously while puffing on another cigarette.

He approached me fast as I walked through the door and asked frantically, "What are we going to do?"

"This train is a fucking local," he spat out.

No shit Mr. Genius of all things Italian, I thought to myself. I calculated that at our current rate we would get to Rome first thing in the morning, around seven.

"Try to get some rest," I offered uselessly, trying to calm Tommy down.

"Yeah, right," he spat out before hurriedly sucking in more smoke from his cigarette. "What are we going to do? Sleep on the fucking floor?" he asked with a look of contempt.

"Don't know," I replied quietly as I began to think about what he just said. That could work, I could sleep on the floor under the jump-seats. It would be a little dusty, but it was worth a try. I was feeling as if I had nothing to lose. Finding a spot to sleep on a crappy local train was not the biggest problem I had ever faced.

My dad had made sure that I had a memory full of really dramatic crap to draw from whenever I would face a really bad situation; nothing and no one could be as scary as my dad. When I was too young to know how to swim well, he would take me to the local pool and hold me under the water while he laughed as I struggled beneath the surface. When I was lifted to the surface, I would scan the sides of the pool for an adult who could help me. I would look to the other adults who were swimming or the lifeguards who sat on their towering chairs to see if any of them would have the courage to come to my rescue. I always determined in my young mind that they would not risk going up against my dad in order to keep me from being drowned without reason and seemingly without end. I struggled to suppress the fear that overwhelmed my whole body like a clawed hand ripping me open from the inside as my mind tried to keep my body from struggling against the impossible strength of my dad's grip on my thin arms, knowing that to struggle would only serve to anger my dad, which would increase the time between breaths and make the entire process last much longer. My mom never went to the pool with us during family swim and my older brother went off to swim while I was struggling to survive by surrendering. This became a standard part of my summers for four years. Each time that the warmth of summer followed the rain and mud of spring, I would silently dread summer and the time at the public pool with dad.

Finding a way to spend time away from Dad became a full-time job for me. The realization that I was safest when I was alone, even at the age of seven, stays with me still. Finding a place to rest on a local train in a foreign country where I didn't speak the language and had no chance of getting any help from the locals seemed to be a relaxing evening to me, at least in comparison to parts of my childhood.

A cold wave of empathy washed over me as I thought about the nightmare that Tommy was living through as his hopes of a *big break* with Fabrizio flew away like a balloon that a child loses hold of, watching helplessly as the balloon drifts and rises into the sky until it suddenly disappears from sight, as if it were never there in the first place. Within a few short hours, Tommy had turned from a cocky Southie into a child hoping and praying that reality was a dream and dreams were reality. He was a far cry from the model that flipped me off a few hours earlier as he stormed out of the agency.

I looked down at the filthy floor and tried to reconcile in my mind that I would be sleeping there for the next six or seven hours. The only space that was not occupied was beneath the jump seats that lined the narrow aisle. I bent down to survey the amount of space under the passengers' legs and decided that it was worth a try. I took off my backpack, pulled out my blue LL Bean pocket anorak, put it on, pulling the hood over my head and pulling the drawstring tight until only my eyes and mouth were exposed. I put on my sunglasses to protect my eyes from the dirt that puffed up from the floor as the passengers tromped by in their rawhide laced work boots. I turned the front of my backpack towards my chest and wrapped the straps a few times around my arms to keep my pack from being stolen while I slept.

I did my best to communicate my desire to sleep on the floor beneath the passenger's legs with a combination of English and an exaggerated form of mime motions, trying to get them to understand that I wanted to crawl behind their legs to sleep on the floor. They all looked at me as if I were a leprous lunatic, with wide-eyed expressions that indicated their disbelief and resistance to my seemingly insane request. The five people who needed to move so that I could squeeze beneath the seats looked at me as if I were crazy, but they eventually complied and allowed me to get under their seats as I smiled graciously while offering a slew of grazies in return for their cooperation. I lay down under the seats, stretched out my legs and folded my arms across my chest. I felt like a corpse in a coffin, but except for the sickening smell of the sticky floor and the bumping of the train axles beneath me, I was quite comfortable. In less than five minutes I had fallen asleep.

It was sunny when I awoke to the commotion of the passengers exiting the train. The cool of morning pushed in through the open windows. It felt good on my face as I rubbed my puffy eyes with my knuckles, trying to speed up the waking process. All of the passengers were getting to their feet. A small group of wrinkled peasant women with dark clothes and sturdy, bowed legs spoke with wildly animated gestures to a slim conductor that stood with his hands on his hips. They all pointed towards me as I struggled to get out from under the seats and stand up in the narrow aisle, my right knee almost completely locked in the straight position. I looked up at the scarecrow conductor from my *bed* and struggled to untie my backpack from my forearms while I scooted sideways on my butt to get out from under the seats.

He started to yell, "al-ey, al-ey!" at me in a loud, shrill voice while adopting a stern look that pulled at all sides of his face. He motioned impatiently with both hands for me to get up from the floor while he continued to screech at me in Italian. I had figured out that sleeping on the floor was probably against the rules and scarecrow wanted to either scare me or levy some stupid punishment that involved holding my passport and shaking me down for fifty thousand lire. He was slim and wore a blue suit with a small fabric covered cardboard hat on his head. He looked at me with disdain as he rained down a string of nasty sounding Italian words that I could not fully understand. I turned my backpack around and slung it over my right shoulder as I slowly stood up in the narrow aisle without talking, but keeping my eyes focused on him as I returned his stare without speaking. He watched me stand up and seemed to abruptly stop talking as he realized that I was much bigger than he was.

I held my hands out with my palms facing him and said slowly in English, "Okay, now what Sergio Valenti?"

He shook his head as if someone had slapped him hard across the face and turned to walk out of the car, either rethinking if it was worth it to continue yelling at me or searching for some beefy reinforcements to punish me for simply sleeping under the seats. I stumbled towards the exit, still more asleep than awake and tried once more to rub the sleep from my eyes. I slowly walked out the door and onto the brick and concrete platform. I scanned the crowd for Tommy and found him hunched over and leaning against the corner of the brick building with his arms tight across his chest. He looked nervous; flicking his fingers up and down, as if playing an imaginary piano. I walked over and quietly stood next to him with my arms limp at my sides and waited.

25

SO MUCH PROMISE...

A stumpy man with an ill-fitting black suit coat, too tight pants and thick, black-rimmed glasses held up a brown piece of cardboard with the word Tommy written on it in pencil.

I nudged Tommy gently with my elbow and said, "I think that guy is our ride," as I pointed to Stumpy holding the cardboard sign.

"Oh yeah," Tommy replied without looking. He looked like he was going to vomit on my shoes at any moment.

Stumpy led us across the narrow parking lot to a white van, and we both climbed in the back. After a short ride in the cargo van without windows, we arrived at a small hotel with a red canopy and flowers growing from large clay pots that were placed on each side of the steps that led into the building. Fabrizio stood at the top of the hotel steps like an army general with his arms crossed over his barrel chest, and his sleeves rolled up to the elbow to expose his hairy forearms. He slowly walked down to meet us as we stepped out from the van. He ignored me and went straight to Tommy.

"Let me look at your eyes my young friend," he said with a paternal look of skepticism mixed with sympathy.

Tommy reluctantly slid his dark sunglasses down his nose and then off his face. Fabrizio looked closely into his eyes and sighed loudly while shaking his head from side to side. He said something to the short driver in Italian, and the driver nodded.

He turned back to Tommy and said in a voice devoid of emotion, "Tommy, you must go back to Milano. Ciao, andiamo."

Tommy *really* looked like he was about to vomit as all the remaining blood drained from his face.

"But Fabrizio, can't I do some photos with sunglasses or something? C'mon! Please, Fabrizio?" Tommy pleaded with a twisted expression of pain stretched across his pale face that pinched his eyes until they were almost closed.

Fabrizio shook his head quietly and rubbed the back of his neck, turned to me, and said without emotion; "Okay, Mr. Chicago. Get your things into your room and meet us in the lobby in thirty minutes."

I looked over to Tommy and extended my right hand, preparing to say I'm sorry and all that feel good crap, but Tommy wouldn't have any of it, and he hissed out quietly through clenched teeth for my ears only, "Fuck you, asshole. You fucking suck!"

I turned to walk away and took the steps two at a time into the lobby. I didn't turn back to watch Tommy leave.

My room was small but clean and elegant. There was a queen-sized bed with a thick down comforter against the wall furthest from the large casement window. Plush green drapes blocked out the early morning sun in my little cloistered space. The bathroom was spotless; small bars of soap wrapped in paper to the right of the small white sink with a shiny brass faucet. A small refrigerator was tucked into the bottom section of a cherry cabinet on the wall opposite the bed, and I opened it to see what was inside. Beer, soda, and small bottles of juice were arranged neatly on white wire shelves. Oversized candy bars, nuts, and small wedges of soft cheese wrapped in plastic sat above the refrigerator on a shelf covered with glass. A thick piece of paper with a printed list of foods and drinks sat on top of the small cherry desk covered with a sheet of glass. I had not eaten for over fifteen hours and wanted to eat all of the food and wash it down with three or four sodas. I settled on one small round-bellied bottle of Orangina and a large bag of salted peanuts. I knew that I would be paying for whatever I ate before we went back to Milano, but right then I didn't care.

I got undressed and walked into the bathroom to take a shower. The water was hot and strong and I closed my eyes as the water warmed my head, back and front, filling the small bathroom with steam. I washed my face, hair, and body with the small bar of soap and stood motionless in the strong stream of water with my eyes closed, thinking about how much better this was than the weak-ass stream of lukewarm water that came from the shower at the prostitute pensione. I grabbed a thick, white towel from a tubular shelf that sat high upon the wall behind the toilet and dried myself slowly, starting with my face and ending with my feet. The towel was soft cotton, and I held it to my face to feel its plushness against my skin. I brushed my teeth with a small blue toothbrush wrapped in plastic and glanced at my reflection in the mirror that covered the wall behind the vanity. I looked dark and tired; there were small bags under my eyes, but the whites of my eyes were clear. I rubbed my eyes with the backs of my hands, hoping to erase some of the puffiness from a lousy night on the floor of the train before meeting with Fabrizio in the lobby. I smiled briefly at the boy looking back at me from the mirror and got dressed in the clothes that lay on the bed.

I walked down to the lobby feeling refreshed and ready to go. Fabrizio greeted me with a warm handshake and a wide smile. He introduced me to the people sitting on the plush chairs that sat in a semicircle in the small waiting area. Carmine smiled, nodded, and waved when Fabrizio introduced him. Fabrizio then introduced the female model, Gia. She was young with smooth porcelain skin and long, dark hair. Her hair lay thick and smooth down to the middle of her back. She stood up from her chair, shook my hand firmly while looking straight into my eyes as she said, "Bonjiorno," with a smile that made my stomach jump as I looked back into her eyes as she squeezed my hand. I silently prayed that this wouldn't be the last job that Fabrizio and I did together as we stepped into the large white box van that sat waiting at the front of the hotel.

I chose to sit next to Gia in the first row of seats and settled my backpack under my seat. Fabrizio turned back from the passenger seat as we started to drive and began talking. Whatever he said to me in English he would then repeat to Gia in Italian. He spoke of what he saw out of the window and pointed to buildings we passed with wide eyes and excited words. I listened intently, instinctively understanding that it was important to him that I paid attention to his words as well as the buildings that he pointed out as we drove through the narrow streets of Rome. Gia listened intently as well with her elegant hands folded gently in her lap. I wondered if Gia and Fabrizio had worked together before. We arrived at a small park with large statues of Roman soldiers with shields, helmets, and spears standing guard on either side of the road. The road was made of white, crushed stone and the tires crunched loudly as we slowly rolled past the stone soldiers standing guard. Soon we arrived at a small pond with dark green water. There were two large swans swimming slowly in circles in the middle of the pond.

The art director dressed Gia in a fitted skirt and sleeveless striped top that hugged her curves. I was dressed in a checkered sport coat, light blue shirt, and skinny wool tie with black wool slacks. A small woman with a spray bottle spritzed my hair and then worked in some gel as she pushed my hair away from my face. Gia's hair and makeup had already been done. She sat quietly on a black, iron park bench with her feet together and her hands on her lap. She was meant to look like Audrey Hepburn. I thought she looked more like a movie star from the sixties than a model.

Fabrizio suddenly appeared between Gia and me and asked me excitedly, "Do you know Gregory Peck?"

"I think so," I replied, trying to remember if I was thinking of a black and white movie with Gregory Peck or Cary Grant. I thought that Gregory Peck was the broad-shouldered, tall actor with a square jaw and a serious look in his eyes when he spoke; the same actor who played Captain Ahab in Moby Dick. He spoke slowly with a deep voice and the unhurried speech of a man who was accustomed to being listened to.

"Well," he continued with bright eyes, "you are Gregory Peck, and Gia is Audrey Hepburn in the movie Roman Holiday. Do you know this movie?" he asked in a voice that expected an answer.

"I think so," I said, hoping that he wouldn't question my knowledge of the old black and white movie. The only old movies that I had seen were on Family Classics early Saturday afternoons, and if it wasn't a war movie or a Western, I probably hadn't seen it.

"It doesn't matter," he said as he shook his head, "we are going to recreate the movie with you and Gia. You actually look more like Gregory Peck than Tommy, and *Lei Magazine* gave me a choice over the male model, sooo, the pictures will not be amazing, but this magazine pays me very well and there will be more jobs, for both of us. Are you ready, Mr. Daryl from Chicago?" he asked with the same warm smile that I had seen when we finished the job for Vogue a few weeks ago.

We shot pictures all around the city. Fabrizio showed me the Polaroid tests and gave me three to keep. I enjoyed seeing the pictures of Gia and me near statues, fountains, and in front of the Coliseum. I wore thick-rimmed glasses with black frames. Gia and I laughed throughout all of the shots and even when we took breaks for lunch or to travel to the next location. There was no heat between us but I enjoyed her company, and she seemed to genuinely enjoy working with me. We pretended to be lovers; smiling, hugging, and even kissing in a few shots. The art director seemed very pleased with the results, and she asked Fabrizio where this young male model came from. I laughed quietly to myself as I thought of how easy it would have been for me to have never arrived in Italy and have never gotten the chance to work with Fabrizio for Lei Magazine. I knew at that moment that my life would never be the same.

I remember seeing the Coliseum for the first time as we drove around the outside walls looking for a place to park. It was much bigger than I had imagined and seemed to be left in its original state; no museum sections or souvenir shops, only a huge stone structure, partially collapsed by the ravages of time. We shot photos outside the Coliseum with the rounded and arched windows showing in the background. I stayed quiet for most of the shooting, nodding when I was told to move to another spot or do something different with my hands or body. The work was easy and the mood was calm and light. We attracted a small crowd shooting at the bottom of a long flight of marble steps near a fountain with stone fish statues spouting a constant stream of water into a deep, round pool carved from limestone. People in the crowd pointed at Gia and me while taking pictures as we waited for Carmine to change Fabrizio's film. A few of the young girls in the crowd came closer to the shooting and spoke to us in Italian. Gia translated their words to English;

"They want to know if we are really in love," she said laughing while speaking to me in English for the first time with a strong but beautiful sounding Italian accent. She explained to the young girls that we were working together for a magazine. I understood the word Americano as the young girls continued giggling and pointing at us. Gia gave me a playful smile with a wink while the camera clicked rapidly as Fabrizio took picture after picture. Gia kissed me gently on the cheek as I smiled before we packed up and headed back to the hotel.

On the second day, we took three pictures in three different locations. We ended the job in the early afternoon under a gray, cloud-filled sky. Fabrizio spent most of the time looking into his small telescope with the dark lens at the sky. He explained that he was watching the movement of the clouds, waiting for the time when the light would change before taking the next picture.

Fabrizio and Carmine sang a song in Italian and celebrated briefly after the last picture was taken. They both looked very happy about what they had accomplished and shook hands and slapped each other on the back. Gia stayed in Rome after the shooting and Fabrizio, Carmine and I rode back to Milan in the white van. Fabrizio talked to me about his next job that would be with Mr. Kane Sicner and me, that started in two days. I was beginning to understand what a big break this Roman Holiday job was as I stared out the window at the trees that seemed to blend into lines of green and brown as we drove quickly by.

Early Monday morning I met Kane, Fabrizio, and Carmine on the sidewalk in front of an old brownstone near the center of town. Kane greeted me with a smile and a firm, enthusiastic handshake and said sincerely, "All right bro! Glad to be working with you again."

Fabrizio and Carmine both smiled as we worked to load the equipment and clothing into the same van that we had used in Rome. Fabrizio asked Carmine to buy pastries and coffee at a small bakery down the street. When he returned, we all got into the van and drove away from the city.

Fabrizio soon turned around in the front passenger seat and spoke passionately about Bologna and the work that we would be doing for the next three days as Carmine drove. Kane and I listened without talking for the first hour of our trip.

Marpessa flashed within my mind as I watched the wheat fields and the vineyards wash by in a blur of color. I pulled up the pictures of her in my mind from our first meeting and felt a pain fill my chest as the understanding that she would never be my girlfriend reconciled with my childish fantasy that could never come true. My mind wanted a girl that was good and sane and stable, but my soul wanted someone who was not available, someone who would make my heart jump from my chest each time I thought of her; who was always new. I knew that it was impossible without having to spend any time thinking out the logic; there was no logic in my heart.

Without warning, the *white noise* took over as the sadness crept up from inside as I drifted away to the place that always waited for me, an inexplicable prison without walls. I tried to reason with it and explain that things were good and I should be happy. I failed quickly and completely as the infinite sadness pulled away the joy as quickly and efficiently as you strip the sheets from an old bed. It left me alone and cold in a dark hole without hope.

The sadness stayed with me in Bologna, even with the realization that the pictures destined for a black and white spread in the pages of Vogue would change everything. I saw a face that I had never seen when Fabrizio handed me the black and white Polaroids to keep. I kept my thoughts wrapped up tightly in my head, as I smiled and laughed at the jokes that were constantly going back and forth between Fabrizio and Kane. All of the pictures were of Kane or me standing alone. I stood in front of abandoned buildings, rusted bridges, and city streams lined with stone walls. The clothing looked like it came from a time of war, giving me a serious look far beyond my nineteen years. My eyes were squinted almost closed against the harsh light of day, even more so when the sun would work its way through the low gray clouds of early summer. The green water iris of my eyes could not block the light of the sun. This squinting had gone on for all of my life. On sunny days walking snow-covered fields I could not open my eyes at all without the aid of dark sunglasses to filter the harsh light of the sun. Fabrizio did all of the photos by himself with Carmine relegated to supplying him with fresh Nikon camera bodies each time he extended his right hand. There was no stylist, no lights, no reflectors; it was all done by Fabrizio. He worked quickly and efficiently to capture each scene on film in under 20 minutes. His unshakeable confidence allowed him to take over while I simply looked at the camera or looked away; putting my hands and feet anywhere that felt right. He guided the picture without controlling every movement, seeming to have complete confidence in Kane and me.

It felt as if I had always done this and would continue to do it for a long time. I was part of something without doing anything. I was different inside. I was someone who existed. Even if I were unnoticed for the rest of my life, I had done something. My critical mind began to soften and relax as I felt that I had some value. Even though no one told me this, I was sure that it could not be taken away from me.

The barren locations mirrored the hole of sadness that surrounded me as I went through the motions for two days. I did not do anything; I only stood or sat, looked at the camera or off into the distance. The two black and white Polaroids that Fabrizio showed me were of a hard-faced man, a man that I did not recognize. Fabrizio was thrilled at how the harsh light and the black and white film turned me from a kid into a man. He told us he was very happy that Kane and I looked nothing like the pretty faced models who posed for the camera with artificially pursed lip and wide eyes that I had seen in the magazines. Fabrizio told me not to change a thing. He wanted me to be who I really was.

After we finished the last photo, we ate lunch at a small restaurant that sat awkwardly in a dusty parking lot near a single lane, paved road. Fabrizio ordered steak for the four of us. He told us that this part of Italy was known for its beef cattle as we waited hungrily for our food.

I finished my thick, rare steak slowly, the juice filling my mouth as I bit into the large pieces.

I allowed myself to feel the pleasure of working and eating with such good people. The *white noise* walked away from me and stood at a safe distance, waiting for the next opportunity to get a boney-fingered grasp on the thin boy that struggled in the deep water.

We took our time with lunch. It was as if Fabrizio had bought the rest of the day by finishing work early. Kane leaned far back in his sturdy wooden chair and clasped his hands behind his head, occasionally reaching for his almost cold beer to take a long drink. Fabrizio began smoking a dark cigar and blew round puffs of smoke towards the ceiling that hung in the air over the table until the slow-moving ceiling fan broke them apart. I looked out the window at the sweeping landscape without buildings and the black and white cows that grazed in the rolling hills that stretched out forever behind the barbed wire fence, looked back at

Fabrizio, and then at Kane and Carmine, and closed my eyes to remember the scene and enjoy that brief moment when I knew that I was exactly where I should be.

We loaded into the van without rushing and opened all of the windows. I slouched down in my seat and stretched out my legs until they were straight, crossing them at the ankle. Within a few minutes, I had drifted off into that indulgent sleep that only happens when you are alone or with those who allow you to be yourself. It was like eating a huge, warm slice of chocolate cake slowly and consciously while you sit alone in a cool, white kitchen on a hot summer's day, closing your eyes to allow your mouth to taste each of the flavors as your tongue feels the textures of the icing and the moist cake.

I awoke slowly to the brightness of the late afternoon sun as I felt Fabrizio shake my shoulder.

"I want you both to come to Paris with me for a shooting," he said excitedly.

Kane and I replied, "Great," at the same time as I rubbed my eyes, trying to get them to focus.

"Listen, Mr. Daryl. Do not show anyone your book," he continued in a hushed tone with a serious expression on his bearded, full face. "I am sending a Polaroid of you to Christian Dior. They cannot know that you are nineteen. They will *never* use you for this campaign if they know your age."

I nodded my head and replied somberly, "I understand," with as much sincerity as I could muster. I tried to imagine what Paris would be like as I drifted back to sleep while we drove on through the day that seemed to hold so much promise.

26

FALLING THROUGH THE FLOOR

The stifling heat of an early summer had moved into Milano while we were away. I spent most nights lying awake and sweating in my bed. There were no fans or small breezes through my open window to move the stifling air and break the heat. Most nights I could not sleep. It was too hot to lie on the damp sheets of the bed, so I sat at the small table near the open windows and read wearing only a pair of white boxer shorts. One hot, starless night when the stone walls dripped with moisture like tears, I met a model named Petra in the lobby of the Pensione Lima. We quietly walked up to her room at the end of the hall and spent hours talking about everything and nothing. She seemed to be casting a spell on me in which time was suspended and the dreamy look in her eyes let me know that she was letting herself go to the place where lust blurs all of the lines of caution that are so clearly drawn in the light of day. I watched her talk and move slightly as she sat on the bed with her back pressed gently against the damp stone walls. Kristina had shown me Petra's card one late afternoon at the agency; she had described her to me as having tits as hard as rock. The image of rock hard breasts stuck with me as we talked quietly about where we came from, how long we had been in Italy and all about the families we had left back home.

Petra complained about the heat with a soft voice and began to pull her light cotton t-shirt over her head and then stood up smoothly and unbuttoned her small white shorts and let them fall noiselessly to the concrete floor before sitting back down on the edge of the bed leaving only her pink panties that rose up high on her hips, showing her long, lean thighs that glistened with a thin sheen of perspiration. She sat back down and covered herself with a sheet on her lap as she leaned her bare back against the stone wall at the head of the bed. I took in her shape in the dim light from the one lamp that sat on the small table at the head of her bed. She returned my gaze unflinchingly, giving me silent permission with her eyes to look at her for as long as I wanted. She looked down at her firm, high breasts and her flat stomach while she slowly stood up and gently pulled her panties down to her knees before letting them drop to the floor. I felt my heart move sideways in my chest and up into my throat as everything in the room around Petra went out of focus. I saw only her beautiful body, full of smooth curves and flat places. It seemed to take hours for her to cross the floor as she silently walked towards me to the chair that I sat on across the room with a slow, tantalizing walk. She stopped with her knees just touching the front of the chair and smiled a closed-lip smile as she looked down at me with large, soulful eyes before wrapping her long arms around my neck and then bending down to kiss me warmly on the mouth, her lips moving and pressing while her smooth tongue gently licked my lips. I returned her kiss tentatively while pulling her by her waist slowly onto my lap. She carefully worked each long leg to the side of the chair until she was straddling me, settling the weight of her hips onto my thighs as she continued kissing me with more passion as each moment passed, running her fingers through my hair and pulling me closer as we explored each other's mouths with our flushed lips and soft tongues. I could feel myself rising up under her as she pushed her hips into mine and she reached her hands around to my shoulders and tilted her head back while pulling me into her full, firm breasts with nipples that seemed to grow with anticipation of my mouth tasting them. I stopped before kissing her breasts and pulled away slowly, gently holding her hand in mine as thoughts of Marpessa drifted through my mind. A mind that would not allow my body to continue in the dimly lit room as I looked to the floor, unable to look directly at Petra as we sat together for long moments before she rose up slowly, touched my face gently with the back her hand and lay down on her bed, with a look of compassion and acceptance on her beautiful face.

She touched her flat stomach lightly with her right hand while gazing at my eyes and then looking down at my front. I wanted to get up and walk out of the room and have a sleepless night in the heat, but my mind was silenced by the lust that coursed through my body. I stood up from my chair as Linda watched me from the bed and pulled my shorts down in the front before letting them drop to the floor. I stood a few feet away from her and stared down at her lying on the bed. She looked at me and lifted her arms up towards me while biting her lower lip softly as I walked towards her. I arranged myself between her open legs and lay with my full weight on her hips and belly as she wrapped her strong arms tight around my waist. We lay together for the rest of the hot night, sweating until the sheets were soaked, stopping to look at each other and laugh gently as we rested between embraces. I felt like I was falling through the floor as time and space stopped moving as we did the things that I had only dreamed of until the soft light of morning pushed through the angled slats of the large metal shutters that covered the window. We fell asleep in a tangle as a cooling morning breeze made its way into the room.

I kept the jobs with Fabrizio to myself, instinctively knowing that the other models in the hotel wouldn't celebrate my newfound success while they struggled for money to pay for food and rent. I didn't want to leave the Pensione Lima, even though the cost for a night wasn't as important as it was when I arrived there four weeks ago. I liked my large room, and I liked that everyone in the hotel was either a prostitute or a model, two groups that had very little interest in bothering other people with demands for quiet, curfews, or the desire to keep track of me in any way. It was not a place that I would want anyone from my Church or my family to visit, but for some reason that I couldn't explain, the vocation of the first-floor residents didn't bother me at all. Everyone just wanted to be left alone; to go about their business. It was easy for me to give up the status of a fine hotel with elevators, air conditioning and a fine restaurant with a piano in exchange for a place where everyone kept mostly to themselves. Pensione Lima was a shit hole, but it was my shit hole.

One uneventful night when the heat continued to push its way into my room long after the sun had disappeared, I heard models talking down the hall over the crackly music from an old radio. The talking grew louder and one voice rose above the others; it was Tommy swearing loudly as the other voices grew silent. His voice got louder and louder as he walked towards my room until I could hear him directly outside my door. He kicked open my door until it banged into the wall, entered and began shouting, "*This is* the fucking guy that stole my jobs!" I turned to face Tommy and saw two men standing slightly behind Tommy to his left and right, each with a beer in his hand.

I looked at Tommy with a smile, certain that he was joking before saying quietly, "Hey, Tommy."

"Go fuck yourself with your *hey Tommy* shit!" he said, as his face went from wet paper white to deep red. His hands were clenched into fists as he leaned forward, putting all of his weight on his toes. The faces behind Tommy looked at me expectantly, waiting; waiting to see what would happen next.

"Take it easy Tommy," I said with another smile and a slight shake of my head, still believing that Tommy was joking and more than a little drunk.

He moved quickly towards me like a bull rushing a matador and screamed with the urgency and pain of a man who has lost everything, "You think it's fucking funny? Huh? I been here for three fucking months waiting for my chance and then you come along and..." he grabbed me by the waist and locked his arms by grabbing each wrist and started lifting and pushing me across the room.

The two faces brought their bodies into the room, standing a few feet away from Tommy and me. They didn't want to miss anything and were leering at the scene like they were witnessing a car crash. I could smell the beer and cigarettes from Tommy's breath on the right side of my face as he tried to lift me from the floor by getting his hips under me and bending back hard. He was stronger than he looked and I briefly thought about letting him wrestle himself out. I was sure he would tire quickly and let me go.

The two faces were floating just behind Tommy now, laughing and smiling with big crazy-ass grins that you see in a crowd drooling on themselves, waiting to see something bad happen. Anything bad will do, as long as it's evil and ends with violence.

"Tommy, okay, I get it, you're really upset. Party time is over, let me go buddy," I said, as calmly as I could, while grabbing his wrists and attempting to pull them apart as the two faces continued to grin malevolently at me, their eyes filled with blood as they moved closer for a better view of the action.

The calm was leaving my limbs as I felt the situation spin into a place that I couldn't control, like a truck heading towards the edge of a sheer cliff. I was calm but could feel the situation getting out of hand quickly. I fought the urge to send an elbow crashing into his face to break his nose quickly and cleanly, but I knew that would bring blood, and the blood would bring more faces with red eyes to my room and maybe even the Carabinieri with their tiny machine guns and tight boots that ended at the knee. I didn't want to lose everything for this Southie, even if I were right and he was wrong. I tried to push back the animal rage and ignore the grim faces floating to my left and right and pull my mind together; to think clearly and calmly while chaos shrunk the walls and spun the floor under my feet.

I turned towards him hard, trying to break his hard boned grip around my waist but I couldn't move. Tommy lifted me as I changed my balance and picked me up off the floor while rushing towards the open window; pressing me against the rusty iron rail. I knew that Tommy didn't have the strength to lift me over the railing and throw me onto the street two floors below, but when I looked at the small screws that held the railing to the stone wall, I began to be concerned. There was a one-inch space between the stone wall and the rail where a screw was missing at the top of the rail. A vision of Tommy and me riding the old railing two floors to the cobblestones below flashed through my mind as I struggled to break his grip around my waist with my hands again. That didn't work, and he pushed insanely with even more intensity than a moment before.

I could feel that I had only moments to act until something very bad happened and my mind sent my body to a place where my strength went from human to animal. It was a phenomenon that my older brother referred to as *bone strength* or *psycho strength* when describing my ability to break free from two or three kids when they were trying to hold me down as the panic and rage mixed together in my blood to create a brief moment of intense strength.

I broke his hands apart by grabbing his wrists, squeezing hard, and pulling as I pushed away from the window with my bare feet on the stone wall. I turned violently towards him as he fell back towards the bed. Quickly hooking his head within the crook of my left arm and scooping up his right leg with my right arm, I pulled my hands together and locked them around my wrists until Tommy was off the ground with his knee pushed into his face in the *cradle position*, the one move I remembered from wrestling. I pressed his balled up body onto the bed and squeezed even tighter, pushing his knee hard into his bleary-eyed face, keeping my weight on him while keeping my bare feet firmly on the stone floor to apply pressure. Looking down at his face, I saw the crab-shell whiteness returned to his cheeks as the red rage drained slowly from his acne scarred skin while he breathed, in short, gasping breaths, struggling to fill his lungs while rolled up into a ball.

"Are we done now?" I said at him with my face close to his white face with as much patience as I could gather. I struggled mightily to resist the almost overwhelming urge to raise up from the bed and punch my hard fist through his face and into the mattress below, viciously taking my place in a long line of brutal fighters that made up my ancestry. I chose instead to keep my rage inside as I watched his white face and pig eyes look up at me while silently pleading for a mercy that even he knew he didn't possess; to let things go and forget about the night.

The floating heads moved quietly to the doorway as the white returned to their eyes. Their expressions transformed into knit brows of faux concern as they hovered in the doorway, expectantly waiting.

"This is over. Right, Tommy?" I said in a softer tone, trying to leave Tommy a way out without taking all of his dignity from him.

"Yeah, Daryl. Yeah," he said between breaths as he closed his eyes hard against the tears of grief that sat just behind them, ready to come out in racking sobs as soon as reality smacked him into sobriety and understanding when he understands clearly all that truly was, and all that truly will be.

I unclasped my locked hands slowly, allowing his head to rest on the bed. I stood up and patted Tommy on the back as he rose slowly from the bed. He slowly shuffled without purpose out the door, quietly following the two floating heads down the hall. I closed and then locked my door.

I woke early and walked over to the open windows to look up at the morning sky streaked with red, thin lines of clouds. A cool breeze pushed the tan curtains around in small circles, dusting the floor with their tattered edges. I washed my face in the small sink attached to the wall and changed into jeans and a blue button-down shirt with a crisp collar and wrinkled sleeves. Kane was sitting alone in the lobby as I came down the stairs. He had his bag at the end of his outstretched legs and was looking calmly out the wide doorway that led down the stairs and into the street. He looked up at me as I slowly made my way down the stairs to the lobby, stiff and sore from the fight with Tommy.

He flashed a white-toothed smile and said, "You ready to do this, bro?" calmly with a tinge of excitement in his voice.

"Yes," I answered, pleased with the thought of leaving the pensione for a few days to work in Paris.

We walked two streets over to find a cab and flagged down a Mercedes taxi with his lights on.

The driver looked back at us in the mirror as Kane told him in Italian to take us to the airport. He flashed his stained tobacco teeth in the rear view mirror as he shifted his gaze from Kane to me. He seemed to be happy to get out of Milan as well.

Kane ended with a sincere, "Grazie," as the cab pulled smoothly away from the curb and blended into the light, early morning traffic.

"I can't wait to meet some French babes in Paris," Kane said while leaning towards me as if he had some really important news.

"Yeah," I said with little enthusiasm, as I thought about the prospect of meeting women while shooting with Fabrizio in Paris. I thought about speaking about Marpessa to Kane, but changed my mind before the words slipped out of my mouth. I felt selfish and jealous about Marpessa and talking about her seemed an easy way to lose what I didn't have. My mind worked hard to deceive my heart into forgetting the willowy siren with some magic trick of memory. I was not successful.

Kane was relaxed with a crackle of raw energy beneath the surface as if he could spring into action at any moment. He rarely mentioned his life in Malibu except when he talked about surfing at the beach from sun-up till sundown. I tried to imagine his life in high school, of surfing and sun, while he tilted his head back and spoke about the California days that seemed to never end. He spoke of the ocean as if it were a living person, a beautiful woman to whom he could not wait to return.

Kane had squared off shoulders that went at right angles to his neck, making him look larger than he was. He had a loosely defined swimmers' build, lacking the six-pack abs that many of the models had. Kane didn't possess a body that would be photographed without a shirt. Fabrizio had shot one photo of Kane without a shirt in the 'Chariots of Fire' shooting, but Kane covered most of his body with a large white towel draped strategically over his shoulders. He didn't have a bad body, just not the cut works of art that I saw in the photos of the male models that were on the walls and cards of our agency. He had long arms that ended with the large, well-formed hands of a professional baseball player, freckled brown from the California sun. He dressed comfortably in faded t-shirts, flip-flops, and well-worn jeans or Op shorts. His blond hair was cut short at the back and sides and left long in the front. The surface of his hair was bleached blond from the sun, leaving the hair beneath the same dark blond color as mine. His long face stopped abruptly at an overly squared off cleft chin, giving him the look of a poorly drawn comic-book superhero. Kane was not classically handsome. I think he was aware of the limitations of his face; knowing that beautiful women would not slide across a crowded nightclub bar to whisper into his ear the things they wanted to do to him. To get there, he knew that he had to do most of the talking.

We boarded the plane, and Kane sat across the narrow Air France aisle and ordered coffee from the slim stewardess with shapely calves and dark hair pulled into a very tight ponytail. She bent over until I imagined Kane could smell her sweet breath as she handed him his hot cup of coffee and then poured the cream and gave him a handful of sugar packets. They got lost in each other's eyes for a moment before she turned abruptly and moved to the next row. His hunt had started already, I thought to myself. I carefully stretched my stiff right leg into the aisle and drifted off into a drooling, dry-mouthed and dreamless sleep as the plane throoshed noisily through the sun-filled morning sky.

27

CHRISTIAN DIOR

Kane and I arrived at The Pin Up Studio near the *Champs de Elysée*, a wide side street near the *Arc de Triomphe*. I had seen the *Arc de Triomphe* on television during the *Tour de France*. It looked much more impressive in real life, except for the graffiti that covered the inside of the arch, as I looked in from the taxi that drove us around the giant turn around that encircled the *Arc*.

Fabrizio approached us quickly as we entered through the side door and introduced us to Chad, a tall, slim model with impeccably groomed brown hair. Chad looked down his nose and over his fine glasses at us as he extended a slim-fingered hand to shake. He held my hand with a limp grip. Kane gave me a look while Chad was looking away with a smirk and a quick tilt of his head. There was no need to talk; I knew exactly what he meant.

Fabrizio hustled around the studio readying the camera, testing the lights, and explaining things in French to a thirty-something woman with a brown clipboard in the crook of her left arm. A new French assistant stood casually near the camera, waiting for Fabrizio to order him into action. He was wearing baggy jeans with holes that were made by machines in strategic places to make them look old and chic, and a loose t-shirt made of material finer than cotton, maybe silk. Fabrizio circled away from the lights and approached Kane and me with wide eyes and fast moving hands. He looked like a sixth-grade teacher giving last minute instructions to the young actors ready to walk on stage for the school play, nervous, and not particularly confident. I was puzzled by the change in his demeanor, but went with it and walked over to the temporary changing room, with the white fabric walls and polished chrome racks filled with men's clothes lined up on the long walls. Within ten minutes Kane and I were ready for the first photo of the day. We met up with Chad in front of the lights and began the first picture standing side by side in our beautiful clothing and looking into the camera, like an old-time portrait from the 1800's.

Fabrizio was very excited when he walked out from behind the camera to show us the color Polaroid of the picture he was shooting. The lighting was dim, and the camera focus was soft as if the lens were looking through a light fog that had settled on a stone bridge in the early morning hours. Chad immediately asked if he could have the Polaroid picture with an attitude of entitlement as he extended a well-manicured hand, palm facing up while waiting impatiently for Fabrizio to hand him the picture. Fabrizio turned his back to Chad and answered *no* as he turned away from us and tucked the Polaroid securely into his photographer's vest pocket. I was secretly happy that Chad had been shut down by Fabrizio with the Polaroid request. I got the feeling that it was more the way that Chad asked that got him rejected than the request itself. Fabrizio was funny that way. I could see that Chad was visibly annoyed.

We shot three more photos on the first day, two with Kane and me together and one with Chad alone. When I was not shooting, I sat slouched with my legs stretched out in front and crossed at the ankle in a metal folding chair near the dressing room. I watched the scene unfold before me, working hard to conceal the yawns that seemed to spread from my mouth to my body with some regularity as I worked to keep my eyes from closing in the darkness of the windowless studio. Kane sat near me and leaned back in his chair with his hands clasped behind his head and looked blankly at the high, dark ceiling of the studio.

We stopped work at about four, and Fabrizio sent us to the hotel with the instructions to meet back at the studio at 7:30 the next morning. Kane pushed the panic bar on the studio door, and we walked from the dark studio into the blinding light of the late-day sun. Within ten minutes we were getting our keys to our rooms in a hotel that was so ornate that I was half expecting to be asked to leave before I could get my laundry bag of clothes safely into my room. We each had our own room with high ceilings and giant beds covered with plush comforters and cylindrical pillows that stretched across the head of the beds. We agreed to meet in the hallway in an hour.

We walked out of the hotel dressed in jeans and button-down shirts with our wet hair combed straight back.

"This is great!" Kane said as he grabbed me by the

shoulders and gave me a playful shake, "We are *definitely* gonna meet some French babes tonight, Doc."

I nodded with a big smile as I thought to myself that it couldn't be that easy for Kane and me to execute his plan for the evening. It didn't help that I didn't really want to meet some babe that I would never see again and do things that my mom had told me over and over was a sin since I was ten years old. It seemed pointless to me.

Deep down I knew that I was a sinner. I knew better than to do some of the things that I did. I always seemed to stumble off the *narrow path to righteousness* that Jesus talked about in the Bible. I seemed unable to resist the voluptuous beauty that made women so irresistible to me. I was rendered powerless when faced with a nude female body, the curve of her hips as they flared out from a small waist, the full, upturned breasts capped with large nipples that pulled me in to explore with my tongue, mouth, and lips as she moaned with pleasure.

I had never been hung-up on perfect tens; I always found beauty in a wide range of sizes and ages, not rejecting a woman for an imperfect face or wrinkles around her eyes, so long as she possessed a quality or feature that made her sexy. This left me with a large portion of the female population to lust after.

I had begun to understand at Monmouth College that some of these so-called average women were not accustomed to getting attention from someone who looked like me.

I saw the confusion in the eyes of Carrie, a redhead with thick round glasses whom I had met at the student union. She had clear, pale skin covered with freckles and walked with the stiff-legged gait of the chronically shy, keeping her books tight to her chest and her eyes cast towards the ground. She wore loose, bulky sweaters and shapeless jeans that were almost successful in hiding her beautiful curves. I asked her out to a movie one quiet Friday night in October. She smiled shyly when we talked after the movie, and we somehow ended up in her brightly lit dorm room. We kissed while standing in the middle of the room. She quickly turned from shy to hungry as she placed her glasses on the desk near the end of the bed and let her thick red hair fall from the pony tail to her shoulders as she shook her hair loose, then pulled her thick sweater over her head to reveal a plain white bra with sturdy white straps that attached to the cone-shaped cups containing her full, round breasts. She watched me looking at her, and we met in the middle of the floor before struggling to take her bra off from the hooks on the back. Her breasts settled onto her ribs, and I silently took a deep breath. Marveling at what had been hidden beneath the layers of clothes and the old-fashioned bra that had held her full breasts unnaturally high on her chest, I drank in her form as she stood in the bright light of her small dorm room looking nervously at the ground, trying to find a place to put her hands.

I held her gently by her shoulders as we sat on the edge of her bed. She was even less experienced than I was; we ended up kissing and holding each other until it was so late that I had to leave, knowing that her roommate would return at any moment. I felt guilt and shame at liking someone that the guys at the fraternity and all the hot girls had determined was an outsider, and left the relationship with Carrie before it even really started, lacking the courage to choose whom I liked without seeking the approval of the masses.

I walked with Kane while looking at the stores with the bright lights as couples and groups of people went strolling by. I felt like a shameless tourist staring at all that there was to see while watching the people walk by, trying to determine who they were and where they came from. I tried to catch everything and everyone that was there, snapping countless scenes and taking pictures to store in my mind. It felt good to pull my guilt-ridden mind away from chewing at the bone that was my self-esteem and value in a world that didn't seem to know that I existed.

Kane stopped abruptly and said, "This place here. This is good," as he gestured towards a loosely defined arrangement of small round tables surrounded by round-backed metal chairs with plastic covered red cushions. The tables were lit by strings of small white lights that hung carelessly from the green and white striped canopy outside the restaurant. Kane chose a table close to the sidewalk as he held up his hand to attract the attention of the lone waiter standing with a round tray at his side.

"This is perfect, my man, we can see every chick that walks by," he continued with the enthusiasm of a ten-year-old boy getting a new bike on Christmas morning.

"Great," I said flatly, as I raised my eyebrows and smiled broadly to make up for my lack of verbal enthusiasm. Kane did not look at my response as he started to scan the people that walked down the street from both directions.

The drinks were expensive. I ordered a Coke with ice. It came in a small, scratched bottle. There was no glass or ice and the Coke was warm. Kane ordered an eight dollar bottle of Heineken and started taking long drinks from his dark green bottle of chilled beer as soon as the slim waiter handed it to him. He ordered another before finishing the first, starting in on it without taking a break. I attempted to choke down the warm, syrupy Coke, but gave up before reaching the halfway point and ordered a Heineken.

Kane called out loudly and clearly to any woman or group of women under thirty that walked by, "Hey, do you want to join us for a drink? Hi, what's your name beautiful? Bonjour, can I buy you a drink?" he would ask with a face-crinkling smile between long slugs of beer.

The sun fell behind the buildings to the west and cast a wide shadow across the *Champs-Élysées*. The cool shadow reached our table quickly as the street lights brightened to push away the darkness that had fallen so quickly on the busy street. Two girls with oversized purses and loose fitting jeans with high-heel shoes paused as Kane extended the same invitation to them that he had used since we sat down.

They looked at each other, shrugged their shoulders and replied *sure* to his invitation. They sat down and ordered a drink from our waiter, then casually turned their attention towards Kane and me.

"I am Simone and this is Jeanne," the one with the black hair tucked behind her ears offered in a strong French accent.

"I'm Kane, and this is Daryl. Nice to meet you," Kane said with too much enthusiasm as he extended a hand to shake, first to Simone and then to Jeanne. I silently did the same.

Kane quickly explained that we were famous models from the United States as I fought back the redness of embarrassment that spread quickly from my ears to my face at Kane's *white lie*. Their faces brightened as Kane continued, telling them about the *Christian Dior* campaign that we were shooting nearby at The Pinup Studios.

Kane spoke directly to Simone and did his best to pretend that Jeanne wasn't there. Simone had a beautiful face and a lithe body. Her bright smile was ever-present beneath bright blue eyes.

Jeanne had light brown hair and a face that just barely sat on the wrong side of beautiful. I did my best to keep her involved in conversation by asking her about her school and the nightlife in Paris, but she only offered partial answers as she sipped her bright colored drink with a look of almost complete detachment. She disinterestedly alternated between looking at me, Kane, Simone, and the people who walked by on the sidewalk. I did my best to serve as Kane's wingman as it became increasingly difficult to talk to Jeanne.

Kane did all of the talking to Simone. After thirty minutes Simone started to steal glances at me while Kane talked. Jeanne had her arms crossed tightly at this point and only loosened them to reach for her drink. By her third drink, Jeanne was smiling and almost seemed to be enjoying herself while Kane was beginning to rush and slur his words as he continued to drink cold bottles of Heineken at a fast pace. He was trying very hard to sweep Simone off her feet. It crossed my mind more than once that both girls were only with us for the free drinks. I quickly realized that they viewed us as dumb Americans who didn't understand the way things worked in Paris.

Kane invited both of them back to our hotel, and to my surprise, they both agreed. Simone gave me a long look from across the table as Kane looked away to summon the waiter to our table to settle up the bill. I tried to give

Kane a fifty-franc note to help with the drink costs, but he refused as he held up his right hand and shook his head from side to side;

"I got this, Doc," he said gallantly with a buzzed, white-toothed smile.

I shoved the wrinkled note back in my pocket and stood up from the shaky table.

We arrived at the ornate lobby of our hotel within five minutes. The girls seemed very impressed; the hotel was well known in Paris.

Kane had a running dialogue going with them as we crossed the lobby; "yes, huh, what do you think, pretty nice, eh? Not bad...am I right ladies?" he said drunkenly as he gestured towards the marble floors with a flourish of his hand and a slight bow towards the statues of nude men and fair maidens standing in the bubbling fountain that took up the center of the uselessly large lobby.

We entered the gilded elevator with the roman numerals and the ornate clock hand that pointed to the floor number and stopped at the fifth floor. Kane slipped his arm casually over Simone's shoulder and pulled her tight to his side as we rode in the elevator. She gave me another look as she tried to lock in something with her eyes. I pretended to not understand what her eyes were telling me as my stomach flip-flopped up into my chest while the weightlessness of the elevator lifted me off the floor. I was struck *dumb* by a beautiful woman's choosing me without words. I looked down at the ground in an attempt to break the spell that was being cast on me by her blue eyes, but knew it was already too late.

Kane unlocked the door to his room and we all walked in at the same time. Kane flopped down onto one of the king-sized beds and said, "Not bad, huh?" as he stretched out on the bed and laced his fingers behind his head, continuing, "C'mon guys. Hop on!"

Jeanne sat down tentatively on the corner of the bed as I slouched down in one of the overstuffed armchairs near the window. Simone sat in the middle of the other king sized bed and leaned back resting on her elbows and looking directly at me while saying quietly in her accented voice, "This *is* very nice." I got the message that she had been sending all night as Kane took it all in stride, starting to notice Jeanne for the first time, as he realized that Simone was no longer available.

Simone focused on me as we talked about and around all of the topics that couples talk about when they have already decided to do something together; a banal, slim-fingered conversation that marks time until they are alone. Jeanne and Kane moved closer together on the bed, then Simone looked over at them and gave me another playful look and asked, "Can I see your room, Darriiilll?"

I looked over to gauge the reaction of Kane and Jeanne. They weren't paying attention to us and had moved closer to each other on the plush bed, looking as if they were about to kiss.

"See you later Kane," I said quietly as Simone and I got up and walked out the door with her reaching for my hand.

In my room, we continued to talk for a few more hours. At around midnight, Jeanne banged on the door, walked in and told Simone that she was leaving. Simone smiled and said, "Okay, chéri."

Jeanne said something in French through clenched teeth, turned and slammed the heavy door.

"Don't you want to go with her?" I asked stupidly.

"No," she said while giving me a knowing smile as she locked her blue eyes into mine.

Simone excused herself and went into the bathroom for several minutes. She came out wearing only her shirt unbuttoned to her waist. She shook the shirt off her shoulders and let it fall noiselessly to the floor. Her body was even better than I had imagined. She brushed her thighs lightly with her hands before running them slowly through her thick black hair, lifting it off her shoulders before letting it drop back down, letting it frame her ivory face.

She reveled in her own beauty, knowing the absolute power she had over me. Reaching out, she grabbed my limp hands from my lap and pulled me gently to my feet. She placed her hands on the back of my neck to pull my mouth to hers as she stood up on her toes. Her kiss was warm and alive and wet and different and completely new. I felt her small hands slide from my shoulders to the small of my back and onto my waist before she gently undid my belt buckle and unbuttoned my jeans in one smooth motion. She then reached down beneath my boxers with both of her hands.

Simone made a low pitched moaning sound that seemed to come from her chest that wiped out most of the caution that still remained in my spinning head. My clothes ended up in a pile on the floor as we lay down gently on the soft bed. Everything in the room disappeared as she moved from place to place on my body, making me feel things that I had never felt before; taking me to a place where I was no longer in control. A feeling of floating and then falling overcame my very being as I struggled to keep a grasp on reality as fantasy overcame me. The fine thread of caution that remained allowed me to somehow keep from entering her; maybe it was fear more than caution.

I awoke early to see Simone making coffee wearing only my button down shirt. She sipped her coffee from a large, white fine china cup that she held gently in both of her hands as if she were holding a fragile bird's nest. She offered the cup of coffee to me as I tried to rub the sleep from my eyes. She was even more beautiful in the soft light of morning than I had remembered the night before, standing half dressed with her front and back visible under the hem of my shirt in the light that filtered in through the open window. It was the first sip of real coffee that I had ever had. It was sweet and creamy, and it went down smooth and hot. I felt the guilty, detached feeling wash over me as I replayed the events of last night in my mind; thinking about the sins that I had committed in the eyes of the Church and Mom while looking at Simone who seemed to be almost *Zen-like*.

In her contentment; she was peaceful and smiling, enjoying the early morning as I sat with my head in my hands, silently admiring her ability to feel joy while guilt and anguish flowed through my veins and clogged my brain. I was jealous of her happiness, thinking it must have been born of ignorance; there could be no other explanation for her state of mind.

I knew that the guilt would only grow inside me as the day wore on. I worked hard to convince myself that my self-loathing view was normal and that I was not as fucked up as I knew I was.

"Simone?" I asked quietly, my deep morning voice breaking the silence, "Did you like doing that thing we did last night?"

"Do you mean that?" she said, as she pointed between my legs.

"Yeah, uh, that," I answered awkwardly.

"Usually, no, but with you yes, very much yes."

I didn't know what question to ask next, so I looked at her deep blue eyes so full of innocence and then walked into the pure white bathroom shaking my head, trying to work out the riddle that seemed to circle around inside my head. I realized that I could have asked her about why she felt no guilt, but I kept silent, trapping the thoughts in the recesses of my mind.

I showered quickly and gave Simone a quick kiss on the lips after I dressed, telling her that she could stay in my room as long as she wanted. As I looked at her sitting on the edge of the bed still wearing only my shirt while sipping her coffee, she looked back at me without getting up. I looked into her eyes one last time before closing the heavy door, listened to the heavy strike click securely into the plate as the door closed, and walked down the long hall without looking back.

The next two days of shooting were very much like the first. Chad was really outclassing Kane and me. He explained to one of his bookers on the other end of a lunchtime phone call that he was really *shining* in this *Christian Dior* shooting and that Kane and I were *not professionals*. Kane flipped him off from behind the dressing room door and made a face as if he had just smelled a big pile of dog shit. Chad was a classic beauty, alright; a kind of thoroughbred working with a couple of dusty plow-horses. I knew that Chad would feel right at home at any country club, while Kane and I would be the guys who cut the grass, emptied the garbage cans and raked the sand traps.

Kane and I were bonded by our immaturity as well as our ability to kick Chad's ass with one hand tied behind our backs. As crowded and bad as it got inside my fucked up head, I still wouldn't change to become someone else, especially a douchebag like Chad. I have never wanted to trade places with anyone. Suffering in my own fucked up head had become a way of life to me; a place where I felt comfortable. Happiness made me feel uncomfortable. It was like walking on eggshells for me or a fine restaurant with three different forks and rules of etiquette to follow. It was not for me. I would always be a greasy diner, comfortable clothes, and a one fork kind of guy.

On the last day of shooting Fabrizio decided to do a family-style portrait of the people who had worked on the shooting. Chad decided that this was not professional and that he would have no part in it. He had his voucher signed by the art director, Caroline, and then walked out the exit door without even saying goodbye, his nose held high in the air as if he did not wish to look down.

Fabrizio had everyone dress in clothes from the shoot, and we stood around him as he sat in one of the ornate prop chairs we used in the shooting. Fabrizio squeezed himself into the same long overcoat that I had worn and held the brass-topped cane in his left hand, looking very aristocratic with his legs crossed at the knee, and his chin held appropriately high for the picture. Even Caroline, and Sophia, who did makeup, wore men's clothing. Brian, from *Dior*, dressed like a newspaper boy from the thirties in knickers and suspenders and held up a newspaper while kneeling on his right knee. Fabrizio gave me one of the Polaroids, and I glued it into my day planner. Kane continued to call Fabrizio *Magic Johnson* while Fabrizio told Kane that he would take his job as a model and fire him, "Your job is so very easy," he said as they both burst into a laughter that filled the studio.

It felt good being a part of this group and for now the desert of loneliness and the *white noise* were far away. I let myself feel something close to happiness as Kane and I took a taxi back to the *Hotel Royal Alma* to pack for our flight back to Milano.

28

WHITE NOISE

Things began to change quickly in Milan after my trip to Paris. Kristina no longer had to convince the clients to see me for jobs; the clients were calling to request me, and booking me *sight unseen*. I worked almost every day and was often double-booked with options to the second job if the first job canceled. Calvin and Kristina called me every morning and spent more time asking me how I felt and if I was happy than telling me about the jobs. Sophie from the First Agency in Paris called Kristina every few days to tell her that a client wanted to book me for a job in Paris, but Kristina would tell her that I was too busy with work in Milan. The money from the Christian Dior campaign allowed me to pay the agency back for the advances and I was able to pay my tab at the pensione at the same time. I was on a ride that continued to go faster and faster while I did nothing but hang on.

I asked Marpessa out on a date the next time I saw her at the agency. We went to a small restaurant that she suggested near the park in the middle of town. She asked me about work and if there were any girls at the shoots. I answered politely, and I ate some really good steak smothered in a cracked peppercorn sauce as she smoked and drank large glasses of wine. After around four glasses she began to speak stupidly, like a child trying to imitate a younger child. I said little and waited to see where our date would go. We finished our dinner and walked down the sidewalk as the heat of an early summer radiated up from the cooling sidewalk, and the cool air pushed down from the night.

She stopped suddenly on the sidewalk and turned to face me, "You like these, don't you?" she asked as she palmed her bra-less breasts with her long-fingered hands, moving them up and down and then squeezing them together beneath the sheer fabric of her blouse. She made a face of exaggerated excitement saying, "Oooohhh," while holding her lips in a circle, as if she were blowing out birthday candles.

I felt a lump rise into my throat as I tried to keep my face neutral. Nausea washed over me as I watched her. My feelings took me by surprise as I silently wondered why her actions didn't turn me on. She continued rubbing her breasts as if it was a big joke and even lifted her top briefly to expose her dark nipples while giving her breasts a small shake from side to side, making them undulate back and forth.

I composed my face and was able to force out a laugh and a wide smile as Marpessa carried on. She grabbed my wrist and pressed the palm of my hand into the soft flesh of her breast and said, "Don't you want this body? Huh?" while pouting and pushing her breast hard against my palm.

The part of me that was aroused was quickly pushed aside by the part that couldn't get past her mocking of the feelings that I had for her. It was as if my feelings were of the least possible importance to her, as if I were an animal that existed only to amuse her and to make her feel that she was the most desirable woman in the world and that I would put up with almost anything for a chance to lie with her for a few brief moments. I pretended to be amused by her actions as we walked side by side to her *pensione*. Upon reaching the stone steps that led up to her Pensione she had begun to sober up as she sensed that she no longer had a hold on my heart and mind. The words of Kristina came back to me as I realized that she was right. Marpessa was a shark, but even the toughest shark can do nothing to harm a heart of stone.

She mumbled, "Ciao, bello," over her shoulder as she turned away from me to slowly walk up the wide stone steps. The night began to cool around me as I turned to walk down the wide, empty sidewalks to the other side of Milan, towards Pensione Lima.

I silently waited for waves of emotion to wash over me as I walked through the heat towards the poor side of town, but there was nothing. I wondered why Marpessa had been washed from my head so quickly; why the pain had not welled up inside my chest like a fiery balloon, burning with pain. I stopped thinking about why I didn't care even before I reached the Pensione Lima, as the cool late night air began to push back the heat of day that radiated up from the cobblestones.

I looked up as I reached the entrance and saw the two large prostitutes sitting like solid-bodied centurions, stoically guarding the entrance to the lobby. They smoked and talked quietly, leaning back as they seemed to absorb the cool of night through their sweat covered pores. Each of them greeted me with an almost imperceptible nod as they looked flatly into my eyes, holding their gaze for a moment. I nodded back and knew in an instant the things that would never be said. I slowly made my way up the stairs and into my dark room and fell into a deep and dreamless sleep as the distant sounds of night floated in through my open window.

I awoke late Saturday morning, and the sun was shining hazy and hot on my feet that stuck out from under the sheets. There was no breeze, and the temperature had already hit ninety degrees. I pulled myself up and sat on the edge of the bed, rubbing my eyes against the knife of sunlight that cut into the room from the open window. I was unable to open my eyes against the assault of bright light. A wave of memory flooded up from my feet as the events of the previous night playing out in my head as I began to wake. I choked on regret for a moment, as I imagined what would have happened if I had chosen to stay with Marpessa. The *white noise* would only have held until morning, and then it would come back, worse than ever, with interest to pay on the debt that would always be due. It hit me like a brick on the side of my head that no one knew what I had done last night, and more importantly, no one cared. I was alone whether I was with someone or not. I slid off the edge of the bed and shuffled to the shadowed corner of the room to slump into my chair.

I silently prayed to be stupid enough to believe that someone or something could take away my pain, but I knew that there was no one at the end of that lifeline that lay drifting on the surface of the cold, calm, deep waters of my overwhelming sadness. I understood that the only way to keep from slipping beneath the smooth surface of the water into the wet darkness was to push away the fear that paralyzed me and to learn to swim—alone.

A warm shower in the bathroom down the hall helped to clear my head. I decided to go to the park at the center of the city. I dressed quickly and walked into the dripping heat of the noonday sun, sweating heavily by the time I reached the street. I slid my cheap sunglasses on so that I could open my eyes and walked to the tram stop, getting on the first tram that stopped. The breeze from the open windows of the fast moving car dried my sweat, cooling me briefly.

I absently watched two young men in their early twenties waiting for the tram at the next stop. For some reason, I felt infinitely older than them. They boarded the tram with broad smiles and wide eyes of hope, speaking with each other as they found a spot to stand together on the crowded tram. They wore black dress pants, white short-sleeved dress shirts, and thin, plain black ties. I immediately guessed they were Americans, most likely Mormons taking their two-year trip to convert others to the world of Mormonism. I wanted to ask them about their Faith, how and why they could commit to a religion, a leader, and a God that they could not see or touch; a faith so powerful that they would commit two years of their lives and travel away from their families. Instead, I stayed silent and watched them talk to each other over the noise of the clanging bell of the trolley and the buzz of the passengers as the trolley swayed back and forth making its way towards the center of town. They were still talking intently to each other as I stepped off the tram and onto the large cobblestones that made up the sidewalk that encircled the park.

It felt like a Saturday as I walked without purpose toward the lake at the center of the park. I passed a stone castle with large mottled rocks of green moss and dark, wet blues and blacks. They were rough on the face and cut smooth and square on their edges, joined together like different sized bricks. It looked ancient and uninviting. Old men with gray whiskers and loose fitting dress pants, white shirts, and cotton caps with short visors played *Bocce* on the long, narrow courts, safe under the shade of towering oak trees, their canopy of leaves starting high above the ground. They clapped their hands slowly as if time were not important and seemed to quietly revel in their time at the park. I imagined them starting early with black cups of sugar-filled espresso and staying at the Bocce courts until long after sunset, leaving their unappealing and angry wives at home to care for the household that they cared nothing about. I wanted to skip the years of my youth to old age and join these old men with their easy smiles and unhurried movements.

I cut across the neatly raked gravel path and stepped over the low chain that was meant to protect the new grass from pedestrian traffic. I walked up and over the grassy hill towards the lake. The thick-trunked trees with lush canopies of green leaves blocked out the bright sun, leaving most of the park in the shade. The brownish water of the lake reflected the midday sun into my eyes. I scanned the groups of Americans that clustered around the water's edge for a familiar face. I saw Brock and Hank sitting on hotel towels near the edge of the water. Brock was wearing only khaki shorts, and Hank was wearing white shorts and a peach-colored v-neck t-shirt. Brock waved to me with a smile and shouted out, "Yo, Daryl," while Hank looked back towards a group of guys playing Frisbee as he pretended that he didn't see me.

"Hey Brock," I said as Brock stood up to greet me.

"Hey Bro," he said with a big smile, "I hear you are *killing it.*"

I looked over at Hank who was busy trying to listen to Brock and me without acknowledging my existence.

"Not really," I lied. I didn't want to make Brock or Hank feel bad about not working.

"C'mon, man," he continued, "I heard from Kristina that you are working almost every day now."

Hank quietly turned towards us, listening intently for my response to Brock's statement.

"I have been kinda lucky, mostly working for Fabrizio with Kane...." I trailed off, unsure of how to continue.

"It's cool man," Brock said sincerely. "Isn't that the reason we're all here? I mean—to work?" He asked as he slapped me on the shoulder and forced out a laugh.

"Yes, *isn't it,*" Hank said as he rolled his eyes and gave me a tight-lipped expression that told me everything I needed to know.

I chose to ignore Hank, saying to Brock, "Kristina said you have some work coming up."

"Yeah," he said proudly with a smile, "It's a swimsuit job for a company called Meyba. I did some work for them the last time I was in Milano—down in Sardinia."

"Well you don't have the job *yet,*" Hank interrupted as he closed the book he was pretending to read for emphasis. He continued, "You told me that they had you on *option,* Brock. Do you know how many models they can put on *option* for every *single* job?" he said with the air of a schoolteacher who had all the right answers.

"No," Brock said as he turned his attention to Hank while still smiling, "How many?"

"I don't know exactly," Hank replied while trying to pretend that Brock's question didn't catch him off guard, "but I'm sure it's a lot. They can do whatever they want to us over here."

I didn't need to ask if Hank had any work; I knew that he didn't. It seemed to me that he should have been working more than I with his classic looks and wavy dark hair, but I guessed that his slim-shouldered build was working against him in a business that seemed to be looking more and more for athletes with sculpted faces and bodies; the *All American*.

Brock mercifully ignored Hank's insult with another forced laugh and turned his attention back to me.

"Well Bro, enjoy it. You're in a very small minority here. I've talked to a lot of models who haven't worked at all since coming to Milan. Some of them can't even get home; they don't have enough money for a plane ticket," Brock said seriously.

Hank turned his attention back to his book with a serious expression etched across his forehead as he pretended that his book was the most interesting book ever written.

"Really?" I answered with genuine surprise. I didn't know that models were stuck in Milan.

As we spoke, two thin, shirtless American men wearing cut-off shorts and flip-flops approached us, and one of them said;

"Hey. Do you guys want some ham and cheese? We just stole it," I looked at their dirty, unshaven faces and then at the leg of pig and the huge red and yellow wheel of cheese with a large wedge missing that they held out in their dirty hands towards us.

"Uh, no thanks," I answered hesitantly, "Did you guys really steal this stuff?" as I pointed to their contraband. I was unable to stop myself from asking the question to which I didn't want to know the answer.

"Hell yeah bro, it's easy," the taller one answered proudly as if it were the dumbest question he had ever heard. "We do it every day dude. Do you want to come with us tomorrow? It's fun!" said the shorter guy with a short, ratty ponytail. He suddenly spotted an unfinished cigarette in the grass, picked it up, and made several attempts to light it with a Zippo lighter that he pulled out of his shorts pocket, putting down the cheese to use his left hand to block the wind that blew across the small lake. He gave up after several attempts and then flicked the useless butt back onto the grass where he had found it. Brock looked over at me with wide eyes and a shake of his head as the two models stuffed their wheel of cheese and leg bone of ham into a grimy looking yellow backpack and walked over to the next group of models near the lake to ask if they wanted to share their contraband with them.

I sat down on the grass and dirt near their towels and tilted my head back to look up at the sun through my cheap sunglasses. I thought about being broke and homeless in Milan like these two guys; it wasn't hard to imagine.

I looked out at the brown-watered lake and watched two swans swim in the shade of a large willow tree. They took turns following each other and often stopped to float, facing each other and rubbing their necks together gently.

My gaze shifted onto two women sitting near the

water's edge. One was very tall with large eyes and mouth and wore a tight bikini top with tight cut-off shorts. Her long blond hair was pulled into a ponytail, and she wore dark sunglasses with oversized frames. The other woman was smaller and her features more refined. Her golden-blonde hair was pulled back and lay on her back. She wore a pair of loose khaki shorts and a loose fitting, white men's tank top with the same type of oversized sunglasses, the kind that movie stars wore. She was a classic beauty. Sitting with her slim legs stretched out in front of her and crossed at the ankle, she caught me looking at her and gave me a short wave that caused me to blush. I awkwardly got to my feet and hesitantly walked over to them.

"I'm Lola," the tall one said when I got close to their blanket before I could even introduce myself. She lifted her big, round sunglasses off her nose and took a lingering look at me.

"Hi, I'm Daryl," I said while extending my right hand.

"What agency are you with?" she continued, staring at me with her eyes opened wide like an owl.

"Beatrice," I answered while I looked away from Lola to the girl that had waved at me.

"I'm Terry," she said while extending a delicate hand for me to shake as she lifted her sunglasses onto her forehead with her left hand. I bent down slightly and held her hand gently in mine for a moment as she gave me a close-lipped smile, as she looked at me with her gray-blue eyes for more than five seconds.

Lola looked at the two of us and said suddenly in a raspy kind of voice, "Don't bother with her D., she already has a boyfriend, and they are *really* in love. His name is

Lucky, maybe you've heard of him?" she said with a great deal of satisfaction.

Terry only blushed slightly as she ignored Lola and asked in a quiet voice, "How long have you been in Milan, Daryl?"

"Around five weeks," I answered while continuing to look into her eyes while holding her hand.

"You're doing well over here, aren't you?" she asked with another wry smile.

"Yeah, I guess—how did you know that I mean about my working here?" I asked with more surprise than I wanted to show.

She chuckled quietly and smiled a white-toothed smile and said, "Don't you know that every model here is obsessed with working and getting tear sheets?"

Lola rolled her large brown eyes and pretended not to listen.

Terry continued, "Everyone checks on everyone else here, *constantly*. They eavesdrop on phone calls from the hotel lobby and at the agency and look at the booker's notes to see who is working and what jobs they're doing. And they ask a lot of questions. You know, about who's working and who isn't. They'll talk to any booker, model, or photographer who will give them the time of day. Some of them probably know more about what jobs you are up for than you do. And of course, they tell *everyone* they know every *thing* that they know, and then it spreads like wildfire from there. It sounds like this is a surprise to you, am I right?"

"Pretty much," I answered, trying to understand why the news of my jobs was such a topic of interest for the other models trying to get work in Milan.

I hadn't told anyone at home or in Milan that things were going well for me. I guess I didn't want to have the modeling jobs slow down or disappear and then be seen as a desperate liar who exaggerates everything that happens to him so that he seems much more important than he really is; multiplying his success each time he tells a story with a kernel of truth, using it to build a big whopping lie on. My older brother and father were masters at this, and it always made me feel a little sick to my stomach, especially when I watched the expressions of disdain and disbelief on the faces of the people to whom they chose to tell their stories to.

"Do you want to go to the swimming pool on the roof of our hotel?" Lola asked, trying desperately to insert herself into the conversation.

"Sure," I answered without thinking, caught off guard again.

Terry gave me a wry smile as she started to pack up her things to go.

We all walked together to their apartment. It was almost a mile from the park. Lola talked without taking a breath, while Terry and I walked quietly, listening to Lola. I wanted to talk to Terry while we walked, but Lola wouldn't allow it. She had wedged herself between Terry and me as we walked and held her center position all the way to the apartment. She was tall and broad-shouldered and a force to be reckoned with; it wasn't worth it to walk to the other side of Lola to be near to Terry, I knew there would be another time.

We arrived at a very modern looking building with new windows and inset doors with an intercom. We took a small white elevator with a small-hinged door to the top floor of the apartment building, then walked up a flight of stairs and out a heavy metal door to the roof.

"We have the whole place to ourselves!" Lola said excitedly as she walked over to the chaise lounges that sat close to the pool. The rails were made of thick sheets of glass, and the pool was small and clean, more a pool to cool off in than to actually swim. I could see over the other apartment buildings that stretched out to the horizon from the top floor. It was the first time that I had seen Milan from up high. It was a much bigger city than I had thought.

Lola placed her small daypack under a chaise and crossed her arms in front and pulled her shirt up over her head in one smooth motion.

"You won't get freaked out if I go topless, will you?" she asked with a wide grin, looking directly at me.

"Guess not," she said quickly, without waiting for an answer. She reached behind her back and untied her top and pulled it over her head and threw it on a small side table.

"What guy doesn't want to see some *American titties*, right?" she asked as she stood in front of me proudly before reaching for a cigarette in her backpack. She lit the cigarette smoothly and began to inhale the smoke with deep, satisfying breaths, tasting the smoke on her tongue and at the back of her throat.

Lola had small, pointed breasts capped with large nipples that were reddish- brown Her waist went straight to her hips, without the flare from small waist to full hips that I liked. There were dark spots on her chest and back from too much sun, and she was already very tan. Her shoulders were broad like a swimmer's, making her breasts look even smaller than they were.

Lola pulled out a towel and lay it on the chaise before lying down, continuing to smoke as she moved around on the chaise until she found a comfortable position. She then lay her head back and closed her eyes to the bright sun.

"C'mon D. Let's go. You *gotta* take your shirt off now," she said while lifting her large sunglasses to look at me standing with my backpack still over my shoulders.

I looked over at Terry, and she gave the same wry little smile that she had given me at the park. She took off her shirt and shorts revealing a conservative robin's egg blue bikini. I swallowed hard taking in her perfect lines as she stood in front of me. She was shy but aware of how beautiful she was. I pulled my shirt over my head and stuffed it under a chair near Lola. I stood for a moment, unsure of what to do next when Lola blurted out;

"Whoa, D! You're blinding me with all that white skin. Get that man some Banana Boat oil, *stat*," she said, giving off a good-natured laugh.

"But first, put some oil on my back, will ya?" she asked casually while sitting up in her chaise. She lifted her long blond hair off her shoulders with her left hand to expose her back. Terry handed me a full bottle of Banana Boat with a greasy paper label and gave me a slow wink. I bent over Lola and poured some of the oil on my right hand and then rubbed it onto her warm shoulders, doing my best to cover as much area as quickly as possible without lingering.

"How's that? "I asked awkwardly, standing up with the bottle of oil still in my left hand.

"Good job D. Now do my front, '*kay?*"

I hesitated and looked back at Terry with a puzzled look on my face, wondering what to do when Lola said suddenly, "Just kidding D...wanted to freak you out a little."

"It worked, didn't it?" She asked rhetorically while reclining slowly and continuing to make love to her burning cigarette.

Terry broke the silence, "Do you want me to put some oil on you?" she asked in a hushed tone that was just above a whisper.

"Sure," I answered slowly, not wanting to appear too anxious as my heart started to pound hard and fast within my chest.

"Remember D; Terry has a boyfriend. Right, Terry?" Lola chimed in while continuing to suck the smoke from her cigarette.

Terry shrugged her shoulders and gave me a mock frown, letting me know that we should ignore Lola's question. I knew better than to ask Terry directly if she had a boyfriend. Inside I knew that she did, but I was enjoying her company and didn't want to cut things short by asking questions to which I didn't want to know the answers.

Terry walked over towards me and took the bottle of oil in her left hand and poured some into her right.

"Sit down, I can't reach you from here," she said with a close-lipped smile.

I sat down on the edge of an empty chaise and waited for her to touch my back with her soft, oiled hands. I could see the oil start to run through her fingers as she positioned herself behind me. She rubbed her hands together slowly and purposefully before gently touching the back of my neck, applying the oil smoothly and gently like a mother rubs lotion onto her only child. She worked her way down my bare back as she hummed quietly to herself. She stopped just above the waist of my shorts.

"You *are* a little pale, Daryl," she said with a hint of a southern accent.

"I know," I answered. "I haven't been in the sun much since I came to Milan."

"Well, you can *always* come here if you want to get some sun," she said with the same wry smile from earlier. "There, all finished," she said as she rested her hands on my bare, oiled shoulders.

"Can you put some oil on my back?" she asked hopefully as if she genuinely thought that I could say no.

"Sure," I said with a calculated indifference that didn't fool her or me.

Lola raised herself up on one elbow and lifted her large round glasses off her nose to look over at Terry and me while shaking her head back and forth. Terry ignored Lola and sat down with her back to me.

"You know," she said slowly and softly, "it's much easier to put the oil on my back if I lay down," as she lay down smoothly on her front, spreading the towel out with her hands.

I loved the way that Terry spoke. She chose her words carefully and was in no hurry to get them out; she took her time and was unrushed and serene in her motions as well as in her speech. I had never been around anyone like her; she seemed to have learned lessons from a faraway place, or maybe she was born into the person that she had become. I wanted to ask her a hundred questions all at once and tell her things about myself that I had never told anyone, but I didn't.

It would be like rushing up on a spring fawn to get a

closer look, while the fawn gets spooked and runs away, never to return to that spot. I knew that if I wanted to watch Terry, I would need to hold still and not rush up to her; not now, and not ever. She slowly positioned herself on her stomach on the flat chaise and seemed to arch her back, pushing her flat stomach into the flat chaise, making the curve of her ass lift slightly off the towel. My heart beat fast within my chest as I soaked up the image of her beautiful skin and her fine curves. I could see Lola out of the corner of my eye as she lay back down with a *humph*, picking up her thick paper-back book with a shirtless pirate on the cover as she began to pretend to read again.

"Can you untie my top, please?" Terry asked with a voice dripping with sweet honey, "I don't want to get tan lines on my back...you know." I was able to steady my hand long enough to get her top untied by grabbing an end with my thumb and fingers and pulling gently, not wanting to seem over-anxious. I then untied the string around her neck and let the two ends drop towards the deck. Terry turned her head towards me and mouthed the words *thank you* with her eyes closed.

I worked the oil onto her smooth skin slowly; starting from the middle of her back and slowly working out to her sides. She rested her head on her hands, leaving her breasts exposed from the side with only her nipples covered by the towel as her bikini top slumped towards the ground. Her breasts were creamy white and pushed out full and round to the sides. I was careful not to rub oil on her breasts; I didn't want her to ask me to stop. I finished with the oil on her back and stopped just above her bikini bottoms and stood up, still holding the greasy bottle of Banana Boat lotion.

"Can you put some oil on my legs too, please? It's so hard for me to get the backs of my legs covered, especially towards the top," she asked with the voice of an angel that had fallen from the heavens.

I answered her by starting to rub oil onto the backs of her thighs slowly, starting just above her knees.

"Don't forget the tops of my legs," she said mischievously as she parted her thighs slightly to allow me to oil the place where her smooth thighs touched together. I poured the warm oil directly onto the backs of her upper thighs and worked it in on both legs at the same time, careful not to touch the places that were covered with her bathing suit. She arched her back again, tightening the smooth muscles of her lower back that lay just below the skin as she pushed her hips with a gentle side-to-side motion into the cushion of the chaise. She had the lithe body of a ballet dancer. I could feel her body vibrate slightly as she moaned quietly to herself, like a purring cat as she stretched in the sun. I reached my rough palmed hands to the fronts of her thighs from between her legs and worked the oil into her skin. I finished rubbing the oil onto her heels and took a very deep breath as I felt my heart punching at the insides of my ribs furiously.

Terry turned and lifted herself halfway up on her elbows and said, "Thank you," while looking directly into my eyes and giving me a full side view of her perfect breasts. "How *did* you get to be so sweet?" she asked with a devious smile.

I smiled back sincerely and stupidly. I silently wished that Lucky wouldn't find his way back to Milan for a very long time.

29

THE LEANING TOWER

I returned to the Pensione Lima as the sun was setting as orange as fire over the dun-colored buildings in the distance. Luigi stopped me from behind the front desk as I walked up the stairs to tell me there was a message for me. I walked over to him and took the small square of paper from his hand that said only *call Calvin* with his phone number written below. I picked up the heavy receiver of the antique style phone at the end of the long marble counter and dialed his number. I drummed my fingers absently on the counter as the phone made that creepy double ring sound like the collect phone call on the end of the Pink Floyd album, The Wall.

"Hallo?" Calvin answered, breaking the sound of the ring with his voice abruptly, catching me off guard.

"Hey, Calvin. It's me, Daryl."

"Ahhh, *belloo*. How are you?" he asked in a completely different tone than the one he answered the phone with. "You have a job on Monday with Fabrizio," he said.

"Great," I answered. "Is it at *Vogue* studios?"

"No, it's in Pisa. You will be riding with another model to Pisa. His name is Wilhelm," he continued excitedly.

"Okay," I replied. I was very happy to be working with Fabrizio and Carmine again.

"You will meet him at the Hotel Trieste at five thirty in the morning. He will drive you in his car."

I wrote down the time and the address in the planner that I had bought at the small cigar store near the agency the previous week.

"How many days is the shooting Calvin?" I asked.

"Only two days. It is a campaign for *Panchetti*. You will come back on Wednesday with Vil-helm."

"*Italian Vogue* called me today," Calvin continued. "They have put you on *exclusive*, which means that you can only do editorial work for *Vogue* in Italy. No more appointments for you, *bello*. They will book you for all of their jobs for *Men's Vogue*."

"That's good, right?" I asked.

"Yes, *bello*, that is very good. I have not heard of them doing this before. I do not think they want you to leave Italy," he said with a laugh.

"Thanks, Calvin," I said as I took in all that he had said.

"Do you feel any different; are you happy?" he asked with hope in his voice.

"No. Not really," I answered honestly.

"Ahhh, *bello*. You are a very strange young man. *All* of the models in Milano would trade places with you in an instant. Even I would have loved to have what you have right now. Perhaps you will feel different when all the campaigns come out in the magazines."

"Maybe," I replied with little energy. I silently wondered why I did not jump out of my skin like a kid on Christmas morning.

I arrived at the *Hotel Trieste* at five thirty-five and saw a young man sitting on a small couch smoking an unfiltered cigarette as he nervously tapped the toe of his right boot on the marble floor. He looked to be almost thirty years old and was dressed in expensive designer clothes. He was wearing leather pants, a loose t-shirt with a gold chain around his neck, and an oversized brown leather jacket that zipped up the side. His straight blondish hair was long on the top and short on the sides. He had small delicate features and looked as if he needed a shave. His dark blue eyes were set deep beneath thick eyebrows that seemed to travel straight across his forehead.

He stood up as I got closer to him and I realized quickly that, even with heeled boots, he was much shorter than I. He gave me a stern look and said brusquely with a harsh German accent, "Let's go. Vee are going to be late."

I extended my hand for him to shake; ready to introduce myself. He looked at me with a dead-stare, picked up his soft-sided leather bag in one quick swoop and walked brusquely out of the lobby onto the sidewalk. For some reason, Wilhelm's rudeness didn't surprise or anger me. I immediately began to wonder what it would be like to be five nine in a sea of six-footers. As I walked behind him, I could see that he wore these tricky little leather boots with three-inch heels that were almost completely concealed by the wide-flaring bottoms of his leather pants.

I'm not sure why I notice all of this crap in an instant. I'm smart enough to know that no one gives a shit about my annoying observations that go unnoticed by others, but it seems to be the way my mind works, full time. I immediately notice everything about everyone.

Although I struggle mightily to keep my mouth shut about all of the things that I see, instinctively knowing that no one wants to hear what it is that I've observed about them. It is one of the many reasons that people think that I am strange and give me puzzled looks of incomprehension. I am beginning to understand that most people's minds do not work the same as mine does. The more I talk, the less people seem to understand what I am trying to say; it's as if I spoke a foreign language.

When I was in high school, I read an article about teenagers who were abused by their parents for most of their young lives. The researchers found that many of the children developed a disorder call *hypermnesia*, the opposite of *amnesia*. They would remember minute details about things that had happened in their lives; people, sounds, places, events. They could remember things with more detail and clarity than most people could who had just seen the event. It was discovered that it was a trait developed by the children for self-preservation; a way of predicting *when* they were likely to be abused by piecing together minute details that would often lead to abuse. They would use this information to avoid the abusing parent. It was a *mnemonic early warning system*.

This seemed to explain some of the things that went through my head about the past. I had never been to a medical doctor, let alone a therapist or psychiatrist, but I knew that all was not well within my head. I read *Dibs, In Search of Self,* in fifth grade for no particular reason. I remember thinking how lucky *Dibs* was to have a patient and kind therapist to meet with him a few times each week.

I started keeping everything in my head after the first few weeks of fifth grade, trying to make sense of things by turning them over and over in my mind, without talking to anyone. I realized that my mom had too many other things to worry about to be bothered with how my head worked, and since I wasn't the type of kid who ate light bulbs or chewed on his arm until it turned red and bled, all of the other adults in my life assumed that I was fine, a perfect kid; happy, content, *normal.*

If I ever did make the mistake of telling my mom that I had these thoughts or that I stayed up all night walking the halls without sleeping she would have told me the same thing that she said to me if I was sick with a fever or had injured myself; "You have to pray about it."

I knew that my mom would also think that I was blaming her for my condition; as if I thought *she* caused it and that I wanted her to fix the problem. To be honest, I am still not sure what caused my problems. Although there are certain events that happened in my life that seemed to have made things worse, I think much of the wiring that led me to where I am at nineteen was already in place on that stormy Wednesday night that I was born a few hours after my mom got back to the apartment after going to a *Wednesday Evening Testimony Meeting.*

My dad said of the night that I was born, "You had these really long fingernails, and you were wrinkly, red and very skinny, like a tiny monkey. You cried all the time, more like screamed actually."

I followed Wilhelm out of the lobby. He stopped abruptly beside a small, chocolate brown Alpha Romeo hatchback. Popping the hatch and throwing his bag inside, he looked at me with a *what the hell are you waiting for* look on his face, so I stepped closer to the car and slung my bag into the back. I was impressed that he had a car. He gave my bag a look as if he was contemplating whether or not he should allow my bag to stay in his car. I settled into the passenger seat and buckled up. Wilhelm started the car while he lit another cigarette. He shifted, steered, smoked, and tuned in the radio all at the same time, settling on a station that was playing *I Can't Get No Satisfaction* by the Rolling Stones. I stared out the open window as Wilhelm worked his way through the early morning streets of Milan. Wilhelm did his best to pretend that I wasn't even there. We were soon outside the city, and I turned to look out the window and watch the green fields and low-lying trees rush by. A farmer drove an old red tractor in the distance, pulling an old-fashioned wood-sided cart filled with hay. I fell asleep soon after and didn't wake until we pulled up in front of a small stone hotel in Pisa.

Fabrizio and Carmine were sitting in the quaint lobby of the *Hotel Arno* as Wilhelm and I walked in. Fabrizio got up quickly and walked over to Wilhelm and me.

"Mr. Daryl from Chicago! How the hell are you, my friend," Fabrizio said with sincere enthusiasm followed by a big bear hug.

Wilhelm looked confused as Fabrizio stepped back and held me at arm's length by my shoulders and looked at me with affection as I replied, "Hey Magic, great to see you," followed by my big toothed, crooked smile.

We shook hands and gave each other another bear hug as he slapped me affectionately on my back. It was good to see Fabrizio and Carmine again.

Wilhelm stood at attention and introduced himself. He finished his introduction with a military nod and a click of his heels. Fabrizio smiled cordially at Wilhelm and told him it was good to meet him and then shook his hand. The expression on Fabrizio's face changed quickly as he continued to look at Wilhelm.

He then paused, took two steps back and looked at Wilhelm and then at me and said with a stern expression on his face, "Mr. Daryl. Please stand next to our good friend Mr. Wilhelm."

I laid my bag on the floor and walked over to stand next to Wilhelm. I knew immediately where this was heading. Fabrizio started to shake his head slowly from side to side and clucked his tongue loudly.

"Your card says that you and Mr. Daryl are the same height," he said to Wilhelm with a school teacher's glare. "Do *you* think that you are the same height?" he asked as he moved closer to Wilhelm with his arms behind his back.

I could easily look over Wilhelm's head as I turned towards him to see how he would answer Fabrizio's loaded question.

"Ja. I mean yes, I think *vee* are almost the same height," he said with complete confidence as he stood up as straight as he could, hoping that his *tricky little boots* wouldn't be noticed by Fabrizio.

Fabrizio got down on one knee and lifted up the hem of Wilhelm's leather pants, exposing his boots with the three-inch heels.

"Even with *these* you are still much shorter than Mr. Daryl," Fabrizio said, dropping the hem of his pants and slapping the side of Wilhelm's boot as he stood back up. Fabrizio had a disgusted look on his face. I knew from the *Christian incident* that Fabrizio hated bullshit...any kind of bullshit.

Wilhelm was surprisingly short for a model. I was shorter than some of the models at Legends, and Wilhelm was *much* shorter than I. I always had a hard time gauging how tall someone was until I got right up next to them, and Wilhelm was no exception. When we stood close to each other, I could see that his shoulders were a full hands-width lower than mine and the top of his head was even with my nose. I wondered how he had gotten this far without his height becoming a major problem. If the clothes fit me, then Wilhelm would be swimming in them.

"Come on. Let's get going," Fabrizio commanded as he marched out of the lobby and down the stairs of the *Hotel Arno*, shaking his head and mumbling to himself as he climbed into the front passenger seat of the big, white van.

We drove out of the city to a small farm with a barn with walls made from very large granite stones. Wilhelm and I stood and waited as Fabrizio worked quickly to get the clothes arranged for the shooting as he instructed Carmine how to set up the camera equipment about ten feet away from the side of the ancient looking barn. Wilhelm watched the action with interest, trying to figure out a way to grow three inches taller before the shooting started. I watched the action without interest and yawned into the back of my hand as I struggled to stay awake.

At twelve thirty we stopped for lunch and ate cold chicken, small rolls with cold butter and a small, chilled vegetable dish with a tangy vinegar-based dressing that reminded me of coleslaw. It was delicious. I finished with a full-size bar of dark chocolate and a bottle of cold Pelligrino.

The lunch had come in the same heavy brown paper bag with brown twine looped handles as the lunches we had at the *Vogue* studio. I was secretly glad that Fabrizio took food so seriously because I was always hungry. Fabrizio spoke excitedly in Italian and English about a job they had just finished. I only partially understood what he said. Fabrizio ended the hour-long lunch with a clap of his meat butcher hands as he said, "Okay my friends, let's get to work!"

Fabrizio had picked out clothes for Wilhelm and me in the morning. He chose a ruffled shirt with a maroon and gray renaissance jacket, and loose fitting black leather pants with extra leather sewn into the legs that looked like kneepads on a pair of motorcycle pants. The shirt had no buttons and no collar; it was tied with little cloth strings in the front like something that you would see at a renaissance fair. I wore boots with low heels that looked like less *tricky* versions of Wilhelm's boots. Wilhelm wore a jacket with padded shoulders and buckles and straps that appeared to be purely decorative. The sleeves were too long and covered his hands almost completely. The shoulders of the jacket were heavily padded and stuck out past his own shoulders, giving him the look of a child wearing his dad's jacket. I was beginning to understand *why* height was so important in the modeling business; all of the clothes we got were the same size. They were made to fit a man that is a slim six feet tall. All of the shirts were size medium, and the pants were approximately thirty-two-inch waist with a thirty-four inseam. The suit coats were 40 regular. I was a 42 regular when I was 170 pounds, so the jackets always seemed a little snug, but it didn't show up in the pictures.

It seemed that Wilhelm could easily fit into a 38 short. Fabrizio pulled Wilhelm's jacket tight from the back at the waist and between his shoulders and clipped it with a metal spring clamp that was coated with orange rubber, clucking his tongue and shaking his head impatiently as he worked, scolding Wilhelm without saying a word. Wilhelm seemed oblivious to just how annoyed Fabrizio was, as he held his head high as if he were the King of Spain. I couldn't tell if Wilhelm was plain old stupid, or if he had that special kind of egomaniacal personality that doesn't allow a person to ever face reality about himself. It may have been a little of each. I could tell that Wilhelm and I would not be friends after the shoot was over; I was not even sure that he would speak to me for the next two days as if it were secretly my fault that he was the approximate height of an eighth grader.

Fabrizio took a few steps back and looked critically at Wilhelm; he squinted his eyes behind his round lens glasses. There seemed to be something that he didn't like about the outfit. After a few more minutes of adjusting he had us both sit down on some old wooden crates in front of a loosely stacked pile of hay that had been pushed up against the barn. Wilhelm sat behind me on my right. Fabrizio handed Wilhelm an old pitchfork and then handed me an ancient rake. I held the rake across my lap. The lights popped a few times as Fabrizio checked the light meter against the readings on his camera. Carmine adjusted the large reflectors as Fabrizio instructed him quickly in Italian. Carmine loosened knobs, tilted reflectors and tightened the knobs back up quickly and efficiently. Fabrizio took a few Polaroids and walked over to show them to Wilhelm and me. He handed me one of the Polaroids and then walked back behind the camera and started shooting film.

"Don't look into the camera, please," Fabrizio said directly to Wilhelm.

Wilhelm turned his head slightly to the side for a few

frames before turning his eyes back directly into the camera.

"I'm sorry. Did you understand what I just said, Wilhelm? I want you to look away from the camera lens. Over there," he said, pointing to a building behind the camera.

I looked back and saw Wilhelm nod severely and then lift his chin up high as he looked away with great effort; as if he were breaking one of the seven cardinal rules of modeling. I simply stood flat on my heels and leaned against the stone wall working hard to keep my eyes opened against the bright sun reflected back at me from the white and silver reflectors that Carmine had set up. I knew that Fabrizio would tell me exactly what he needed, and if I were doing something that he didn't like, he would tell me that, too. To be honest, I felt no pressure at all.

Fabrizio started to take pictures quickly using the auto-wind as the Nikon camera with the big lens *ke-chered* loudly with every new frame. Within half an hour we were done with the picture.

I thought we would move to the next shot, but Fabrizio told us that the light was almost gone and that we would finish the other shots on Tuesday.

I started to take off my jacket and shirt as Wilhelm walked confidently over to where Fabrizio was cleaning off the lens of his camera with a small hairspray sized can of compressed air.

"Can I get a Polaroid?" he said without using the *magic word*.

I knew that this would not end well as I listened for Fabrizio's response.

"No," Fabrizio answered without looking up from his work.

Wilhelm looked as if he had not been heard and started to complain about not getting a Polaroid to show his agency....

Fabrizio had already stopped listening as he finished cleaning his camera and turned to load it into the hard black briefcase with the egg carton gray foam inside.

The next day was more of the same. The outfits were loose fitting and very well made. We did one more shot with Wilhelm and me together. He stood on an old wooden crate, and I stood on the ground. After lunch, we shot two more pictures with me alone. Wilhelm was impatiently waiting for his next turn in front of the camera, but it never came. I was relieved when Fabrizio offered to give me a ride back to Milan, saving me from a silent ride with *Big W*. I imagined Wilhelm would work hard to freeze me out with his Germanic version of the cold shoulder.

As we were leaving, Wilhelm did a lot of headshakes and hard stares towards me. He made continuous comments in a guttural, rapid-fire German under his breath, none of which I could understand. I knew Wilhelm would not be throwing any birthday parties for me this November.

30

CALVIN DIRECTS

The weather had turned cool and rainy in Milan while we were away, the gray-cloud ceiling matching my mood which had taken a turn towards unreasoning sadness after my trip. I tried to hide out in my room, but the other models had started to greet me with a reverence that I couldn't understand, and I had no success in hiding. I continued to keep the jobs to myself and pretend that nothing had changed, but they wouldn't allow it. I was doing something effortlessly and without passion that they had been unable to do with intense effort and unyielding passion. From my perspective it seemed easy and uncomplicated; from their view, it seemed an impossible puzzle that I had solved. All of the decisions that had been made about my future in modeling were made by others, and from my perspective on the sidelines, they seemed very arbitrary. I did not allow myself to believe that there was something special within me that separated me from the others who spent their days looking for work to validate their long and expensive trips to Italy. My view that I didn't think I was doing anything special seemed to make the distance between myself and others even greater. It might have been better for me to brag continuously about my jobs and make a complete ass of myself by telling others the story of my greatness behind a pair of Wayfarer sunglasses while sipping a glass of white wine at a sidewalk café. The nicer I was, the more normal I acted, the more they disliked me. I had found a whole new way to be isolated and alone.

Calvin asked me to do a test shoot for him on Sunday as a favor when I returned to Milan. It was a *test* for his portfolio as a stylist. A girl named Kit with bad skin and too much makeup and her model boyfriend met us at a very dirty park with a large, rundown parking lot with litter scattered around, pushed up against the curb by the hot and lazy summer wind. Calvin was a nervous wreck, pacing back and forth without purpose as he gathered up clothes in his arms and hurriedly called for us to get dressed while he spoke in broken Italian to the young photographer. He explained how he wanted the photo to be set up.

The photographer listened without paying attention, his tired eyes half closed as he fumbled carelessly with his cameras. He nodded his head dismissively, as if all that Calvin was saying was a major pain in his ass.

I wanted to walk up to him, chuck him under his scruffy chin and say, *Hey cut the shit. How about some respect for Calvin, dirt bag?* but I kept my mouth shut and my thoughts to myself. I felt very strange. I could feel the awkwardness of the dynamics between the photographer and Calvin, Kit and her boyfriend, and her boyfriend and me. It was no secret to me that he was upset that he wasn't chosen to be standing beside his *lady love* for these wonderful pictures. I tried to listen carefully without getting involved with the action, adopting a relaxed attitude that I hoped would not add to the pressure cooker that was already simmering on the gray Sunday afternoon.

Calvin handed me a lemon-yellow outfit made from a sheer, linen fabric. Kit wore a polka-dot skirt and a bright purple top with a fluffy collar. The shirt was tight around her waist and was made from the same sheer material as my outfit. Her boyfriend, Tyler, was a model who appeared to spend most of his time working on his biceps at the gym; every time I looked over at him, he was either in full flex mode or had his arms folded tightly across his chest. He was about the same size as Wilhelm and had a perfectly styled head of hair with just the right amount of blond frosting on the top. He had that movie star look, a cleft chin, square jaw, and small, deep-set eyes. He reminded me of an older version of Kurt Russell back when he did the Disney movies.

He stayed on Kit's hip at all times, whispering in her ear when the shooting stopped or rubbing her arms with his hands as he turned her towards him to look into his eyes as he spoke to her. I didn't know if Kit was annoyed by Tyler's over-confident display of ownership, but Calvin seemed ready to throw a rock at Tyler's head at any moment. In most of the shots, I wondered how *Shaggy* the photographer was able to keep Tyler out of the picture. I wondered why Calvin had *not* chosen Tyler to model with his girlfriend; it would have made everything much easier, I thought. As the shoot dragged on with one crappy photo after another, I asked Calvin that question as he hurried back and forth waving his arms theatrically to no one.

"Why didn't you use Tyler for the shoot?" I asked as non-confrontationally as possible

He stopped his rushing long enough to turn to me and answer; "Oh, no. No *bello*. He is not right for these pictures. Look at him," he said while he pointed a long finger towards Tyler as he shook his head with a look of pain wrinkled across his brow; "I need *you* for these pictures, *bello*. Don't you know that you are going to be famous?"

Actually, no I didn't, especially not today. I felt like a fool. The pictures were forced and fake, and nothing felt right. I could see the pictures in my head without seeing the prints. Today did not feel right. I felt like an organ grinder's monkey, dancing for loose change for the crowd of people while my master cranked the handle and played a carnival tune. I did not think Calvin could tell that this type of shooting didn't come naturally to me; that the pictures were destined to be complete and total crap. He was too wrapped up in his project to notice anything but the obvious. I shrugged my shoulders laconically and dropped the subject, not really caring why Tyler was not in the pictures or why I was in the pictures. I didn't care. I also didn't feel like making myself care or even pretending to care. I was all out of caring for today. Judging by the lemon-sucking expression on Tyler's face, I was sure that this same question was burning a hole in his frontal lobes as well.

The whole experience was awkward. Everyone there was keyed up and hopeful, waiting for some beautiful pictures for their portfolios. I knew that there would be *no* pictures even worth printing and that the whole shooting was a big waste of time. Georgio, the droopy, cigarette smoking photographer, ran out of film after only three rolls and I silently mouthed *thank you God* as I looked up to the sky.

Calvin became borderline hysterical as he screeched like an over-stimulated parakeet, pleading with Georgio. "You *must* have more film, man!" he screamed as he struggled to control his anger and frustration.

"I am-a sorry Calvin. I forget the bag that keeps all my film cold. We can do a shoot again. Maybe next week, no?" he offered unconvincingly as he chopped up the words with his thick Italian accent while sucking the smoke from his burning cigarette before pushing the smoke forcefully out his nose; looking like a thin bearded dragon ready to breathe fire at any moment.

"Can we do another test *soon?*" Calvin turned to me and pleaded, his pink-palmed hands reaching out to me like a black priest offering benediction at a Sunday morning service. Tiny beads of sweat had pushed out of his skin on his forehead, and his neck was completely slick with sweat. There was a draining of the color from his purplish lips, and his eyes had turned almost completely red as his black pupils seemed to fill all the space not filled with red.

"Sure," I said with a big smile of faux-confidence and calm while wanting only to take off the lemon yellow outfit and go back to the *Lima* to lie down and read...alone. I felt sorry for Calvin. Although he was in his early thirties, I knew that his modeling days were long over.

His smile was as bright as ever, but his hair was thin in the back and had receded over his ears. He kept his hair very short, but it was obvious to me that there were already places where hair didn't grow. He appeared tall with his lean frame, but in reality was only about five-ten. His arms looked like flesh-covered broomsticks coming out of his fashionable shirts, and I knew that he didn't have the build that most of the clients were looking for now. The modeling business had changed almost overnight right under his nose, and there was no indication that it would ever change back to the slim-bodied sophistication of the seventies. I didn't know exactly *how* famous he had been when he modeled, but I knew that right now Calvin couldn't *buy* a job modeling. Looking less than perfect and trying to continue as a model seemed to me to be a very depressing lifestyle to put yourself through. It was something that I did not want to try.

I knew that any more pictures of Kit and me from another shoot would be a waste of time for everyone, but if Calvin wanted to do another shoot in a week or a month or a year, then I would be there. Calvin gave me a shot when a twenty-two-year-old receptionist rejected me after seconds of pretending to look at my book. Heads of all the major men's divisions were all but laughing in my face at the prospect of my becoming a model. Calvin had taken a risk on me; he had trusted his judgment, and he had trusted me. If I had not worked when I arrived in Milan or if Fabrizio hadn't liked me, then Calvin would have been on the *chopping block* at Beatrice, having wasted both her time and her money. This would surely have jeopardized his job. Calvin chose me from some bad pictures over hundreds of other models who had portfolios infinitely better than mine and who others thought deserved to be flying to Milano more than I did. I would do as many tests as Calvin wanted. I just wished there was a way to help him come up with better pictures for his portfolio. I was starting to understand how very good Fabrizio was and how lucky I was to have started with *him* five short weeks ago.

"What did you think?" Calvin asked expectantly as

Georgio began to pack up his cameras as he lit another cigarette.

"About what?" I responded stupidly as I peeled off the lemon yellow outfit in the middle of the parking lot.

"About me being a stylist. Did I do a good job?"

I reached for my shorts that sat on a soft-sided suitcase that held all of the clothing for the shoot, zipped them up and snapped the button and answered instinctively as I stood awkward and shirtless in the dirty parking lot.

"Great, Calvin. Really great," I said as I smiled broadly while reaching for my shirt.

I knew that compared to the stylists that I had worked within the last five weeks Calvin sucked. The other stylists were cool, calm, organized, and tough as hell. They were not mean, but they were there to get a job done, and if anyone got in their way for *any* reason, they were gone before the next picture started. Whatever they said was *law* on the set. They didn't care what the photographer or the models thought of them; they had a job to do, and nothing was going to get in the way of that.

Calvin was a *people pleaser* and wanted the people around him to like him. I did not want to kick Calvin when he was down, but in my head I knew that he would never be a great stylist.

"Is this what you *want* to do?" I asked with genuine interest as I pulled my t-shirt on.

"Oh yessss," he said in his melodic Caribbean island voice, "I have always wanted to be a stylist, to work with beautiful people, beautiful clothes, travel to beautiful places."

"It would be wonderful," he said with a faraway look in his eyes and a white-toothed smile on his face.

"Really?" I asked with genuine surprise.

"Oh, yes, *bello*. I need to make more money as well. I do not make enough money looking for new models and working as an agent with Beatrice."

I was totally confused now. I had thought that Calvin was part owner of Beatrice and that he made good money; not great money, but decent money.

"Why don't you take the pictures?" I suggested without really thinking about what I was saying. His frustration with Georgio's lack of enthusiasm seemed to be a major factor in the shoot not going well for Calvin. If Calvin took the pictures, there would be no photographer to fight with; it would only be Calvin. I thought the photographer sucked as well.

I knew I wouldn't be seeing any of his pictures in any of the major magazines. He thought that we were all losers, but in reality he was the biggest loser of all; not only did he lack talent, but he squandered whatever chance he had of making it with a bad attitude and a crappy work ethic. I could imagine his going home to smoke some Moroccan weed in his tiny room in his parents' apartment while deluding himself that he was a great photographer that would someday be recognized for his talent by his peers.

It always seemed to me that those with the least talent did the most talking about how great they were, and when they weren't talking about their greatness, they were busy trying to make those around them feel like crap by being rude to them or insulting them for anything and everything. It was a way that I was trying hard not to be. "Oh no, bello," Calvin replied with a worried look wrinkling his face as he spoke, "I am no photographer." He shook his head from side to side while lacing his slim fingers together in front of his chest, appearing to be deep in thought. I started to walk across the dirty parking lot, passing Tyler as he talked to Georgio intently about getting the pictures of his girlfriend right away! Their voices faded behind me as I turned the corner and walked in the general direction of the Pensione Lima, my home.

I spent the next week going to appointments that Kristina had set up for me. I saw Terry whenever I could for lunch or dinner or to hang out in the sun on her apartment roof. We went to the park at the end of the week. I had fallen quickly and deeply in love with her and Barbara had become a faded memory from long ago. Terry smiled sweetly at me whenever we were together and even held my hand in both of her hands a few times. We talked for hours, and I felt something inside me soften a little each time that I saw her. We did not talk about Lucky or when he would return to Milan, but I knew that our times together would be over when he returned. Terry was a very good girl, and although she was very fond of me and cared for me, she was not in love with me. Lola was right.

I wrote a long *love letter* to Terry while sitting on a low-slung park bench in between appointments, cautiously disguising the significance of my words by signing it *your friend*. I dreamed of her leaving Lucky and deciding to spend the rest of her life with me. I never gave her the letter.

Lucky returned to Milano on a hot and humid Friday night. Terry told me at lunch that he would be returning to his fancy-assed hotel that night; she was very excited and could hardly contain her joy. I was happy for her as I felt something break inside me, a fragile glass vial filled with a dulling poison that shut everything down in a matter of minutes. Numbness blocked the pain, and the white noise seemed to be waiting in the distance, ready to move in slowly under the cover of night. Terry wanted to introduce me to Lucky. I stupidly agreed to meet her at eight in the hotel lobby.

Terry was standing close to Lucky and hanging on his arm like a beautiful groupie when I arrived in the hotel lobby at 8:30. He was tall, broad-shouldered and slim; dressed more like a wealthy businessman than a model. He shook my hand firmly and then casually looked away as he effortlessly ignored me within seconds. He wasn't threatened by me. Hell, he didn't even acknowledge that I existed.

Terry and three other female models listened intently as he told stories of the jobs that he had done in Morocco, Spain, and Paris. He reminded me of Rock Hudson from the television show *McMillan and Wife*, except for his voice, which was a little on the high side. Terry held on tightly to his right arm and listened intently while looking up at him with a *love-sick* expression that I had never seen on her face. He seemed to be accustomed to being the most interesting person in the room, telling story after story without even pausing to catch his breath. I probably would have liked him fine, if he were not Terry's boyfriend, but the truth was that I was working hard not to say anything that would embarrass Terry and make me look like a bigger *ass* than I already felt. After about thirty minutes of politely listening to embellished stories of his global travel and success as a model, I tapped Terry lightly on her shoulder and told her that I had to go. She looked up at me with a slight smile, nodded her head slowly without speaking, and then turned her full attention back to Lucky. I walked out of the open glass doors of the hotel into the warm night. Lucky's voice was soon drowned out by the sounds of the street rolling up the steps as I descended to the street below.

The *white noise* began to fill my head, flooding through my body, thick and heavy; a wall that blocked out the world and took me back to the special kind of self-loathing that sapped all the strength from my limbs and numbed my mind like a giant shot of Novocain. It was far more overpowering than it had been the day I had met Terry in the park. I thought of all the reasons that a woman like Terry would never be with someone like me. I was a hopeless, depressed kid without much to offer, strong when angry, but hopelessly weak the rest of the time. Reality gave way to delusion as I dreamed of being the man that Terry would listen to intently as he spun tales of his brilliant modeling career in the lobby of a fine hotel while wearing a custom-tailored sport coat with custom slacks that matched perfectly. Nope; I could not even sell that one to myself.

I quietly whispered, "Fuck it" to myself as I tried to pretend that I gave a shit about anything or anyone as I walked down the dark sidewalk away from the lights that lined the streets. Thoughts of disappearing like a raindrop hitting a hot sidewalk flickered through my brain like an old black and white movie as I tried to smile against the pain and dullness that tried to push its way out of my head through the backs of my eyes. Silently I accepted the pain that had nowhere else to go. I tried to find some relief in thinking about the few things that could never be taken away from me; my name, my face, and my mind. It helped—a little.

31

"EVERYONE WAS YOUR FRIEND..."

Paul called from New York and left a message with Calvin for me to call him. Kristina set up the long distance call from the phone in Calvin's office. His office was cool and dark and had the look of a place that was seldom used. There were no pictures on the desk or walls, no pencil and pen holders; just a black phone on a dark wooden desk with a comfortable chair that tilted back so far that I thought that I was going to fall. I closed the door and sat at the desk without turning on the lights. Paul answered the phone after a few creepy long-distance double rings. He asked me how I liked Milan and then asked me if I thought that I was a big star, stuff like that. I did not know how to answer the star question.

He abruptly changed the topic of conversation to agencies in Paris. "There's an agency in Paris that wants to sign you," he said with certainty and confidence.

"I thought I was going to sign with First Agency in

Paris. They are expecting it, and Sophie has already called Beatrice a few times to tell them about jobs for me in Paris."

"Well, Beatrice doesn't really care *which* agency you join. Anyway, I want you to join *Paris Planning*; we do a lot of work with them, and they already have some jobs lined up for you."

They do? I thought to myself. *What the fuck*; "Do *I* have a choice?" I asked, trying to keep the frustration that I was feeling out of my voice.

"Not really," Paul lied with a tone of indifference, "You need to work with an agency that we have a relationship with...."

"Okay," I interrupted, "I might not be going to Paris anyway." For the first time, I was uncomfortable with Paul and with the whole conversation. There was something in his tone that I had not heard before, a cold calculated distance as if he didn't know me as if he were preparing for something that he knew was going to happen.

"What does that mean?" he asked as the pitch of his voice raised sharply as he struggled to contain his anger.

"It means I want to come home at the end of this month," I answered without hesitation.

"You can't," he said flatly. "You haven't even worked in Paris yet."

"What about the *Christian Dior* job with Fabrizio?" I asked defiantly, unwilling to let Paul take control of the conversation or of me.

"That doesn't count; that job was booked through Milan," he countered, no longer trying to camouflage his irritation. "Sylvan at Paris Planning told me that they have a lot of jobs for you in Paris."

"What if I don't go to Paris?" I asked, knowing that this would light Paul up like a *Roman candle*.

He launched into a long speech about *owing* him and the agency and that he was only doing what was best for me and all that kind of crap. I could tell that all of this had nothing to do with me. Everyone was your friend and happy as shit *until* you disagreed with them, then their true feelings came out. I was sure that there was an arrangement between Paris Planning and Legends; money changing hands for models, or favors that would be returned sometime in the future. I wasn't sure. I hadn't figured it all out yet. Maybe I was wrong. But it didn't make sense for me to change to Paris Planning when I had already committed to First Agency. *Technically* the agencies worked for the models; they took a percentage from each job and then gave whatever money was left to the models. In Milan, the agencies took almost 50% of the total job. The reality of the situation was that the agencies ruled the business relationship with their models with an iron fist; they had complete control of the money *and* the jobs, they even determined how long a model could stay in Europe. They would often refuse to buy a plane ticket back to the United States or not allow a model access to his *own* money to prevent the model from buying a ticket home until the agency was ready for him to go. No models had their own bank accounts; the agencies kept all of the money that they earned. They were very polite about it and all warm and fuzzy with big smiles...but make no mistake about it, it was always *their* way.

We finished the conversation before I could ask him when I could return to New York. I heard the long dial tone that let me know that Paul had hung up on me.

Slowly placing the receiver back in its cradle, I leaned back in Calvin's chair. I closed my eyes and tried to make a list of all of the people in my life that I could trust. I couldn't come up with one.

Kristina smiled broadly at me as I walked slowly out of Calvin's office, telling me happily that I was on option for a big swimsuit job that started at the end of the week. I spent the rest of the week alone walking to all of my appointments, sitting in my room reading anything that I could get my hands on, and writing long-winded and stupid letters to people back home.

Most people started writing me when they learned that I was modeling in Italy; they all thought that I had made it to the *big time.* When I was at school or in Connecticut struggling to survive I rarely got any letters from anyone; sometimes my mom would write, but not very often. My older brother Stokes wrote letters asking for things. He started one letter by asking if I could get him some modeling jobs in Milan and if I could get him some *wine, cheese, and simple leather clogs*. He was going to school at a small college in Illinois and wanted to take some time off *to model* as if it were the easiest thing in the world to do. He even enclosed a cheesy picture of himself wearing a fancy polo shirt and raspberry colored shorts that was taken by the water and asked me if I could show it to my agency in Milan to get him some work.

I showed the picture to Calvin and Kristina and they both said, "No, no bello, he is not right for modeling."

"This is *your* brother?" they both asked quickly and curiously. We didn't look much alike.

Stokes and I were like oil and water...but he was still my older brother. I had started to understand that Stokes and I were very different when we became counselors at a summer camp in Missouri. My friends were shocked that we were brothers because we were so different. After I was promoted to director of Junior Leadership, Stokes would give me impromptu speeches any time that he saw me. He told me I needed to dress and act better now that I was in a position of *power*. He told me to stop wearing black concert t-shirts and old jeans with holes in the knees. He added that I should consider wearing a nice pair of *Sperry topsiders* instead of the same ratty sneakers that I wore every day, that they weren't *professional* looking. He was always wearing a bright colored shirt with the collar *popped* and some preppy tennis shorts. He seemed to think he was at a country club and not a sweltering summer camp in the middle of Missouri.

My response to him was a basic letter with all the stuff that people put in when they don't know what to say, things like, *having a great time, you would love Milan, it's really beautiful here, can't wait to see you and the family.* I felt like an even bigger phony than before I wrote the letter. I was beginning to wonder why I even bothered.

The distance insulated me from my family's opinions and theories about how I should live my life. My mom was especially interested in telling me how to live, which apparently should be parallel to the Dalai Lama's, especially in regards to sex. I had decided a few years ago that the only opinion that really mattered was my own. Not only did I not think my family was qualified to guide my life, I also had a difficult time trusting their motivations; it always seemed that they had an angle, a vested interest in guiding my life to suit their needs. I mostly ignored their advice with a touch of sadness. It was not lost on me that people that I spent the first seventeen years of my life with did not know me at all.

The only bright spot in my family was my relationship with my two baby brothers, Jayson and Andy. They were twelve and thirteen years younger than me, and we had a relationship that was more like a father with his two kids than brothers. I loved spending time with them and would put up with any amount of crap from Stokes and the rest of my family to be able to spend some time with them when I visited home. Andy was six years old, and Jayson was seven when I left Connecticut for Milan. I thought about them often and wondered how much time I would be able to spend with them in the next ten years until *they* left home and went to college. They were the only reason I ever regretted leaving home. Maybe things would be better when I returned home again, and it would not be so difficult to spend time with the rest of the family. I daydreamed of a happy barbecue in our backyard with delicious food and real laughter as we each told funny stories about our summer. I knew it was only a dream, but it made me smile and warmed me for a moment.

Kristina told me on Wednesday morning that the Meyba swimsuit job had been confirmed. It would start the fifth of June and run until the eleventh. She was very excited and told me that the job paid cash, almost five hundred dollars per day. The client would give me the money in *lire* when the job was finished. I was happy; happy to get away from Milan and my own thoughts that seemed to be dragging me further and further down with each passing day.

I met the photographer and the art director for the Meyba job at nine-thirty Saturday morning in a small, narrow coffee shop near the agency. They were talking excitedly in Italian to each other while drinking small cups of dark coffee and smoking thin, dark cigarettes.

Two mousy looking women stood with their backs against the wall with their luggage at their feet. I introduced myself with a smile and a handshake and immediately forgot everyone's name except for Sergio, the photographer. He had a squared off and stocky build with thinning blond hair, and a wide face with a matching smile. He smiled widely and shook my hand firmly and began talking to me intently in Italian. I was certain that he thought I spoke Italian. A very small woman with a boy's body and large, random curls of dark hair cut short over her ears and at the back walked towards me and began to speak to me in English. She had a strong Italian accent and a surprisingly deep voice. I found myself liking the way she talked and listened carefully to not only what she said, but how she said it. She had a large gap between her two front teeth and looked at the ground or to the side whenever she spoke to me, avoiding direct eye contact as if she were too shy to look directly in my eyes. She introduced herself as Alesandra and explained that the trip would include me and two female models. She then took me gently by the hand and walked me to the end of the bar. A medium built man that sat at the other end of the bar, smoking a small brown cigarette with a cup of tea steaming on the counter in front of him.

She told me that he was the owner of the Meyba swimwear company; Carrero Robli. He had dark hair and an air of sophistication. Very *put together* and coordinated, from his sock-ess feet in loafers, to his gold chains, he was dressed like a wealthy businessman going on vacation; styled and ready to go. He smiled warmly as he smoothly switched his cigarette to his left hand to shake my hand; he seemed excited that he was coming with us.

He spoke English haltingly but with confidence and said to me; "This is gonna be a fun trip. You like fun, no?" as his eyes wrinkled as he laughed genuinely.

"Yes, Carrero. I like to have fun," I said with a stupid grin that would have made the village idiot look smart.

I had no idea what to expect from the trip. I knew that we were traveling to an island off the coast of Spain, but I had no idea how far it was or what the island would be like. I thought it might be an island paradise in the Mediterranean. I honestly didn't really care, it was out of Milan, and there would be sun, sand, and water. Sergio kept slapping me on the back and began speaking to me in Italian again. I smiled and nodded often, not wanting to offend him or break up his little *happy-fest*.

Marpessa arrived late with a large leather bag and her signature leather backpack strapped to her broad, boney shoulders. She smoked languidly, and her face looked as if she had partied all night. Sergio immediately pulled her close to him and gave her a big hug, lifting her off the ground with his hips. Marpessa smiled without opening her mouth and held her burning cigarette in the air away from Sergio. She caught me looking at her over Sergio's shoulder and gave me a *cat that ate the canary* smile. I looked away quickly pretending that I wasn't watching her. Sergio asked her if she wanted a coffee.

"*Grazie*," she replied knuckling the sleep from her puffy eyes as she turned to the bar to order a coffee. She strode over to me and stopped a few inches in front of me, looked me straight in the eyes and said, "*Ciao bello*," slowly and deliberately as she held her cigarette behind her ass and smiled her crooked little smile. I was amazed at how disarmingly beautiful she looked, even when she was bleary-eyed and puffy from the night before.

"*Ciao,* Marpessa," I replied quietly while looking directly into her liquid yellow-gold eyes before looking away. She stood defiantly in front of me with her shoulders back and her hard-nippled breasts pushing against the sheer fabric of her blouse. I stole another glimpse of her as she tilted her head back and coaxed more smoke from her cigarette. I felt myself growing hard as I did my best to ignore her. This was going to be a long trip.

A blond woman with broad shoulders wearing oversized sunglasses walked through the door and immediately greeted everyone with a hug and a kiss on the cheek. She seemed to spark an immediate infusion of excitement to everyone in the small café. She was wearing white espadrilles, white shorts and a loose fitting, v-neck t-shirt with a tight men's tank top beneath. She was taller than Marpessa and had the look of an athlete; strong shoulders and arms with full, round, muscular thighs. Her thick hair was pulled back in a ponytail, and she was perfectly tan. As she walked over to me, she took off her sunglasses and introduced herself, extending her hand for me to shake.

"I'm Sara," she said confidently while looking directly into my eyes and shaking my hand as firmly as any man.

"I'm Daryl," I said while looking into her clear blue eyes.

"How long have you been in Milan?" She asked with some interest.

"About six weeks," I replied, noticing out of the corner

of my eye that Marpessa was looking intently at Sara and me as we stood between the bar and the wall.

"Isn't he cute?" Marpessa interrupted in her thick Dutch accent to Sara as she stood up and walked towards us. She reached up and ran her fingers through my hair, trying her best to be endearing.

Sara looked over at Marpessa as she continued; "Can you believe he didn't want me? What does a girl have to do?" she said with a cutting laugh that seemed as if it would never end. I put my eyes towards the ground and shook my head slowly from side to side.

Sara put her hand on my shoulder and left it there as she said; "Hey, it's nice to meet you. I think this is going to be a fun trip."

When I looked up from the ground and into her deep blue eyes, she smiled warmly and gently lifted her hand from my shoulder as Marpessa strutted back to her coffee at the bar.

Alesandra announced that the van was ready to take us to the airport. Everyone grabbed their luggage and loaded it into the back of the van and then climbed in.

Sara and I sat together near the center of the plane. I took the aisle seat on the left side so that I could stretch out my stiff right leg and Sara sat by the window. Marpessa and the others sat in the far back of the plane and lit up their cigarettes as soon as the plane took off.

Sara was even more beautiful in the morning sun that pushed through the small window of the airplane. She wore no makeup and her clear skin and freckles were the picture of health. We talked about her family and her two brothers. She pulled a picture out from her purse of her mother and brothers. Her mother looked like an older version of her; small waist, full breasts and hips, and a bright smile. Her hair was blonde, and she wore a skirt with a sleeveless top. Sara leaned into me as she spoke about her family as I did my best to listen without interrupting. I was not looking forward to talking about my family and was hoping that we would land in Ibiza before it was my turn to talk. I knew better than to ask where her father was; if she wanted to tell me about him, she would. After thirty minutes of talking, Sara leaned her head on my shoulder and fell asleep, breathing noiselessly, as the plane moved through the morning sky. I did my best to keep my shoulder from moving and not waking Sara.

It felt good to have her asleep on my shoulder, and I began to daydream about a life with her. I thought of us living near the beach in California and having two kids; a boy and a girl. We would walk on the beach as the sun set in the west, looking for sea-shells and laughing as the water gently lapped at our feet as our children ran up ahead and splashed playfully in the surf. Something good and safe, that was my dream. Good luck with that.

The plane landed smoothly on the asphalt runway, the only indications that we had landed were the flaps angled at ninety degrees from the wing and the sound of the engines being reversed to slow the plane down quickly. Sara awoke from the noise and looked at me to determine what was going on, I smiled and told her that we had landed. She smiled sleepily and rubbed her face with her hands.

After everyone had gathered their luggage from the baggage claim, we loaded into four taxis and left the airport on the one-lane road that exited the airport. The air was still cool, and Sara and I rolled the windows down to let the breeze in.

We arrived at a hotel that rose high above the neat, low buildings in the city. The lobby was beautiful, and I wished again that I had some luggage other than the purple laundry bag that I lugged up the marble steps into the lobby. A round fountain with two angels spouting water from their mouths filled the center of the high ceilinged lobby. The front desk stretched for at least fifty feet. Alesandra was at the front desk speaking to the concierge in Spanish and turned to motion towards the group with a sweep of her hand. She walked over and handed each of us a plastic card with a black stripe on the back and explained that this was our room key. The name on the card was *Royal Alma #427*.

We all rode the elevator to the fourth floor, and I followed the sign to my room. I swiped the key a few times, but the door didn't open. Sara walked up behind me and took the card from my hand, turned it over and ran it slowly down the vertical slot. The light turned green, and the door clicked. I pushed the lever down and opened the door.

"Thanks," I said as I turned to face her before walking into my room.

"No problem," she replied as she walked back down the hall to her room.

The room was beautifully decorated with dark mahogany cabinets, a white couch, and king-sized bed. I couldn't believe that they would get a room like this just for me. My bag looked even more out of place in the elegant styled room as it sat in a lump on the dark, plush carpet. I kicked off my shoes and lay down on the soft bed as I sank into the impossibly soft down comforter. I looked at the ceiling and let the softness of the bed sink in as I smiled at how lucky I was to be here. I drifted off into a dreamless sleep.

I was disoriented as I awoke to a banging on the door, having completely forgotten where I was. As I looked around the room, then back to the door, it started to come back to me as I struggled to get up from the bed quickly and I started for the door.

"Coming," I said as I approached the door.

I opened the door quickly and saw Sara standing in the doorway with only her white tank top and a pair of dark men's boxers with white anchors on them. She wasn't wearing a bra, and from the looks of things, the hallway was very chilly.

"What have you been doing?" she asked as she walked into my room.

"I must have fallen asleep," I said while rubbing my eyes to clear them to take a closer look at Sara and her t-shirt.

"Didn't you hear the phone?" she asked.

"No. I must have been really tired."

"Well, don't worry about it. I volunteered to come get you. We're eating dinner at the hotel restaurant in thirty minutes. Do you have anything to wear?" She asked as she turned towards me and placed her hands on her hips.

Man, she *must* have known what she looked like and that she drives men crazy. I shook my head to concentrate on answering her question instead of staring at her with my jaw open in amazement.

"I think I brought a white shirt and one pair of pants that aren't jeans."

"Let's see them," she said with a look of mock impatience.

I walked over to the closet and dumped the clothes in

my laundry bag onto the bed. Sara reached for the white shirt.

"This is *really* wrinkled. I'll take it back to my room and iron it. You get ready, and I'll be back in twenty minutes.

I nodded and mumbled, "Okay," as Sara walked out the door. My eyes followed her as she walked on bare feet to the door. I didn't know why she was only wearing the shorts and tank top, but I knew better than to ask.

After quickly showering in the sparkling white bathroom, I looked at my face in the brightly lit mirror and noticed the dark circles that curved beneath my eyes, settled into the deep sockets above my cheekbones. I quickly brushed my wet hair off my face, put on a white t-shirt from the pile of clothes on the bed, then pulled a pair of khakis over my boxers. They were impossibly wrinkled and fit like crap.

I dug through the pile and found a pair of jeans that almost fit, pulled them on, found my cheap leather flip-flops, put them on, and then started to fold the clothes that lay sprawled out on my bed. I heard another knock on the door.

"Are you decent?" Sara asked from the other side of the door.

"Yes," I called out as I walked over and opened the door.

Sara stood in the doorway in a white dress that seemed to hug every inch of her body. She couldn't wear a bra or underwear with that dress even if she wanted. I found myself standing in front of her forgetting to breathe as I took in the vision that stood before me.

"Can I come in?" she asked with a laugh.

"Oh, yeah. Sorry," I stammered as I backed into my room.

"You *can't* wear that t-shirt," she said bluntly as she tossed the white shirt she had in her hand onto the bed and walked over to me and began to pull my shirt over my head like a mother would undress her child. She threw the t-shirt on the pile of clothes on the bed and stepped back. I stood shirtless in front of her as she stopped and stood still, letting her eyes linger on my body. I felt a tingle travel up my spine as she boldly stared at me without blinking.

"I can see why they hired you for this job," she said as she tilted her head back slightly and ran her fingers down from her chin to her chest as she continued to stare at my shirtless body.

I blushed at the attention and looked down at the ground and said, "I can see why they hired you, too."

"Well, *you* haven't seen me without *my* shirt on. Not yet, anyway."

I wasn't sure if my heart could take seeing Sara without her shirt on, I was hoping to find out soon.

I put on my white shirt and unbuttoned my pants to tuck in my shirt as Sara silently continued to stare at me with a closed-lipped smile on her face. There was something very sweet, and innocent, and honest about Sara; I felt good and safe with her. We walked out the door and down to the first floor for dinner.

Sara and I were the last to arrive at the restaurant. Everyone was seated at a long table with a white tablecloth, and round, fat candles were placed on the table every few feet. There were two seats near the end of the table where Sara and I sat as the others talked excitedly to each other.

"What do you want for dinner?" Alesandra asked us from across the table.

"Oh, I like meat. Do they have any steak?" I asked, trying to speak loud enough to be heard but not so loud as to draw attention to myself over the noise.

"Yes," she answered loudly, as she raised her voice over the noise. "I'll order you something from the menu," she said with a broad and sincere smile that made me feel good and important. I wasn't used to anyone thinking about me and what I wanted. It felt good.

Sara joined in on a conversation with Sergio and Carrero, and I sat back to listen to them. Everyone was speaking Italian, and except for reading their expressions, I had no idea what they were saying. I slumped down in my chair and watched and listened. I wasn't at all unhappy as I sipped my ice water and waited for my food to arrive.

The food was delicious, and I ate everything on my plate. The conversation never died down as Marpessa continued to *hold court* at the far end of the table, and Sara listened and laughed at whatever Sergio and Carrero were saying, while everyone sipped wine and smoked their cigarettes. I felt as if I were watching a movie, more a part of the audience than the action. I had become invisible, and it felt good; it felt like I was where I needed to be.

Everyone straggled up to bed around midnight except for Sergio and Carrero, who went through the lobby to the elegant bar with the piano music floating out from the darkened door. We would be leaving at six-thirty in the morning, and I was still very tired and wanted to get some sleep before then. I walked into my room without turning the main light on, undressed and got into bed. Before I could consider the events of the night I was asleep.

I woke to the loud ringing of the heavy phone that sat near the bed. The bell inside the phone was louder than any phone I'd ever heard, sounding more like a fire alarm than a telephone. I groped for the receiver in the near darkness and put it to my ear,

"Buenas dias! Buenas dias!" a woman's' voice sang out from the phone. I listened without answering, still mostly asleep and more than a little confused. The voice continued without pause, only louder, "Buenas dias! Buenas dias!"

"Yeah, Yeah, I get it," I answered impatiently as the voice on the other end of the phone stopped abruptly and hung up the phone.

I rubbed my face hard and shook my head in an attempt to wake up quickly. I turned on the light near the bed and realized that I wasn't wearing any clothes. I looked at the red numbers on the clock and realized that I had only fifteen minutes until I needed to meet the others in the lobby. I rushed into the bathroom and ran a shower. I held my hand under the high-pressure stream of water and thought that it would have been nice to wake up early and have a leisurely, hot shower before leaving the best hotel that I had ever stayed in. I washed myself and brushed my teeth in the shower. I dressed quickly by the bed and turned all of the lights on and double-checked all of the drawers and the closet for my clothes before hurriedly throwing everything into my laundry bag. I placed some small items into my backpack, shoved the plastic card-key into the front pocket of my military shorts and walked into the hallway. The hall was silent, and I knew that I would be the last to arrive in the lobby.

Everyone except for Sara and Marpessa was on the front steps of the hotel smoking. Sara sat on a couch in the lobby, hunched over a diary that she was writing in. I slowly walked over to her, trying not to catch her attention as she wrote intently in her leather-bound diary. She had her hair in a ponytail and wore small, round glasses without frames. Marpessa was not in the lobby or outside. Alesandra efficiently put out her cigarette in a large clay pot filled with sand that sat near the front door and walked across the lobby to Sara and me.

"Andiamo, andiamo," she said with wide eyes accompanied by rapid gestures of her tiny hands. Sara looked up at Alesandra and noticed me, as I stood like a statue with my purple bag over my shoulder. Sara smiled warmly at me as she closed her dairy and placed it carefully in her leather backpack. She wore loose fitting shorts and a loose, hooded sweatshirt with long, jumbo-sized strings coming out from the hood.

"Hey D," she said with a smile and a twinkle in her eye, "How'd you sleep last night?"

"Fine," I answered as I placed my laundry bag on the marble floor, "and you, how'd you sleep?" "I slept okay," she replied, "I was a little lonely though. And my bed was *so* cold."

I imagined Sara sitting in her cold bed with no clothes on, then shook my head back to reality and the thoughts out of my head.

"Oh," I replied stupidly, unsure of how to respond.

Marpessa walked out of the elevator with the golden doors followed by a bellboy sweating and lugging her bags behind her. She held a lit cigarette in her right hand and walked like a queen, even though her hair was flat on one side and was an exploded mass of curled tangles on the other side. Alesandra gave her a look behind her back and shook her head from side to side. It was easy to see that she didn't like Marpessa's shit.

32

THE SUN IN IBIZA

We all loaded into three white Mercedes taxis and pulled away from the curb of the hotel in one smooth line. The morning air was cold as it blew through the open window at the front of the cab. The driver smoked a foul-smelling cigar that filled the small cab with a pungent, heavy smoke that overwhelmed the cool, clean air of the morning. I did not like cigarettes, and his cigar was worse than any cigar that I had ever smelled. I silently crossed my arms to warm myself and leaned out of the window to get some fresh air and to avoid puking from the smoke.

I did not like breathing his nasty smoke the first thing on a Sunday morning. I didn't like it at all.

The buildings of the city gave way to wide-open expanses of sand, rock, and scrubby bushes that sat low to the ground; as if they were hanging on to protect themselves from being uprooted by a strong wind. Soon there were no buildings, only a kind of featureless desert that reminded me of the plains of Wyoming before they rise abruptly into the snow-capped Rockies.

The smell of the sea began to filter through the open windows as we continued to drive. I looked ahead and saw a cove of dark water stretching out before us as the land slowly turned from sand to green, the shrubs giving way to trees that looked like smaller versions of the palm trees that I had seen in Santa Monica last summer. They were prehistoric looking, low to the ground with gnarled trunks that followed no particular growth pattern. We drove through a large gated entry and rumbled down a curved driveway made of stones set into the ground. As we drove down the long driveway of our destination, the wheels shuddered loudly as the cabs slowed to a crawl to keep from vibrating themselves to pieces. We parked in front of a stone wall that stood six feet high with a gently curving arch that said *Casa del Rey* at the top in large, carved wooden letters. I jumped out of the cab as soon as we came to a stop, and took a deep breath of the rich, fecund, ocean air.

I walked towards the arch as I felt the sun at my back and the moist breeze from the water buffet my face.

We ended up at a small pool that seemed to be carved out from a flat spot on the cliff that came up from the water's edge. The small rectangular pool was surrounded by grass that was cut so close to the ground that it looked like a green carpet; not made up of individual blades of grass. I was so fascinated by it that I knelt down on one knee and touched it with my hand. It felt as soft as a short-nap carpet.

Alesandra called us over to a shady spot under a wooden pergola at the end of the pool. We sat down in comfortable, curved iron backed chairs and waited. A chubby man with a bright smile and a full head of perfectly combed hair stood up and spoke to us in a thick Spanish accent.

"My name is Miguel. Welcome to my *paradise by the sea*. I hope that you enjoy your stay here. If there is anything you need to make your time more enjoyable, please, let me know. We want your stay at the *Casa del Rey* to be a wonderful *experiencia!*"

A beautiful woman sat behind Miguel. She was slim and wore only bikini bottoms. Her breasts were small and upturned with puffy, dark nipples. She had a baby on her lap. After Miguel spoke, she turned the baby towards her and held his head towards her breast. He began to suckle as she continued to smile as if this were the most natural thing in the world. I looked away and tried to think of anything but the bare breasts of this beautiful woman.

Alesandra called Marpessa, Sara, and me over to her and handed each of us a bathing suit.

"These are the suits that you will be wearing in the first picture. You can change now, and Sergio will start taking pictures later this afternoon. Just stay around the pool. We'll eat lunch at 12:30 twelve-thirty at the bar, over there," she said as she pointed to a large thatched roofed cabana with tables and chairs scattered on a stone patio behind her.

I nodded, took the bathing suit from Alesandra, and walked over to the men's room that sat behind the open bar and restaurant near the pool. I changed quickly, stuffed my shorts and shirt into my backpack, and walked out wearing only my flip flops, shades and my Meyba suit.

I sat down on an empty chaise near the pool and shoved my backpack underneath the chaise. The sun was high in the sky, and it warmed my skin quickly as I stretched out on the cloth chaise. I pulled out a book about a woman who killed her three kids and herself in the United States. It was meant to be fictional, but I knew that it was based on some sick shit that really happened. It was written from the husband's perspective as he returned home after work on a Friday only to discover everyone dead and scattered in the rooms of his house. The story chronicles how he reacts to this gruesome discovery. It was really a sad story, and I didn't know why I was reading it. I really didn't need any more depressing shit to fill my brain with dark thoughts. I did not need to view the world any darker than I already did.

There was nothing redeeming about the book and the story. The husband slowly went insane doing crazier and crazier things as the weekend unfolded, unable to sleep and unable to come to grips with what had happened to his family, let alone understand *why*. I continued to read and soon forgot about where I was, pulled in by the husband's chilling, unemotional narration. It was a really bizarre story that seemed to have no end.

I fell asleep right after the part where the husband decides to hit golf balls barefoot from his backyard pool and hits himself in the foot, breaking his big toe. He takes some painkillers and chugs some whiskey until he can no longer feel the pain.

When I awoke, the sun was hot and high in the blue sky. I could feel the sweat dripping on my face and beading up on my chest and legs. I sat up spastically and blinked myself awake as I looked around the pool. The pool was empty, and most of the guests sat under a large pergola that blocked most of the heat from the midday sun.

I got up from the chaise and slid into the pool quietly, letting myself sink below the surface. The water was colder than I thought it would be and it cooled me almost instantly. I swam underwater slowly and came up on the far side of the pool. I could taste the salt in the water as it dripped off my face and lips as I realized that the pool was filled with water from the sea below. I ducked back under the water and swam a few laps before lifting myself out of the pool. The soft grass was warm as I sat with my feet in the pool. I reached for a white towel from a fresh stack that sat atop a dark wooden table and dried myself off.

Sara and Marpessa were sitting across from each other playing chess over at the tables near the bar. Sara and Marpessa had taken off their bikini tops and their full breasts were on display for all to see. I tried to breathe naturally as I walked over to the other side of the pool, looking at them while I worked hard not to stare. I stopped and sat down at a table near Marpessa and Sara.

Marpessa knowingly looked over at me and said, "You like big titties, don't you?" as she arched her back and leaned back in her chair to give me a good view of her breasts that jutted proudly from her slim rib cage. She took a deep drag from her cigarette and smiled mischievously, looking into my eyes with her yellow cat eyes that were anything but human.

I looked away, unsure if I had broken some rule about looking at a woman's breasts when they were right in front of your face.

Sara looked over at me with a sympathetic smile and said; "It's okay. I don't mind if you look. For me it's the same if a guy with a good body is walking around with his shirt off I will look at *that*, and so will most girls. So I think it's natural for you to look at our boobs."

I couldn't believe what I was hearing. Not only was Sara giving me *permission* to look at her breasts, she was encouraging it.

"Well, I can see why they hired you and Marpessa," I said as I looked at both of them at the same time. They were a study in feminine contrasts.

Marpessa was all long lines and angles except for her full, round breasts. Her waist was high and tight and impossibly small as if it were too small for her body. Her stomach was flat and tight. Her shoulders were hard right angles, and the bones in her arms were thin and long, almost devoid of muscle, and ended with long-fingered, elegant hands. She looked as if she would be unable to lift a ten-pound weight with one hand. The long, slim toes on her feet continued the line of her long slim legs. Her skin was the color of browned marshmallows that had been held near a flame, just before they catch on fire and are ruined.

Sara was broad shouldered and had a small waist that flared into strong hips and round, powerful thighs. She weighed at least twenty pounds more than Marpessa and had a body sculpted from years of sports. She had a swimmer's build, a swimmer that mostly did sprints. I could see the power of her muscles that sat just below her skin. She was tan and had a healthy, red-cheeked glow on her face.

"Hey, Mr. American Tittie Lover. Who has bigger titties? Me or her?" Marpessa asked out of nowhere cupping her breasts in her hands and lifting them up slightly as she stood up from the table and gave her breasts a quick side to side shake until they quivered like a firm Jello ring that had been bumped on a dessert table.

I blushed, looked down at the ground, and remained

silent, unsure of what the right answer to Marpessa's question was.

"C'mon Sara," Marpessa encouraged. "Stand up. Let's give Mr. Americano something to *really* stare at."

Sara pushed back from the table and stood up with her arms at her sides. Marpessa walked over and stood right in front of her and moved forward until their breasts touched. I could not believe what I was watching. Sara had full, teardrop-shaped breasts with large, round nipples the color of milk chocolate. They looked to be heavy and full. Marpessa had large breasts that seemed to be almost perfectly round with dusty, dark nipples that were half the size of Sara's. They were each spectacular in their own way, and they were standing right in front of me.

"Whose are bigger?" Marpessa asked as she turned her head to look into my eyes with her yellow cat-eyes.

"Your breasts are about the same," I lied diplomatically, knowing that Marpessa was the only one who really cared. Sara smiled understandingly, backed away from Marpessa and sat down at the table. Marpessa gave me another hard look that ended with an attempt at an innocent smile.

After lunch, we shot film for three and a half hours until the sun began to sink close to the horizon. Sergio was happy with the shots, and we did little more than stand and talk or interact casually while he snapped photos from far away. It was easy and low stress; I should have been happy with a situation that most men would kill for.

The next day started out with more pictures in the morning until eleven. We stopped and hung out by the pool before we ate a light lunch of salad and lots of breadsticks with butter, sitting at the little wooden tables with the glass tops that were scattered under the thatched roofed cabana that shaded the bar. Marpessa started to spend her time with the others from the shoot. They were a good audience for her, and all of their attention was focused on her, just the way she liked it.

Sara and I began to spend all of our free time together, more by default than for any real reason. She was easy to talk to, and I had begun to realize that she was already spoken for. Our relationship was doomed to friendship before it could ever really get started. For some unknown reason, I accepted this without any internal drama. I wanted to be more than friends with Sara, but I knew it wasn't going to happen, so I enjoyed the time with her for what it was; a friendship with a beautiful woman who spent most of the day walking around without a top on. I could live with that. I knew from many years ago that you could never make a girl *like* you if she has decided you are not the *one* for her. Sara was beautiful and kind and fun, and I remembered all of the things we did with fondness. I knew that Sara *liked* me, but she was not *in love* with me. She seemed to accept me for who I was instead of something that she needed to change. I was close to happy during the day but felt the happiness fade with the dimming of the sun as the cloak of night extinguished the light of day along with the dream of holding Sara through the long, silent night.

33

LONELY TOGETHER

On the third day, we drove to a ferry a few miles from the hotel. We rode for an hour on the slow, flat-bottomed boat that seemed to smooth out the chop of the sea with its massive weight, thudding into the waves as we seemed to stop in the air for a moment and then crash into the next wave through the trough of water that was formed between the waves. I stood at the bow of the boat with my hips pressed against the low iron rails. I closed my eyes to the strong wind that pushed steady on my face and body. The early morning sun was bright and blinding as it reflected hard off the surface of the twinkling water. Even with my dark sunglasses, I could see little more than the harsh light of the sun.

Sara walked up noiselessly behind me and pushed at the back of my right knee with her foot, buckling my knee awkwardly as I lurched to catch my balance by grabbing onto the rail. I turned around quickly as Sara laughed at me.

"Nice view," she said as she looked out over the water towards the horizon.

"Yes," I answered as I looked away from Sara and out over the water.

"Do you know where we're going?" Sara asked as she turned to face me.

"Not really," I answered. "Alesandra said it was another island, but didn't tell me the name."

"We're going to Formentera. It's a really beautiful island."

"Is it like Ibiza?" I asked

"Not really. There are no cars allowed on the island and no large buildings. It's kind of like a deserted island with a few places to sleep and eat. It's pretty cool."

"My booker told me there are only beaches, no clubs or stores," she continued as she gave me a playful shove with her shoulder. "Sounds like fun, doesn't it?"

"Yeah," I replied, caught in another daydream of Sara and me living happily ever after together. I shook my head hard while Sara was not looking. I needed to get these stupid thoughts out of my head.

The ferry docked at a barren piece of land made up of sand and rock with a sign set on two tall, round wooden posts with the word *Formentera* carved into its thick wooden surface in large block letters. We grabbed our bags and walked down the heavy metal ramp they had unfolded until it rested on the concrete dock that disappeared into the endless sea of white sand. A small parking lot defined by logs set into the sand lengthwise was filled with small golf-cart-like vehicles, Vespas, and a few motocross style motorcycles. Sergio and Alesandra waved us over to the parking lot.

"We need to ride these Vespas and motorcycles to our shoot location. I'll take the bags in this car," Alesandra said as she pointed to an oversized golf cart with a striped yellow and white cloth canopy.

"Does anyone know how to ride a motorcycle?" she asked.

"I do," I replied quietly while standing next to a red Bultaco that sat high and looked as if it had been poorly maintained. It had a ripped seat, black dirty oil on the pegs and foot shifter and the rubber was stripped from the throttle, hand clutch, and brake. All in all, it was a greasy piece of shit.

"Okay, you and Sergio can each take a motorcycle. Everyone else will take a Vespa."

I walked over to the beat-up looking motorcycle that looked as if it were leaking oil everywhere, swung my right leg over, and settled into the seat. There were no helmets, and we all wore shorts. I threw my backpack over my right shoulder and cinched up the straps, so it sat high in the middle of my back. Bending over, I turned the stopcock on the left to open the fuel line and looked at the clear plastic tube to make sure there was fuel. I turned the key to the *on* position, flipped the choke, then pushed hard on the starter with my right foot. She coughed to life and ran with a sharp bang on each stroke of the two-cycle engine as if she were struggling to stay running. I turned the throttle hard a few times to feed her fuel as she smoothed out and started running with a steady cadence of sharp bangs as I eased off on the throttle. I held the throttle steady at two thousand RPMs until I was satisfied she was warmed up, then switched the choke off. I looked over at Sergio and the others and gave a thumbs-up signal. They all stared blankly at me as if I had just given them the finger. Judging by the fact that I was outnumbered, I was beginning to think that it was me, not them. Sergio smiled awkwardly to nobody in particular as he struggled to start his motorcycle by pumping hard on the kick-starter while turning the throttle hard after every kick of the starter. I motioned with my right hand and yelled over the banging of my motorcycle.

"Turn the fuel on!" I shouted to Sergio over the loud banging of my motorcycle.

Sergio nodded without comprehension as if his nod was meant to *shut me the fuck up* as he smiled his meaningless smile and continued to pump away at the starter like it was his job. I shook my head from side to side, cut the engine on my Bultaco, put her on the kickstand, and walked over to his bike. Reaching behind his left leg, I turned the fuel cock a quarter turn to the left, then held up my index finger and said, "Wait."

Sergio must have understood what I said. He stopped pumping the shit out of his kick-starter and sat red-faced and sweating on his motorcycle with his hands still holding the grips on the handlebars.

He looked at me expectantly. I waited a minute and then nodded and said, "Try now."

I looked to make sure his left hand had the clutch pulled tight to the handlebar, and his right hand had the front brake on, but could not tell if his bike was in neutral. After three herculean kicks from Sergio, the bike sputtered to life, bogging down as it threatened to stall when Sergio fed an ass-load of gas to the carburetor as he revved it like a madman. I bent down to turn the choke off and then turned to walk back to my bike. He popped his bike into first gear with the clutch only partially engaged and lurched forward quickly as his legs trailed behind in the dust for a few feet, leaving a low cloud of brown dust. He got his feet onto the pegs with some effort and pulling onto the hard packed, dirt street, winding up his engine and roughly shifting gears as if he were in a mythical race against lightning fast opponents. What an asshole, I thought to myself as I shook my head from side to side.

I walked back over to my motorcycle and climbed on. I was beginning to realize that Sergio was not as cool as he thought he was. The rest of the group were on their Vespas and pulled onto the road and followed Sergio. I started my Bultaco up again and took up the rear, thinking only of the ride as I stayed close enough to see their tail lights, but far enough back to feel that I was all alone and riding free with the wind against my face and the sun warming my arms and legs as we sped off to our first location.

The sun was hot, and the temperature had quickly reached over ninety degrees. The wind was noticeably cooler as we approached the water on the west side of the narrow island. The road narrowed to a flat path about four feet wide and began to wind aimlessly up a barren hill littered with rocks and small scruffy bushes that looked to be dead. A very large lighthouse sat at the top of the rise and the smell of the sea filled the air.

The lighthouse was a hard angled octagon at the base that rose into a very large rounded column of sandstone as it tapered towards the glass top that housed a light that looked like a giant light bulb made of thick glass. The group parked their vehicles on the land side of the lighthouse and used the base to block the wind from the sea to light their cigarettes. I walked past the smoking group to the edge of the cliff on which the lighthouse sat. There was no rail, and the water appeared to be about two hundred feet below the lighthouse. The whitecaps of the waves seemed like little parentheses, and the gulls looked like white mosquitoes as they soared near the rocks and water at the edge of the cliff.

The water at the bottom of the sheer cliff seemed to pull at my head and body, like an increase in gravity as I had an almost overwhelming desire to float off the edge of the cliff and fly to the water and rocks below. I took a hasty step backward and shook my head to clear the thoughts that would lead to a quick, painless, death. I walked back to the smoking group and waited silently while resting on the seat of my Bultaco.

We took pictures the rest of the day until eight-thirty. The sun was still bright as it sunk towards the horizon when we started back down the road towards the center of the island. After five or six miles, Sergio pulled off the side of the road suddenly and got off his bike. There was a burnt oil smell and the thick smoke that a motorcycle rider does not want to see was billowing out of the right side of his engine. Sergio looked at his motorcycle with an expression of shock and bewilderment. I looked down at the choke and saw that it was all the way on. Mr. S. had been riding just a little bit *hot* in the ninety-degree heat. The group leaders talked amongst themselves and decided we should push the motorcycle up ahead to a small building housing a restaurant that sat near the road. Alesandra told me to push the motorcycle while Sergio rode my motorcycle to the building up ahead. I was sweating in the late day heat as I put Sergio's motorcycle up on the kickstand in front of the building. Alesandra and Sergio spoke rapidly in Italian to each other as I stood by his motorcycle.

"We will take your motorcycle ahead and get some

help. You stay here with Sergio's motorcycle." She said to me before climbing on the back of my motorcycle.

I didn't have time to respond. The rest of the group hopped on their Vespas and mopeds and quickly pulled away. Sara gave a melancholy wave as she turned to look at me as they rode off. I raised my hand and gave her a weak smile. I sat sidesaddle on the torn seat of the motorcycle, crossed my legs at the ankles, and stretched out as I tried to relax. I looked down the road at the sun nearing the horizon and thought of how long it would be until they returned. An hour? Two hours? My stomach was empty, and I decided to leave the motorcycle and get something to eat at the restaurant.

I shuffled up the stone steps with my backpack loose over my right shoulder as I reached into the front pocket of my shorts to see how much money I had with me. I fanned out the bills with my right hand, looked at them and then folded them and placed them back in my pocket in one motion. A full-figured waitress with food stains on her white apron that sat just below her breasts motioned with her head for me to have a seat without speaking to me. I found a small table for two in the corner, pulled out a chair and sat with my back to the wall facing the sky that could be seen from a space in the old latticework that defined the outside dining area. My waitress appeared with a stub of a pencil and a piece of white cardboard in her hand to write down my order. I ordered a Coke and pointed out a dish on the menu that seemed to have some meat in it. She nodded her head impatiently and turned and walked away from the table.

She quickly appeared with the soda in a glass etched with scratches from years of washing. The iceless Coke was almost cold, and I took a long drink that left the large glass half empty. I looked down the road towards the horizon and watched the sun burn its way through the dark line where the sky met the land. The sun was soon gone from view, and the soft glow of the light from beyond the horizon lit up the sky like a small campfire atop a hill approached in the dark of night. Paper lanterns were strung over the posts and rails of an old fence made of rough strips of wood and worn posts that surrounded the hard packed dirt patio. They provided little light, but they gave a warm and festive glow. A smile pushed at the corners of my mouth as I stared at them until they became only blurred spots of bright colors, melted together into a nighttime rainbow in my unfocused eyes. I slouched in my wooden backed chair and absently looked around the dining area. There was only a young couple huddled together over a small white candle that sat in the middle of their plain white table. They murmured quietly to each other and looked deeply into each other's eyes. Their smooth-skinned faces were made even more beautiful by the soft glow of the candlelight.

Agitated voices interrupted my daydream. I looked down to the road and saw Alesandra and Sergio arguing with each other in Italian while a slim, shirtless man was crouched over the engine of Sergio's bike with a flashlight between his teeth and a small wrench in his right hand.

"Hey guys," I offered from the patio.

Sergio glared up at me and spoke rapidly to Alesandra in Italian. She turned to me and said,

"Sergio did not want you to order food; he wanted you to stay with the motorcycle. He is very angry."

"He's angry with *me?*" I questioned with too much emphasis on the word *me*.

Sergio must have understood what I said or just inferred it from my tone. He started screaming in a high pitched voice as if I had just run over his foot with a steamroller. Alesandra was shaking her head back and forth as she listened to Sergio's rant and looked at me through the lattice that surrounded the patio.

I finished my Coke with one long drink and left enough money to pay for the drink and my uneaten meal on the table under the glass. The waitress looked at me as if I were crazy as I walked past her and said "adiós" with a half smile and a slight wave of my hand.

I knew that it wasn't worth arguing with Sergio. Within twenty minutes the mechanic had fixed the bike. He gave Sergio a ride on the repaired motorcycle, and I gave Alesandra a ride on the back of my motorcycle. She squeezed me tight around my waist and pressed her face against the back of my neck as we rode through the dark, hot night.

The next morning I woke early and took a ride on one of the Vespas to avoid waking the others by taking my loud, two-cycle Bultaco. The sun rose slowly over the water and the day felt fresh and new as I sped down the road with no destination in mind. Gulls flew overhead, and I could hear the waves crash against the rocks at the base of the cliff.

I stopped and sat on the Vespa in the shadow of the smooth stone base of the lighthouse and looked out to sea. I saw a small ship trailing nets and puffing smoke from an oversized stack as it crept across the water. I had forgotten my sunglasses, and my eyes involuntarily shut almost completely against the sun as I made a visor with my hands to shield my eyes. I took one last look at the paradise that stretched out before me and locked it into my memory, a bright moment to think about when things got dark, and the *white noise* blocked out all that was good in life.

We shot pictures in the morning until the sunlight was too harsh and directly overhead. Sergio said that we could not make beautiful pictures in this light. We stopped for lunch and Sara and I sat together at one of the small tables near the bar and ate a delicious and moist crab salad with a refreshing, chilled bottle of Kronenbourg beer. After we had finished, I slumped down low until my head rested on the back of my wire-backed café chair. Sara pulled a tattered paperback book with a pink cover from her leather backpack and held it up so that I could read the title.

"Have you read this?" she asked with a somewhat serious expression on her face.

"No, I've never even seen it. Is it any good?"

"Oh, yeah, it's really good. I'm reading it for the second time," she said as she placed the book on the corner of the glass table.

I pushed at the book with my index finger and spun the book on the table so that I could read the title once again and read aloud; *"Zen and the Art of Motorcycle Maintenance.* Sergio could have used this book the other night," I said with a laugh.

"Well," she said as she stifled a laugh with the back of her hand, "it's not *really* about motorcycles." She took her large sunglasses off and settled them on top of her head, "It's about this guy and his son, and his friends, and they take a trip on motorcycles. It's hard to explain. Everyone I know has read it. It's one of those books that changes your life, you know?"

"Yeah, I think I know what you mean. Do you think

that I can borrow it?" I asked hopefully as I looked up from the book into Sara's impossibly blue, sincere eyes.

"Oh, sure. You can *have it*, actually. I have the hardcover version in my room," she said.

"Thanks, Sara," I replied sincerely as I took the tattered book carefully into my hands and placed it into the front zippered pocket of my backpack.

After lunch, I walked alone to the red rocks that met the surging waves of the Mediterranean Sea. I took off my flip-flops and put them in my backpack and pulled the straps tight over my shoulders to keep the weight close to my body for balance. I carefully made my way through the sharp rocks until I reached a spot that was flat and smooth and large enough to sit and place my pack at my side. My legs hung over the edge, and the blue water surged twenty feet below my feet as I pulled *Zen* out of my pack. The water pushed at the rock ledge, and the water rose fifteen feet and then dropped back down with little or no sound. The weight of the surging water seemed to pull at me to jump as I started to read my newly acquired book.

I was immediately pulled into the story by the voice of the man who spoke unhurriedly of his motorcycle trip across the western United States. I read of Chris, Sylvia, and John, and a man he called *Phaedrus* who was somehow linked to his past. The narrator faded in and out, talking of the present as much as the distant past. He started talking about ideas that got Phaedrus locked up in the *nut-house* and hooked up to some serious amounts of electricity. They wanted to erase the crazy thoughts about *quality* that seemed to make him even crazier than me. I soon figured out that *Phaedrus* was actually the narrator before he got zapped, although he pretended that even *he* did not know who the fuck Phaedrus really was.

His thoughts and views of the world and philosophy cut through something deep inside me. He said things that I had only thought of in dreams. Phaedrus was much more intelligent than I and crazier as well. The thing that seemed to make him crazy, I mean *really* crazy, was that he thought that he could actually make people listen to his ideas and philosophies about the world and adopt them as their own. The only reason he thought they would listen, and even be *grateful*, was that he was speaking the *truth*. Since when does speaking the truth mean that people will actually listen to what you say? Actually, it's just the opposite. If you lie to people, they will eat it up with a spoon. If you tell them the truth, well, they will hate you before the words are even out of your mouth. All Phaedrus got for his efforts was a partially erased memory, a failed marriage, and a mildly screwed-up son who had signs of mental illness at the age of twelve. I was smart enough to keep my crazy assed *true* thoughts to myself. I lacked the conviction to tell the world the *truth* that I knew. I wanted to, *believe me*, but I wasn't stupid enough to imagine that anyone would listen to me. I knew what speaking the truth would get me in the end.

I spent the rest of the trip either reading *Zen*, sleeping or shooting pictures. Sergio didn't speak to me after the motorcycle incident, and Alesandra only gave me the suit for the next shot with a tight-lipped smile and a nod of her head. Sara and I did most of our shots together, and Marpessa did the more glamorous bathing suits alone; sequined one-piece numbers that looked more like ballet costumes than bathing suits. Sara wore the *all American* bathing suits and the light color bikinis. I blocked out most of the static created by the tension of dealing with Sergio by reading. I was able to keep the *white noise* at bay and found hope in Robert Pirsig's book that seemed to never end. On page 153 he wrote, "What does it all mean? What's the purpose of all this?" Exactly, I thought to myself. Fucking *exactly*.

Marpessa had stopped flirting with me, and Sara and I became the kind of friends that would never spend time with each other after the job was over. I talked to some of the guests at the *Casa del Rey* and even made a few friends. A German man named Boris came to the pool every day with a dog that looked like a giant German Shepherd. I mistakenly called his dog a *German Shepherd* before he quickly corrected me in his thick German accent,

"No. Max is an Alsatian. They are much different than a German shepherd. Stronger, bigger, *and* smarter."

I sagely nodded my head as Boris talked and then dropped the subject.

Later that afternoon I went for a swim in the pool and was looking at the sky as I sat on the smooth steps with just my head above the surface of the water. I watched an impossibly tall, slim, white Afghan strut onto the short-cropped grass that surrounded the pool. He had a long, snippy nose and pure white fur that hung down almost to the ground. He pranced in like a *Lipizzan stallion* and headed right towards Max. I went underwater and swam to the other side of the pool. When I came up, I heard the vicious snarling of a dogfight followed by an ear piercing and pathetic yelp of pain and fear. I looked over and saw that Max had flipped the Afghan on its side and had his teeth locked around the white dog's throat. I pulled myself out of the water and rushed over to the two dogs. Boris had tried to pull them apart and had been bitten on his hand by the panic-stricken Afghan. Boris's face was filled with panic. I could see that Max would kill the Afghan soon if we didn't act quickly. A woman screamed in a loud shriek of fear as she ran down the rock steps to the pool. She must have been the Afghan's owner.

I yelled to Boris, "Throw them in the water. Pick them both up and throw them in the water!"

He looked at me as if I had lost my mind and then his face changed when he understood what I was saying. On the count of three, we flipped the heavy tangle of dogs into the water and they began to sink as one. Soon Max let go and came to the surface, unable to breathe with a mouthful of the Afghan's skin in his mouth as he sank to the bottom of the pool. Max coolly swam to the side of the pool and Boris and I pulled him out by his collar and haunches. The Afghan whimpered as he swam slowly to the side and Boris and I lifted him out as gently as we could. With his mass of wet hair, he weighed more than Max. I quickly looked him over and discovered that he was bleeding from bites on his neck and back leg; it could have been much worse. His owner came over and dried him off with a towel while screaming in French at Boris and Max. I stood back and watched. After everyone had calmed down and the dogs were removed from the pool, I sat down on a chaise near the edge of the pool. Boris came over and said; "Thank you, I think you saved that poor dog's life."

I nodded my head and said "Probably. Why did Max attack him? He seems like such a calm dog."

"Oh, you do not know the story, my friend. Max *is* a good dog and as you say very calm. But even a good dog has a limit to his self-control, just like a man. Every day this bitch of a dog would come up behind Max and bite him on the back leg, hard enough to make Max jump and turn to face the dog that bit him. This went on for almost three weeks, and Max did nothing, he only turned and looked at the Afghan after each bite. Today was the same as every other day for the last three weeks; this bitch bit him in the same spot and this time Max did not turn and just look at the Afghan. He grabbed him by his back leg and flipped him on his side. He then grabbed him by his throat in his strong jaws. You saved that poor dog's life and probably Max's life as well. It would not have been good for Max if he had killed him; not good at all."

He extended his soft-palmed hand for me to shake. I shook his hand without speaking. "You have a hand like a peasant farmer," he said absently as he turned to walk away.

Thanks, Boris. I should have thrown *your* soft-assed body into the water. I started to read again and forgot everything after a few pages of *Zen*.

Sara and I did some fashion shots for Sergio in the town of Ibiza on Thursday. Sara wore a dress with a gold necklace and matching earrings; those big looping hoops that looked as if they could be worn as bangles around her wrist. I wore an open, white linen shirt with beige linen pants. Sergio seemed excited about the pictures he was taking and smiled as he spoke in Italian to his assistant. I followed Sara's lead since I had no idea what Sergio was saying. We finished as the sun set and had a late dinner in town before heading back to the *Casa del Rey* by taxi. It was cool and breezy by the time we arrived. I hugged Sara and kissed her on the cheek as we went to our rooms for the night. She smiled meekly over her shoulder as she walked away.

I woke early Friday morning and walked to the pool. The grass was cool and damp with morning dew. Everyone stood around smoking while Alesandra looked frantically through her bags that sat on the ground. "I cannot find the passports," she said with a rising panic in her voice. I rubbed my face awake and said,

"Did you leave them at the bungalows in Formentera?" I asked, still half asleep.

She looked up at me quickly with an expectant look on her face as she seemed to be working out the possibilities in her head.

"Shit!" she said as the truth of my question lodged in her head as she thought of the consequences of her mistake. "I think I did. We need to be at the airport in two hours."

"I think I can get the passports and come back in time," I said without thought.

Alesandra had insisted on keeping our passports to make sure that they wouldn't be lost since she apparently viewed all models as idiots who couldn't seem to keep track of their own shit.

I took a cab to the ferry and borrowed one of the Bultaco motorcycles from the young mechanic at the rental place who had fixed Sergio's bike. I gave him a five dollar bill for the use of the bike. I raced along the dirt road going too fast, with no helmet and only my flip flops on my feet. I was unsure of exactly how much time I had to get the passports and get back to the hotel since I didn't have a watch and there was no schedule for the ferry. The dark-skinned gypsy woman at the bungalows pretended she didn't know me as she held up her calloused palms as if to apologize for my problem. I persisted in English speaking louder and slower, thinking that this would get my point across to her. After a long five minutes of this, she shook her head and went into a room behind the rough-hewn plank that served as a counter and came back with all of the passports in her hands.

I blurted out "gracias" as I turned to rush out the doorway through the hanging beads. I shoved the passports deep into my backpack and hopped onto the still running Bultaco. Within ten minutes I was back at the dusty parking lot thanking the mechanic with exaggerated nods of my head while I pumped his hand up and down with a maniacal handshake. A ferry was pushing across the chop of the small white caps in the distance, heading for the deep water dock. I sat down on a rock near the wood post that held the sign for *Formentera*, trying to hide in the narrow band of shade behind the post as I waited. I looked around to find a place that sold cold drinks or bottles of water. There was nothing.

Alesandra called us over to a secluded corner table near the grass-roofed bar one at a time and gave each of us the money we were owed in lire. I was meant to get four hundred thousand lire each day, but Alesandra cut off Friday and last Saturday, paying me for only five days of work and no travel days. I didn't complain; it was still a lot of money, and I needed every single lire. I took the wad of cash and carefully hid it in my laundry bag in a roll of socks at the bottom. I kept fifty thousand lire in my wallet.

I instinctively decided to stay apart from the group at the airport, watching from a distance, thinking that there was a chance they would check our bags at customs and find the money. I had heard from some of the male models that most countries did not like people taking money out of their country, even if it wasn't their currency. I didn't want to take any chances. I would rather lose the money in my checked laundry bag than take the chance of the money being confiscated by customs and being deported or arrested. I looked like a student and did not want to draw attention to myself. Staying far away from the group that was acting as if they were superstars, I watched as two customs officials in blue uniforms and military hats with shiny black visors took Marpessa by each arm and led her behind a screen. They took all of her cash, which it turns out was almost twice the amount I got. She was crying, shaking and smoking as she sat down on a scoop-backed chair bolted to the floor. She waited with her head in her hands to board the plane.

We arrived in Milano at 3:35. I waited until everyone exited the plane from behind me before standing up to get my bag from the overhead compartment. Sara, Marpessa, and the others were long gone by the time I reached the slow-moving conveyor belt that carried my purple bag around in circles as it waited for me to claim it. I got my money out of my laundry bag, shoved it in my front pocket and walked out to the street to hail a cab. I took a smelly ride to the *Lima* and tipped the driver more than I should have.

34

ZEN FOR ONE

My room was just the way I had left it. I turned the bright light on and flopped onto my bed with my copy of *Zen* in my right hand. I read in the harsh light until the darkness fell outside and the noises of night started to filter in through the open window. I had no desire to leave my room. I fell asleep as the narrator of *Zen* met up with a painter friend from the past, some guy that lived in the pine trees in the mountains near Bozeman named DeWeese. I slept dead through the night and woke up early. I started to read where I had left off but reluctantly rolled my feet onto the floor with the room becoming uncomfortably hot as the morning sun filled the small room with its hot brightness. Remembering that it was Saturday and that I had the day to myself, I decided to kill the time alone and walk the streets near the Lima.

I left without showering and walked with my eyes towards the ground with only my copy of *Zen* and some thousand *lire* notes stuffed in the pockets of my cargo shorts. Finding myself near the small stone bench by the broken fountain with a thick layer of pond scum and a few inches of stagnant water, I sat down to read and was soon traveling across the plains with *John and Sylvia*. I absently thought about taking a trip across the United States alone and meeting people along the way. I calculated the cost of a used motorcycle and the expenses for the trip. I could camp out on the side of the road, or at the rest stops with the *semis* that pulled over and lined up with each driver sleeping in their cabs. It would be a chance to change, to get rid of the *white noise*; find a different voice or sound to fill my head, some form of happiness as I made new memories to erase the old ones. I knew that even this fantasy was bullshit, but it felt good to dream; felt good to have some hope. Maybe I could change and be more spiritual, and find some kind of happiness that would last more than a day.

I realized that I had read a few pages, but had no idea what I had just read. I went back through the worn pages until I found a spot in the book that I remembered and started to read again. I looked up at the sky when the words became difficult to read in the light and saw that the sun was low in the sky ahead of me. I searched to find a clock for the time and then stopped looking. It didn't matter, it was late, and I didn't give a shit; the day was burned and it was time to go back to the Lima.

I walked the long way home and stopped at *Fat Brothers* for a large bowl of spaghetti carbonara and ate all of it as soon as it was served. My stomach pushed out against my shorts as the heavy food filled my stomach. I drank a frosted bottle of Kronenburg and slouched low and comfortable in my chair and watched the brothers serve food to the other customers who sat at the plain tables. Michael walked over to my table with a small plate with three chocolate mounds covered with dripping chocolate.

"Profiteroles for you, signore Daryl," he said with a smile that filled his face and crinkled his eyes with happiness.

"Grazie, Michael," I replied as he placed the plate on my table and handed me a small spoon with a flourish and a small bow. I tasted the chocolate, ice cream, and pastry on my tongue as I ate the desert quickly. I did not stop until the chocolate sauce was cleaned from the plate. Michael came back to the table and asked;

"You like?"

"Yes, I like them very much. They're very good, Michael. Thank you."

My stomach became even more distended as I drank another beer that was so cold it made my teeth ache as it went down smoothly and crisply. I continued to sit and watched the activity in the restaurant for almost an hour with thoughts coming in and out of my head as the clatter of dishes and the hum of conversation lulled me into a state that could almost be described as happiness. I was reluctant to make the trip back to the *Lima* as the brothers began to clean up the tables and place the chairs upside down on the tables to mop the floor. They all smiled and waved through the plate glass window as I walked down the street with my hands pushed deep into my shorts pockets. There was a chill in the summer night as I walked back with long, slow strides to the *Lima*.

It was late and *business hours* were over for the prostitutes sitting in the sturdy wooden chairs on the sidewalk on either side of the steps that led up to the *Lima*. They raised their chins as they smoked long, slim cigarettes and looked down their noses and through the smoke as if to study me. I felt they wanted to figure me out the same way that I wanted to figure them out. Good luck with that one, ladies. I nodded slightly, and they nodded back slowly, in unison, taking another long drag on their cigarettes. I walked into the lobby and then up the stairs to my room, hoping not to meet anyone who would want to talk. My wish was granted, and I made it safely into my room, closed the door quietly, locked it, and got into bed.

Sunday I woke early without purpose and with a feeling of hope that surprised me. I showered quickly and came back to my room and dressed in jeans and a black t-shirt with a picture of *REO Speed Wagon* on it. Calvin called up from the lobby to my room phone and told me that he wanted to take me out to lunch and introduce me to someone. Calvin smiled broadly, opened his arms and said, "Ciao, bello," when I walked down the stairs to the lobby.

"Ciao, Calvin," I responded awkwardly. Calvin changed his opened arms ready for a hug to a handshake when he saw that I wasn't coming in for a hug. I never was much of a hugger. We walked and talked, soon arriving at a small restaurant with dark wood paneling and small windows that let in almost no light. There were a few waiters leaning on the counter of the bar with crisp white shirts and ties covered by neatly fitted vests that were buttoned from bottom to top. We walked to a table near the back corner and a man with a deep tan and white teeth stood up to greet us.

"I'm Scott Copeland," he said as he extended a hand to greet me.

"I'm Daryl," I replied as I shook his hand firmly while he smiled without getting up from the table.

"I know. That's why I'm here," he said with a laugh as Calvin reached out his right hand and said,

"Hello, Scott."

"So you're the big time model that Calvin has been telling me about," Scott said before we had settled into our seats.

"I am?"

"Well. Calvin said that you are getting almost every job you are up for and that Italian Vogue has put you on exclusive for editorial work. I'd say that qualifies as *big time* in the fast-paced modeling world."

I looked at Calvin to see his reaction, and he smiled and said, "This is true, *bello*. This does not happen often. Things are going well for you. Soon we will no longer be able to keep you to ourselves in Milano. Paris calls for you every day for jobs that they want you for."

"I guess things are going well," I agreed tentatively. I did not understand exactly why things were going so well and was stuck in my head that everything could evaporate as quickly as it began.

"I'll get right to the point," Scott said as he leaned across the table and flashed some of the whitest teeth I had ever seen. "I would like you to work for me. I *manage* between eight and ten male models, that's it. I will serve not only as your agent but your manager as well. If you follow my instructions, I can guarantee you a six-figure salary the first year and the cover of GQ. I not only book jobs for you, but I also guide your career, help you make decisions on what direction to go."

"Really?" I asked, surprise and doubt filling my voice.

Calvin grinned like a parent watching his child walk for the first time and said,

"Scott is the best in the business. He would not make the offer to you if he did not believe in you."

"First thing you need to do is get those teeth cleaned, filed, and filled. They need to be perfect if you want to make the big money. You'll be working in Japan and Germany; they are kind of obsessed with perfect teeth."

I suddenly became self-conscious about my teeth and the calcium deposits that were on the front of my top teeth. They were there since my adult teeth came in and looked anything but perfect.

"Whatever works," I said with a shrug, trying to cover how I felt inside. "When do we start?" I asked.

"After you finish getting as much work in Europe as you can. I'm based on the West Coast, near Los Angeles. You'll need to come to LA. Calvin told me that you would be in Paris and Milan at least until the middle of August. We'll get together when you get back to the states," he said with a big smile.

"*Six figures,*" I said quietly to no one in particular as I looked over at Calvin as he smiled maniacally. I was still trying to grasp how much money that was and how much my life would change if it were true.

"Yep, six figures," Scott said with a slight laugh. "Most of my guys make well over a hundred thousand dollars per year."

I shook my head from side to side as thoughts of working at Table Works for $4.75 per hour drifted through my head. I still had a hard time believing that I would ever make a six-figure income.

Scott left after eating only half of his appetizer and Calvin and I had a leisurely lunch at the almost empty café. Calvin was very excited and could not stop telling me how great my life was going to be working for Scott. I ate and listened and held my excitement inside, not wanting to believe what Calvin already saw as immutable fact.

35

SOPHIE CALLS

I did a small campaign for Carlo Orsi on the outskirts of Milan on Tuesday. At the end of the day, Kristina told me about a job in Paris that had been booked by First Agency. I asked if I would fly to Paris and Kristina said that I should take the train. I didn't even know it was possible to take the train from Milan to Paris. They gave me money from my account to buy a ticket and two hundred thousand lire for the trip. I traveled by tram to the train with an overstuffed small bag that I had bought at a department store for the equivalent of twenty dollars. It was a piece of crap that wouldn't last, but it was much better than the laundry bag. I left Wednesday night on a clean train with chrome sides and clear windows. It was a beautiful train with sleeping compartments, large windows, and blackout curtains.

My ticket had a number that corresponded with a sleeping compartment. I found my compartment after some back and forth searching for it, the numbers did not make sense to me, and I ended up passing my compartment twice before finally figuring out how the numbers worked. The sleeping compartment was spotless, and there was plenty of room between the bunks that hung from the wall with slim chains that were bolted to either end. I was on the top bunk, and I climbed up to settle in for the ride as the train jumped gently as it began to move slowly down the track. There was a lone fat man on the lower bunk across from me that was asleep with his arms crossed over his round stomach, hugging himself with a flimsy blanket bunched up at his feet. I turned towards the wall and started to read *Zen* in the dim light from the small ceiling fixture in the middle of the compartment. The train rocked slightly as it started to pick up speed. The lights that bordered the track flashed closer and closer together. I thought that this seemed like a much better train than the *local* that Tommy and I had taken from Milan to Rome. I quietly drifted off to sleep as I read about Phaedrus spending ten years of his young life in India.

I awoke as the sun threatened to rise up from the horizon. The sky burned red where the land met the light of the sun with the sky still hanging onto the dark cloak of night. I rubbed my eyes and looked around the compartment and saw that my chubby travel companion was gone. His bed was turned up, and all traces that he existed were erased. My right leg was stiff as I climbed down the shiny chrome ladder. I could feel the train start to brake as I found my balance and heard a faint metal on metal squeal as the engineer applied the brakes slowly, causing the train to slow down smoothly without the jumping and jerking of the cars like my trip to Rome. Soon the light from the sun rising over the strip of horizon pushed through the open window with a bright orange light like a campfire at night. I grabbed my bag and placed *Zen* in my backpack. The light of the sun disappeared suddenly as the train pulled slowly into a tunnel that led into a loud and cavernous station with impossibly high ceilings and voices that echoed off the metal and glass walls and ceilings as people bustled out of the train and onto the wide concrete platform that led up to the ticket booths and tiny shops that sold books and food in the station.

I took a cab to a photographer's home studio on Rue *Dest Michelle* on the outskirts of Paris. It looked like a tightly packed suburb more than the city. I knocked on the door and was met by a small woman with a tan face and hair that was dyed dark and cut in a bob. She smiled professionally and bowed slightly as she invited me into the studio. She introduced herself as *Marianne*. We shook hands, and I followed her with my bag in hand and my pack still on my shoulders into the studio. A small man with a tan face that sagged from below his eyes to his sallow cheekbones walked out from behind a glass block wall and introduced himself as *Alain Laurrue*. We took a cab ride together with all of his photography equipment stowed in the trunk of the cab. He did not have an assistant; Marianne was the art director for the shooting for *Le Officiale* magazine. We arrived on the west bank of the *Seine* and shot all day in the same location, changing the camera angle and the background for each shot. We were shooting winter sweaters, jackets, and pants for the November edition of the magazine. Marianne seemed very pleased with the pictures and asked me about doing another job the end of July with Fabrizio Gianni. We finished shooting as the sun worked its way towards the horizon and were packed up and ready to leave by eight.

The next day we met Jeff, a model from First Agency, on the east bank of the *Seine*. He was dressed fashionably and seemed much older than I. He walked slowly and spoke softly, almost whispering with his lips held close together over his teeth. He smoked languidly between shots and had a way of pursing his lips when Alain was taking pictures as if to suck in his cheeks to make his cheekbones more pronounced in photos. I don't know if he was aware that he was doing it. We did most of our shots alone except for a few shots where we sat together against a stone wall made of smooth gray granite, fit together without spaces. Jeff seemed to be very concerned about his position in the pictures. Whether we were standing or sitting, Jeff would position himself in the foreground and look directly at the camera. I did not get the feeling that the pictures would be very good and simply looked at the camera or away, I didn't care how well I was featured.

Short-armed Alain handed me a Polaroid of one of the solo shots. I hadn't realized that my hair was such a freaking mess. It was frizzed out and damaged from using harsh soap to wash it instead of shampoo, and it sat atop my head like a nest more than a hairstyle; it looked like a bad perm. I nodded diplomatically to Alain and carefully stored the picture in my backpack. Alain smiled to show off his nicotine-stained teeth and went back to shooting.

I got the feeling that Jeff had been in Paris forever and wanted to be a model for another ten years at least. His demeanor was that of a man who was trying hard to let everyone know how bored he was with being a model; too cool to enjoy sitting or standing in front of the camera. I decided that he must be full of shit.

The shoot ended with my sitting alone in a layered outfit that was tight across the shoulders and arms. What size do they think models are at six one? I figured that a slim 165 pounds with narrow shoulders would be the perfect size to fit the clothes that we were given to wear. That's pretty fucking thin. Alain and Marianne gave synchronized smiles as Alain raised his hands in the air and said something in French clapping his hobbit-hands together. They were very happy, and I gave a smile and I clapped my hands as well, unsure of what the protocol was in this situation. Jeff was working on a Camel cigarette and looked over with a half-lidded expression meant to show his contempt and boredom for all things un-cool. I changed into my clothes and tried to arrange the clothes from the last shooting in a pile that was easy to handle and gave them back to Marianne. She sang out, *merci*, as she gently grabbed the pile and started to load it into a garment bag with a zipper that went all the way around the bag, allowing the top to be removed like a can of sardines. Jeff walked over to me and handed me a voucher that he had torn out of his book.

"Evelyn wants you to get this voucher signed and come back to the agency with me," he said flatly without interest as he continued to smoke with a look of disinterest without focusing on me. I watched Jeff fill out his voucher and copied the words and numbers that he wrote. I only knew that seven francs equaled one dollar and couldn't do the math in my head very well. The number that Lee wrote seemed to amount to approximately *shit dollars and fifty cents* for the two-day shoot. I thought that I might end up owing the agency money after they took out their complicated bullshit *tariffs* and *made up fees* that made the *shit pay* even more insignificant.

Jeff ambled over to Marianne and held out his voucher

for her to sign. He did not speak. She placed the floppy voucher book on the stone wall and signed it quickly with a flourish. She tore off the white copy of the voucher from Lee's book and placed it on a small clipboard that sat on the stone wall. She looked at my voucher as I handed it to her and said; "Would you mind signing my voucher?"

She looked up at me and said, "*Absolutmont*," which sounded a great deal like *absolutely*, so I took it as a yes. She smiled kindly at me and took the top copy of the voucher and put it on top of Jeff's on the clipboard.

"Merci," she said with a genuine smile as she extended her small hand for me to shake.

I shook her hand gently and responded, "Merci."

Jeff interrupted with an impatient tone, "Come on, let's go. Evelyn wants you to come to the agency with me before they close."

I turned and started to follow Jeff trying to catch up. *What's the deal with these fast-walking models?* I thought. Jeff moved more quickly than I did and unless I jogged, there was no way that I was going to catch up to him walking. He was a fast walker who wanted me behind him, not beside him. He stopped at the main road and placed his cigarette in his mouth and signaled for a taxi with his right hand. A Peugeot pulled over to the curb, and the light at the top of the cab turned off. Jeff opened the door and got into the passenger side of the cab and closed the door behind him. I was beginning to think that he didn't like me. I climbed into the back with my two bags and rolled down the window. Lee and the middle-eastern cab driver spoke in French, both smoking happily as we pulled away from the curb and into the fast-moving traffic.

Within ten minutes we had traveled to the *Champs-*

Élysées and were driving around the biggest turnaround that I had ever seen which encircled the *Arc De Triomphe*. All of the cars on the road were small and nicely maintained. I did not see rust or bald tires or confederate flag stickers on any of the vehicles. We turned abruptly onto *Rue Richepanse* as the cab smoothly came to a stop in front of an elegant sandstone building that was visible from the *Champs-Élysées*. Lee paid the cab driver in francs as I stood on the sidewalk and waited, I held a twenty-franc note in my hand and offered it to Jeff, but he ignored the gesture.

I felt foolish as I followed Jeff across the wide sidewalk while the pedestrians looked at me as if I were something hideous to behold. Jeff walked through a narrow concrete-walled entrance to a building that was all stone and glass. There was a small elevator that was open on all sides except for some slim iron bars that completed the cage. It traveled in the middle of the stairs that wrapped around the cage of the elevator, which contained the heavy braided cables and the electrical wires. Jeff pressed a worn looking solid brass button that was mounted on the ornate iron frame of the first-floor entrance to the elevator. A loud buzz echoed in the metal and stone stairway. The cables began to move quietly and quickly as the elevator descended from above in the narrow, open shaft. The elevator was operated by a young man wearing oversized clothes and a cap similar to the men who played *bocce* in the park in Milan. He smoothly slowed the elevator to an almost silent stop and pulled the accordion style gate open with a hard pull of the handle with his right hand.

"Hey Jeff," he said with an accent that sounded like a combination of French and west coast-American. It sounded strange and almost comical, like Steve Martin and

Dan Akroyd when they played *the wild and crazy guys* on *Saturday Night Live*. I could tell that he thought his accent was more American than French.

"Hey, Michel," Jeff offered with an enthusiastic handshake and a warm smile.

Jeff did not introduce me and Michel was busy staring at the floors whipping by.

"I'm Daryl," I offered as the elevator suddenly arrived at the seventh floor.

"Hmm," was all that Michel said as he jerked the gate open and stepped back to allow Jeff and me to exit the narrow doorway.

I felt lost and confused, like coming to grade school halfway through the day when I was sick all morning when I didn't understand what the teacher was talking about, and had missed all the best classes; gym and lunch, making me wish that I had stayed home. All of the other kids in the class were no help; they simply stared at me as if I had broken some unwritten rule, as if I had done something wrong.

I did not feel like I belonged in Paris, and it seemed that Jeff and Michel thought the same thing. I was starting to understand the difference between Milan and Paris. I was certain that I would never be completely comfortable in the *City of Lights*. Scratch that. I would never be *close* to comfortable in Paris; Paris rejected me like a bad organ transplant. We were not compatible.

The agency stretched out without partition walls to divide up the space into offices and conference rooms. Everything was in one room in the corner of the building with two long outside walls with large casement style windows. There were plain square posts two feet square that held up the floors above. The agency was one big room with desks arranged randomly in the bright light that poured in through the dusty glass from the late afternoon sun. Jeff walked over to a desk where a round-shouldered woman in a shapeless dress with small frameless glasses and short brown hair sat.

"*Bonjour* Evelyn," he said with a big, face-cracking smile. He fake-hugged her and kissed her on both cheeks without actually touching his lips to her skin. She hugged him hard around his waist and closed her eyes as she pushed the side of her face into his chest and her body against his. Jeff reached down with one arm and held her tentatively as he looked towards the ceiling until she stopped hugging him. He gave her another *larger-than-life* smile when she looked up at him adoringly as they both sat down at the same time.

"*Bonjour Chéri*," she gushed as Jeff gave her a great fake smile. "We have not seen you for almost a week. How was your trip?"

"Good, good Evelyn. It's good to be back, though. I missed you guys," he said in that full of shit way that made me want to puke on the carpeted floor.

Evelyn blushed and smiled shyly, stealing a glance at Jeff, as she pretended to get some papers together on her desk. Jeff flopped his backpack onto the floor near Evelyn's desk, stretched out his legs and sighed.

I continued to stand with my heavy bag in my hand and my backpack still on both shoulders. I felt like a slack-jawed idiot as Evelyn looked over at me.

"Hey man, how's it going," an energetic female voice said from behind me with the same attempt at an American accent that Michel had. I turned to face a short woman with wild dark hair smoking a fat cigar. She wore cowboy boots, a snug pair of 501 Levi's, and a man's pink Polo button-down shirt. The top three buttons of her shirt were undone, and I could see the tops and sides of her bra-less breasts without even trying to look. She wore a bright gold chain with a large *Star of David* that ended somewhere near the top of her cleavage. Her face was pinched and drawn like a dried out apple making her dark, raisin eyes look even smaller than they really were. There was something sexy about this imperfect creature with her man's clothes and tight body; it was as if the contradiction made her more attractive than if she dressed as feminine as her body. I could tell that she worked hard at trying to dress like a man.

"Um, good, I guess," I answered as I stared at her with a confused expression on my face.

"You are a fucking hottie, man!" she said as she punched me in the front of my right shoulder with more force than I expected. "I'm Sophie, welcome to Paris, dude! We got *a lot* of work for you here, and we are *not* going to let you go back to Milan," she said with a full, belly laugh that made her breasts jiggle beneath the fabric of her shirt. I stared at Sophie with a half smile and thought silently how much I liked her. I hoped that she would be my booker and I wanted her to like me. Staying in Paris sounded good to me all of a sudden. I liked Sophie. I liked her just fine.

"Great," I answered as I let my bag drop to the floor.

Sophie sat me down at a little dark-stained wooden desk without drawers. She tried to explain the *tariff system* in Paris and showed me a copy of a black and white chart that had numbers in columns with strange symbols after the numbers. I thought about Sophie's breasts and nodded my head at appropriate times as if I were listening to her talk about the complex list of deductions, where the money seemed to go to everyone but me. She had me fill out and sign some forms that, for all I knew, could have authorized all of my money to go directly into her own personal bank account. I gave her all of my passport information and then put my passport back into my backpack. I had learned from the raid by the *Carabinieri* at Beatrice that the safest place for my passport was with me. The tariffs confused the shit out of me, and I tuned out the detailed information she was giving me after she finished explaining the second tariff. It did not take a genius to figure out that I was *not* going to make any money from the jobs with so many bullshit tariffs. The only purpose of the tariffs was to separate models from their money. I knew the drill, so it didn't really bother me too much; as long as I had enough money for food and rent, and for a few token presents for my family, I was good.

Sophie leaned into me from behind, pushing her firm breasts into my back as she put her arm around my shoulder and pretended she needed to be this close to help me with the paperwork. I didn't mind at all and pretended that this was the most normal thing in the world. I could smell her *Old-spice* after shave and the strong-sweet tobacco smell of her cigar that she had left burning in a small green glass ashtray on one of the empty desks. Her hands were small, and her nails were clipped short, like a man's. Her sleeves were rolled up to the elbow to expose tan, hairless arms with a chunk of a man's diving watch on her left wrist. I finished the paperwork quickly and stacked the papers on the corner of the desk.

Sophie grabbed my small-backed office chair and spun

it around until I faced her as she leaned over me with her feet set wide apart. She looked me square in the eyes and climbed onto my lap as if we had known each other forever. She moved her hips onto my lap until she was comfortable. She felt warm and light on my lap and a pleasant warmth spread from my lap to my stomach. My brain fuzzed over as the pleasure took over rational thought and I sat without speaking, not wanting the feeling to end. She smiled at me and ran her fingers through my hair. I returned her gaze. Her eyes were small, deep-set, and almost completely black. She was very tan and deep lines had formed around her dark eyes. I was pulled in by her differentness and felt comfortable staring at her intently as she seemed to be doing the same with me. She sat surprisingly light on my legs, and I drifted off to a daydream of her and me sitting in a room, on a bed without clothes looking at each other. Sophie was not a classic beauty. I reached around her small waist and clasped my hands together slowly as if it were the normal thing to do. I could not tell if she was playing with me or if there was a note of seriousness in her actions.

A voice broke the silence from across the room, "You know she is a *lesbi-anne*, don't you?" a man asked with a familiar and condescending tone as if he had known me for years. There was sarcasm and irritation mixed with a hint of a joke in his French-accented English words.

"Bonjour Monsieur Ja-nney," a small man said as he walked across the room and stood in front of Sophie's desk with a sweet as pie voice. He presented himself and clicked his heels together as if he were a direct descendent of Napoleon Bonaparte, fresh from the front lines.

I looked up at him blankly as he continued to talk, "I am Paul Hagenauer, the direc-*tor* of First Agency." His voice seemed designed to broadcast his importance while he reminded himself of the same thing as if he needed a reminder more than the person to whom he spoke. He was a short, tan, slim man in his early forties. His too tan face looked crispy and damp with moisturizer. He had bulging eyes that seemed to be propped wide open at all times. He was dressed in the same style 501 jeans as Sophie and had a white polo shirt that was pulled tight across his manboobs. The stiff collar of his shirt was turned up. He wore dark loafers without socks and had the look of a man that took his appearance *very* seriously. He stood as if he were at attention with his hands at his sides, his feet together and his butt cheeks clenched tight.

"I'm Daryl," I said, as I tried to stand up with Sophie still on my lap. I offered my hand, and he reached over the desk and gave me a firm and efficient handshake as he nodded his head in my direction.

"Hey Paul, you know I like *some* men," Sophie said defiantly as she wiggled her firm ass into my lap and draped her arms around my neck.

"Oh, Oui?" Paul said mockingly, "When is the last time you slept with a *man* Sophie??" Paul asked with a good-natured smile and a few scolding clucks of his tongue. "You know you like the women with big bottoms and big soft breasts and a warm space between their legs, *mon chéri*. This is nothing to be ashamed of," he said with a twirl of his right hand as he turned on his heel as if he were planning on walking the runway.

Sophie gave Paul the finger behind his back, moving it up and down for effect, and said coyly, "*Sometimes* I like guys, Paul. Maybe not as much as you do, but there are some guys that I like." She smiled and, standing up, pretended to kick Paul in the ass. I took everything in as I stayed seated and watched in silence.

"Sure Sophie, sure. Okay. Let us ask Eve-lyn. *Eve-lyn-a*, does Sophie like men or women?" Paul turned and asked from across the agency. Evelyn turned her attention to Paul as Jeff smoothly pretended to be examining the fingernails on his right hand.

"Oh, *merci* Paul, please do not get me involved in this conversation," she said dismissively.

I leaned back in my chair, stretched out my legs, and crossed them at the ankle, listening and watching.

"Maybe I would change my team for *this* one, you fucking queen," Sophie said as she looked towards me. What the fuck did I have to do with this conversation? Everything, apparently. I slouched in my chair and tried intently to act indifferent to the discussion between Paul and Sophie.

The late afternoon sun had started to work its way behind the buildings across the street, and a light breeze floated its way through the open windows, scattering some of the loose papers from the desks to the floor. Paul looked at the papers as if there were no fucking way he was picking them up. Paul sat across from Sophie and me with his legs crossed at the knee. He pulled a small silver case from the back pocket of his jeans, selected a small brown cigarette, and lit it quickly with a very shiny lighter.

It looked the same as the cigarettes that Calvin smoked and the spicy smoke soon filled the area that we sat at. It wasn't the disgusting burning-shit smell of Marlboro cigarettes that everyone else smoked. It reminded me of the cigars and pipes that my grandfather smoked when Stokes and I would go to visit him and grandmom in their old, white farmhouse on the fast-moving highway in New Jersey.

Paul told me how great First Agency was and how good it would be for me to stay with their agency. I didn't bother to tell him that I had no intentions of changing agencies. Hell, I didn't even know how to use the phones in Paris even if I did want to find another agency. I was here; I liked Sophie, and as far as I was concerned First was my agency from this point on.

"Paul, I want to work with First," I interrupted quietly.

Paul smiled like the Cheshire Cat. I was certain he had spoken to Paul Rackley in New York and knew that Paul wanted me to sign with *Paris Planning*. I knew that Rackley told me to sign up with Paris Planning, and I was sure word would get back to New York that I had ignored his instructions before I had a chance to speak to him, but I didn't really care what he wanted. It felt as if he were a million miles away, and living in a different time in a different world.

Paul abruptly told me that I could stay at his apartment in Paris until they found me a place to stay. I shrugged my shoulders and nodded my head, said goodbye to Sophie and waved to Evelyn as we walked out of the agency towards the cage elevator. Jeff pretended to look down at his planner as I tried to get his attention with a wave.

36

FRENCH ADVANCES

Paul and I ended up below the agency in a cool and damp parking garage. The concrete ceiling was wet and cool a few inches above my head; the cars in Paris must be smaller than those in Chicago. Paul had a small Peugeot that was the color of a flesh colored band-aid. He took my bag from me and placed it in the trunk, and we both got into the car. I had no idea where we were going and didn't really care. Paul seemed intentionally cool, acting as if he had all the answers; that kind of cool that high school kids adopt when they want to impress someone, not a real cool or *grace under pressure* cool. I think he thought he had me fooled and I was impressed with him. He was not correct. He seemed genuinely interested in my staying with his agency. Although I only knew Paul for about an hour, I could tell that he was somewhat of a joke, the titular head of the agency that was really run by Sophie and Evelyn. It seemed to be very important to Paul that I thought well of him, which I did to a certain extent, I just didn't take him seriously and saw him as someone who had little or no power to affect my life.

Paul drove skillfully through the streets of Paris as if he were a professional rally driver. He talked rapidly about the agency, the modeling business, and about Thierry, the wealthy owner of the agency. I learned that Thierry was an impossibly wealthy heir to a pharmaceutical empire and was engaged to Christina Onassis. Paul insisted that we go to his castle in the country one day soon. We arrived at a small row of peaceful brownstones with trees planted every 20 feet on a cobblestone sidewalk. Paul maneuvered his *Peugeot* skillfully into a tight spot between a *Citron* and a red turbo *Le Car*.

"Alles, we have arrived!" he said from the driver seat.

"This looks great, Paul" I replied, not knowing the right thing to do or say.

We both got out of the car at the same time, and I walked to the back to grab my bags. Paul insisted on carrying one of the bags and I backed away slightly to let him grab it. I followed him through the small swinging wrought iron gate that led to the front of his home. The shrubs and flowers were perfectly placed and looked like a miniature botanical garden. He opened the old-fashioned front door with a key and opened the door for me to enter first. I walked into the marble-floored entrance. The hallway was not large and opened into a sitting room on the left, but it was very well kept, everything looked fresh and clean. A small man with dark hair and skin with a small mustache entered from the other end of the hallway. He was dressed in black pants and a crisp white shirt with a black vest.

"Bonjour Master Paul," he said with a smile as he bowed slightly.

"Bonjour Jute," Paul replied without looking at him. "This is my friend Daryl," he continued as he put down my bag and turned to face me. "He will be staying with us for a while."

"Very good, Master Paul," Jute bowed slightly and quietly slipped out of the room.

"He is my servant from Tunisia," Paul continued." He makes very good *cafe* and keeps everything clean and tidy while I am working."

"Wow," I said quietly as I took in the rest of his house.

"Follow me, you will stay in the guest suite, on the other side of the dining room."

He said as he gestured for me to follow him down the hall and to the right, through the dining room.

He opened the door, and I looked at a tidy room with a small bed, dresser and writing desk and chair that faced the window. I carefully placed my bag and backpack near the foot of the bed.

"My room is at the end of the hall, and the bathroom is the next room down," Paul said. "Relax and unpack your things. I would like to take you out to dinner to celebrate! I am Tres joile that you have joined our Agency!"

"Ok, thank you," I replied while looking around the room, unsure of how to reply to Paul.

Paul walked out of the room, and I closed the door and began to put some of my clothes away in the dresser. I took off my sneaks and lay down on the bed and took *Zen* out of my backpack to start to read.

I was awoken by Paul's voice from down the hall. "Darill, Darill!"

"Yes, Paul," I responded through my closed door.

"Come here; I want to talk with you," he replied.

"Ok, be right there."

I opened the door and walked down the hallway towards his voice.

"In here," he called out from the open door of what seemed to be the bathroom. I walked over to the doorway and looked in. Paul was lying in the bath nude. The water was completely clear. I immediately walked out of the bathroom and stood in the hallway.

"I want to talk with you, mon ami," he called out from the bathroom.

It was an awkward moment for me, the only thing I could think to do was to stay in the hallway and talk to him from the other side of the wall. I replied with a laugh in my voice, as if I were not offended by his actions.

"I'm good here, Paul. I can hear you fine."

"Oh, but it is so much better to speak face to face. Oui?" He pleaded with a drippy and dramatic voice as if he were truly wounded by my actions.

"I can hear you fine, Paul."

"Ah, well. If you insist, chéri...I want to tell you that you are destined to be a *big star*. Milano was only the beginning for you. Kristina and Calvin are wonderful, but they cannot provide the big jobs for you that come out of Paris. We are going to have a long and wonderful relationship. You are already booked for another job with Alain Larue in a few days. And Sophie told me that Knut Bry is in town and wants to meet you for a job. Knut works every day and is one of the very best there is."

"That sounds great, Paul," I said from the other side of the door, feeling better that he did not continue with the requests that I stand in the bathroom and talk to him while he was touching his unit in the bath.

It was not lost on me that there was a paradox going on. In high school, I took showers with guys after every practice… but it was different. They were not looking at me in a sexual way, and they did not want to "show" me their *units*, like Paul was trying to do right now. I was disgusted, but not really surprised. I was confident that the work that I had done would offer me some degree of protection from Paul retaliating against me for not complying with his request. I decided to ignore his sexual advance. I had the feeling that I was not the first male model to get this treatment from Paul, and definitely not the last.

We left his brownstone at about eight and went to a small cafe on the corner a block and a half away. I ate some amazing steak with a delicious cream sauce. Paul offered wine, I declined but had one glass of cold Kronenbourg beer in a tall glass. Paul insisted that I try their specialty, an apple filled pastry with vanilla ice cream for dessert. I tried to focus on the food and not on the company and was able to enjoy my meal very much. I knew that Paul and I would never be close friends. He wanted something from me, and I wanted nothing from him. The evening played out quietly, and we walked back to his home at about ten thirty. I tried to use the skills I had learned in Mr. Tillmans sixth grade class, pretending to be interested in what Paul had to say. It seemed to work, Paul seemed upbeat and happy, putting the bathtub incident behind and moving forward.

"Good night Paul," I said with a quiet finality as I walked into my room. I waited until I heard him go into his room and close his door before I quietly removed the skeleton key from my door lock and turned the thumb latch from the inside to lock the door.

I removed my sneaks and slept on top of the covers.

Hoping for the best, but planning for the worst as I drifted off into a troubled night of sleep.

37

MALLORCA

I awoke early and walked to the kitchen. Jute was busy preparing breakfast and coffee. I had only tasted coffee once in Paris with Simone, but I was tired and thought that coffee would wake me up and clear my head.

"Cafe?" I asked Jute with my hands out in front of me.

"Oui, Oui Mr. Da-rulll. Five minutes."

"Merci Jute," I replied with a smile. I walked into the sitting room with the walls of books. I sat on a stiff looking chair with green velvet upholstery and stretched my legs out.

I looked around absently and rubbed my eyes with the backs of my hands. Jute came into the sitting room with a silver coffee pot and a small white china cup with a creamer that matched the coffee pot. He placed the whole tray on the low table in front of me and poured a steaming cup of coffee. He bowed slightly and walked out of the room. I added cream and two teaspoons of sugar and mixed it together. I sipped the steaming cup of coffee and closed my eyes, thinking about Sara and how I would probably never see her again. Calvin told me that she had an Italian boyfriend that she would "never leave."

Paul slipped into the sitting room wearing a silk robe and carrying a cup of coffee.

"Bonjour Dareell," he exclaimed with a smile too big for early morning.

"Bonjour Paul," I replied while taking another sip of my coffee.

"How did you sleep, my prince?"

"Fine Paul. Thank you." I replied cautiously, instinctively wondering if he was bothered by the events of last night. If he had, I was in no mood to deal with it. I hoped that he was not heading in that direction.

"I need to get you to the agency in one hour to meet with the great *Knut Bry,* can you be ready in thirty minutes?" he asked, as he tilted his head to the left.

"Sure Paul. No problem, I'll get ready right now," I said as I stood up to walk back to my room.

I showered quickly, put on some jeans and a concert t-shirt and my sneaks and combed my out-of-control hair straight back, hoping that it would dry better than it did for the *Renoma* pictures with Alain. I could really use a haircut.

We arrived at the agency at around nine thirty. There were a few models standing over by Sophie and Evelyn and a very tall man with a camera around his neck standing apart with his long arms at his sides.

"Ah, hallow Darill. Knut, this is the model that I was telling you about! Darill, come meet Knut." Sophie said as she sprang up from her desk.

I walked towards Knut as he strode towards me. He

reached out a large hand attached to a long, thin arm for me to shake. I shook his hand as he smiled warmly at me with a twinkle in his light blue eyes.

"Nice to meet you, Daryl," He said with a Norwegian accent.

"It's a pleasure to meet you, Mr. Bry," I replied.

"Oh, please call me Knut. I'm not ready to be Mr. Bry!" He said with a hearty laugh.

He was the tallest person I had met since coming to Europe. He was at least six foot six inches tall. He had a mop of blond hair and was clean-shaven with a boyish expression on his face. He seemed kind and gentle, without a mean bone in his body. He was so thin that I wondered if something was wrong with him. I learned after working with him many times that he would get so involved with taking pictures that he would forget to eat...sometimes for days.

"Man, you are going to have so much fun on this job with Knut! I want to come, man! Daryl can get a look at my perfect titties at the beach, ha!" Sophie exclaimed as she pushed me with her shoulder in my ribs.

"I think he will be perfect," Knut said to Sophie as if I were not standing right in front of him. "The job is in Mallorca, near Ibiza. Do you know it?" He asked me in a voice that sounded more suited for Yoda than a giant of a man.

"I know Ibiza and Formentera," I replied. "We went there a few weeks ago for a swimsuit job for Meyba."

"Ah, then you know how beautiful it is."

"Yes, it is very beautiful. It would be great to go back there again," I said.

We talked about some of the places that he had worked

and what the shooting was for. It was an *up and coming* designer named *Jacques Loicq* from Mallorca. We would leave on July third, next Saturday. Paul had retreated to his office and did not get involved in the conversation with Knut, Sophie and I. I liked Knut very much, he appeared to be a giant with a gentle soul. I was not sure what made him tick, but I knew that he was a good person that I could trust.

 I did a few jobs until the weekend and then flew out of *Orly Sud* on Air France to Mallorca. I arrived around noon and was met at the little one-room airport by Knut and Jacques, a small dark man with wild and long dark hair. He was as soft-spoken as Knut, only with a strong French accent. They drove me in an open-sided cart that looked like a larger version of a golf cart, with a bigger canopy and more seats. We went directly to an ancient Turkish bath in town. The two other models were already there. The girl was Lynn; a tall, angular, older model with high cheekbones and a smokey-eyed look. She was very dramatic and seemed to have the ability to make the most average picture look dramatic. Our first picture together was with me standing in the background leaning on an ancient pillar inside the bathhouse in loose linen pants with stripes and a beautiful leather jacket with a contrasting leather collar. Lynn was wearing a leather bathrobe and posed with her arms above her head and with her hands and fingers extended, as if she were going to fly away. I was looking at the ground for most of the shots and had my hands in my pockets and my feet crossed at the ankle. I had learned from Fabrizio to always be natural and not pose for the picture. Knut seemed to like this and took pictures before, during and after the picture was set up. I was not really interested in whether the pictures were "great shots" of me, or not. I was only interested in not being phony in front of the camera. If it didn't feel natural, then I wasn't going to do it...unless the photographer requested it.

I walked over to meet the other model after Lynn and I finished our picture together.

"Hi," I said as I offered my hand for him to shake.

"Nice to meet you, I'm Kevin," he said, with a hard glare and an iron handshake.

"Great to meet you, my name is Daryl, or Dareell, if you are French," I offered with a smile. Nope, no smile back.

Kevin was all business and would not smile for the camera for some reason. I had never seen him before, and he spent most of his time in front of the camera with his chin down and his eyes raised up to look at the camera. He seemed to have gotten the same advice that I received from Ron and Ken Haak a few months ago; to keep my chin down and my eyes up.

Kevin joined in with Lynn and me inside the Turkish bath. We shot pictures in the front, seated on some ancient stones on the side of the building and in a narrow alleyway. We must have done thirty different shots in the afternoon. Knut was very quick and very efficient. He seemed to do everything with his camera without even thinking, as it if were an extension of his hands. He was very different from Fabrizio. He would not "set up" his shots; he just kept following the action wherever it was and made little comments to guide us. It seemed like the more relaxed I was, the more pictures he took of me.

We ended the day as the sun sunk into the sea which was a few miles to the west of the Bath. Jacques, Kevin, and

Lynn all lit up cigarettes and enjoyed themselves in the fading light. I walked towards the crimson-colored sky to get away from the smoke and feel the moment of the changing of day to night. Knut was busy packing up his cameras and then taking pictures of the sunset as it it washed the the ancient buildings with it's ever-changing light. I felt a sense of momentary peace and smiled to myself as I looked forward to the new day that would come when the sun rose in the east.

We ate dinner at a quiet, open restaurant near the Turkish baths with arches and a long row of flowers that looked like bright red carnations. After dinner Knut asked Jacques to hold one of the reflectors to shine the light up from an open flamed lantern near the ground. Knut had me put the leather tunic on without a shirt underneath and stand in the center of the stone archway with the flowers behind and to the sides of me. It was a very dramatic picture of me looking directly into the camera with the soft light from he open flame reflected onto my face and chest. Knut showed me the polaroid of the shot, and I knew that Knut had created an amazing shot. We drove a few miles away to a low stone building that was a friend of Jacques house. Knut and I talked on the balcony that was completely open to the night sky. There were no street lights, allowing us to see millions of stars in the moonless night.

Knut told me about growing up on a farm and leaving because he wanted a different life. He had come into photography because he loved capturing things on film and making them look even more beautiful than they looked in real life. After a few hours I tried to go asleep, but it was too hot for me inside the house. I decided to drag my mattress out to the large balcony and sleep in the cool of the night as the temperature dropped until I could get to sleep. As I drifted off to sleep, I thought back to first grade in Palatine with the humid heat of the summers. My mom would not allow air conditioning and would not allow a fan in our room. She insisted that the fan that she put in the hallway would suck the cool air of the night into our room through the small window and cool us off. It never worked. My solution was to sneak out into the hallway with my pillow and a sheet and lay at the end of the hallway with just my face in front of the fan, invisible from the door to my parent's bedroom. I would wake early in the morning and sneak back into my room before I was discovered.

The next morning I awoke on the balcony stiff and with mosquito bites on my face and arms. My eyes were puffy, but at least I had gotten some sleep. Knut came out to the balcony and immediately started taking pictures of me, I was not ready, but didn't really care. We all had a quick breakfast of rolls, orange juice, and hot coffee before loading up and heading to the beach.

The beach was wide, and the sand was white and fine. We set up near a small bar with a thatched roof that also served food. We took pictures all throughout the day. There were many topless beautiful women all around us. There seemed to be the same dress code in Mallorca that was in Ibiza and Formentera.

Knut was shooting me sitting on a row of rocks near the dirt road that led to the beach. A woman in her late twenty's came over to get a closer look at the scene. She was directly in my sight line about ten feet away from me. She sat on the rocks with one leg over the edge and the other knee up with her foot close to her body. She was very blonde, completely naked and disarmingly beautiful. I had a very difficult time paying attention to the shooting. She smiled directly at me. I had no idea what to do, so, I did nothing and walked back to the group after the shooting was over.

We shot dozens more pictures that day at the beach and did a few shots the next day at a castle before leaving in the early afternoon. Knut mentioned that he thought I was the best model he had ever worked with. My face turned red as I downgraded the compliment in my mind, thinking that he was partially trying to make me feel good. He continued telling me that he wanted me to do a campaign for Wrangler in Cyprus in a few weeks. I quietly thought of what the job might be like. It seemed that the *white noise* had taken a vacation for the last few days and for the moment, I was happy and content with my life.

38

DAMNED IF YOU DO....

We left Mallorca on a small jet plane and flew into Orly Sud towards the end of the day. I grabbed my luggage and took a cab to the agency. Sophie was the first one to notice my arrival, and she jumped up from her chair walked quickly over to meet me and gave me a big hug.

"Knut said that the shooting went great and he wants to use you for the Wrangler campaign. Man, what a stud you are! Can you believe this guy, Evelyn?!" Sophie said, as she turned towards Evelyn.

Evelyn looked towards Sophie and slowly pulled her glasses down her nose and replied, "Oh Oui, Sophie, whatever you say, mon ami," she said without emotion before turning back to her papers on her desk.

I was not sure what I was missing with Evelyn, but I didn't really care. For some reason, I was not Evelyn's cup of tea. I don't think she disliked me; I just think she didn't like me that same way that Sophie did.

"It sounds like a really cool job," I said enthusiastically to Sophie.

"Oh it *is* man, Knut has been talking about this job for a month, and now all of a sudden he decides to use you. This is great, man!"

"Let's go get something to eat, we're almost finished for the day, anyway. Ciao Evelyn, by Paul!" Sophie said as she stuck her tongue out in the general direction of Paul's office. Sophie did not give a shit, and I liked this very much about her. She motioned to me with her hand to follow her and we walked quickly to the elevator. She may not have been polished, but Sophie was definitely *not* boring. I smiled as I looked towards the ground as we rode the elevator together to the first floor. It felt like we were cutting out of school before the final bell, it felt good.

We walked down Rue Richepanse until we arrived at a small cafe with a green awning that covered three tables. Around the tables stood the standard metal backed cafe chairs with the plastic seats.

"Let's sit here, man," Sophie directed, as she lit up a cigarette and sat down. She then leaned on the table with both elbows, like a truck driver from Des Moines.

I sat across from her and put my bags under the table, close to my feet.

I looked across the table at her wavy hair, loose blue t-shirt with no bra and skin-hugging Levi jeans that were snug all the way down to her worn cowboy boots. She was a complete character, but she had her own sex appeal at the same time.

"Man," she said to me while looking me straight in the eyes. "You get my heart going, Dareel."

I looked down at my hands folded on the table, not

knowing how to respond to her statement. It seemed genuine, but it conflicted with the fact that she was a lesbian.

"But I thought that you liked women, Sophie?" I questioned, hoping not to offend her with my direct question.

"Yeah, I do," she replied with a smile that pushed into her eyes. "But there are certain guys that just have something that turns me on, like, without even thinking about it. Do you know what I mean?"

"I guess," I replied, as I realized that I had no idea what she was talking about.

"You know Brock, from Milano, right?"

"Yeah, we came over on the same flight from New York. Great guy."

"Well, Brock is also with First Agency, and I would *definitely* sleep with him. There is something about his skin, so smooth and perfect...and the rest of him is not bad either," she laughed.

"So where do I fit in?" I asked boldly, not sure if I wanted to hear the answer to my question.

"You, Dareel, are different. I want to sleep with you for everything. It's kind of hard to explain. You are just so different, and the package is not too bad, either!"

I swallowed hard and did not have anything to say. My mind jumped to a place where Sophie and I were together in a white room with a soft breeze blowing through the open window as the waves crashed against the shore of a nearby beach. I got lost in the fantasy of lying on the bed with Sophie as she did things to me that I didn't know existed. I shook my head to clear the thoughts as I came back to reality with Sophie sitting across the table. I decided that she was only joking and that we would never, could never, be together.

"What do you want to eat, man?" She asked.

"Huh?...Oh, maybe one of those steaks with the thin french fries and some cold water with bubbles."

"Ok," she ordered steak frites for me and something that I could not understand for herself. We sat and ate quietly, looking at each other often and commenting on how delicious the food was.

"You're going to stay with us, I mean First Agency, aren't you?" she asked as she finished her fish and put her utensils on the plate.

"Yes, of course," I replied. "Where else would I go?"

"Yeah, I guess you're right," she said a bit sadly. "You know that you're working with Alain Larue for *Foncel* tomorrow" she added quickly, changing the subject abruptly "and *then* you are going to the Alps in Laplagne for eight days for French Vogue...you are going to be a busy dude," she said with a smile.

"Wow, that sounds great," I responded, still chewing my steak and looking up from my plate at her.

"You can stay at my place tonight, and I will drop you off at the studio in the morning for your shooting...unless you want to stay with Paul?" she asked with a mischievous grin.

"No, no, that sounds great. Thank you, Sophie," I replied, trying not to sound too eager. We finished our dinner as the cool breeze of night blew from the west as the light changed slowly, as the shadows lengthened and then disappeared.

I slept on the couch at Sophie's tidy one bedroom apartment. She was within walking distance to the Agency. Don't ask why we didn't sleep together because I don't have a reasonable answer. I *never* had good luck with these types of things...that place where the lines are blurred between a good idea and a very bad idea. I don't think sleeping with Sophie would have been a mistake, it just didn't sit well with me. I knew that it would affect our friendship, or even worse, have been really bad, which would of course ruin our friendship forever. The other possibility was that it would be amazing. Which would lead us to a place that neither one of us could even consider. Sophie woke me early with a hot cup of coffee on the counter of her kitchenette as we smiled awkwardly at each other. She drove me the studio in the suburbs to the west of Paris and then drove away slowly in her black Le Car. I walked into the small brick building with ivy stretching it's way up the sides and across some of the windows. I pushed the brass buzzer and waited for an answer with my bag in my hand and my backpack over both shoulders. A 30 something woman with black pants and heavy legs opened the door abruptly and said,

"Come in, you can put your bags over there," she said absently, as she pointed to a corner with a row of coat hooks with a thin wooden shelf above them. She turned and walked away without waiting for me to respond. I placed my bags under the coats and stood in the middle of the floor, waiting for someone to let me know what to do next. Alain walked out from a door near the seamless backdrop and quickly walked over to where I was standing.

"Bonjour Dareel!" he exclaimed as he put his hands on my arms.

Alles, Alles...over here," he walked me over to two racks of clothes on wheels.

A young woman with thick glasses and an oversized men's shirt walked over from behind a small table set up with water and some breakfast food.

"Bonjour, I am Natalie," she said with a genuine smile, as she extended her hand to me.

I squeezed her hand gently and said;

"My name is Daryl, very nice to meet you."

She got me dressed in some casual sports clothes with dull colors, the kind that old men wore at the golf course. Pale blues and greens and salmon colors. It was only me at the shooting. I shot outfit after outfit, smiling and posing as Alain kept the lights popping and his camera clicking. It was mindless and easy work, I got the feeling that they had a lot of pages to fill in the catalog, and volume was more important than quality. Nothing we shot was *high fashion*.

We broke for a light lunch at around one. They had sandwiches that tasted like a light and fluffy egg salad on fresh baked bread. I liked them and could have eaten five more if they gave me the chance. We continued shooting through the afternoon and into the night. We ended at around seven. I put the clothes from the last outfit on the rack and got dressed in the corner since there was no dressing room.

After I was dressed, Natalie walked over to me and explained that I would stay at Alain's apartment tonight and that a car would pick me up in the morning and take me back to the Agency in the morning. Alain listened intently and asked Natalie a few questions in French, to which she replied to him in French as he nodded his head emphatically with a smile on his face.

"Doesn't it make more sense for me to go to Paris tonight?" I asked.

"Oh, no," she replied quickly, "There are no more cars to take you. You will leave early in the morning and get to Paris before eight o'clock." she said casually.

Alain and I left the studio and got something to eat at a smokey bar near the studio. I ate a toasted ham and cheese sandwich and had a Kronenbourg beer. Alain was staring at me the whole time, and it was impossible to communicate with him because he spoke no English, and I didn't speak French. It was more than a little awkward.

We left the restaurant and walked a few blocks to his first-floor apartment. It was the same place I came to earlier in the summer from Milano. It was a surprisingly small apartment with an office, a very small sitting room and a bedroom. He did his best to show me around and then explained to me with gestures and broken English that I would sleep in his bed with him. I looked at him like he had lost his freaking mind. I said, "No, merci Alain," with as much restraint as I could manage and went into the little office area to set up a place to sleep on the floor. I slept in my clothes with some rolled up pants for a pillow and my jacket on the floor as a makeshift mattress. I drifted off to sleep quickly.

At about one thirty in the morning, Alain came into the tiny office wearing only a shirt and standing near my pillow with a *semi* and talking very animated in French. I jumped up and said, "What the fuck!" and started to get my shit together as fast as I could. I wanted to punch him in the face but knew that no one would believe me, because I was American, it was his house, and I was almost twice his size. If I hurt him, *I* would be the one arrested and taken to jail, and he was *definitely* not worth it.

He started talking louder and louder, making what sounded like threats to me. I ignored him and knew that I would never work for him again. I was so pissed that I was actually shaking. I tried to think quickly what my options were, and my only choice was to get the *fuck* out of his house. I walked to the front door, and he tried to stop me and said, "No," but I simply opened the door and pushed past him. Maybe he thought I would come back when I had no place to stay; not likely. I walked for about thirty minutes until I ended up in a place that I didn't recognize at all. There were people on the street corners playing guitars and singing, prostitutes and a few transvestites talking to small men. I saw a three-story building with neon sign that said *Hotel.* I walked in and asked how much a room was for the night. It was over 400 francs for the night. I only had a few hundred francs with me. I got some change from the hotel clerk and went to a payphone across the street and called Margaret in Indiana and told her what my situation was. She was able to pay for the hotel with her credit card by phone. I got into my room by about three thirty. I was so amped up that I didn't fall asleep until around five in the morning. I woke late and stayed at the hotel until check out time, wanting to get my money's worth. I didn't tell anyone at the agency what had happened, as I thought it would get around like wildfire and *somehow* reflect badly on me, like *I* did something wrong. It was an awkward situation that there seemed to be no antidote...as if it would happen no matter what. Like the sun rising in the east and setting in the west, I was powerless to stop it from happening. And the *one* advantage I had over shrubs like Alain, my physical strength and size, would work against me if I ever did strike him down and *actually* hurt him. A Catch 22 more devious than anything in Joseph Heller's best-selling book. Damned if you do, damned if you don't. Well, fuck it, not with me, not today...I don't care who you think you are and what you think I owe you.

39

HOTEL LOTTI

For the next few weeks, I did more work in Paris than I had ever done in Milano. I worked for French Vogue in Laplagne with Francois Deconinck. We skied on the glaciers at the top each morning and early afternoon and came back down to the hotel in the afternoon to swim and play tennis. There was only one model working with me, a guy from Australia named Warren. He was a solid built twenty-five year old with capped teeth that took over his mouth with their massive size. He played the same part as Mel Gibson in Road Warrior on a TV show. He had a picture of himself sitting on a cop car that looked just like the one in Road Warrior. He was game for anything and funnier than anyone I had ever met. He was constantly referring to his *stuff* as; *my "twig and berries."* He would hit on any woman under the age of forty. His accent was bracing, like getting hit in the face with a block of ice. He literally never stopped talking, all I had to do was watch and listen and I would hear and see more things in a day than I would see by myself in a week. One day we were sitting by the packed hotel pool, and he noticed a beautiful young woman in a bikini with an old, bald, fat man. He said loudly to me, "Shit, look at that fat bastard with that young *sheila*. What the fuck is that all about?"

I turned to look and saw a fifty-something man laying down and talking to a beautiful woman. The woman heard what he said, but Warren thought she did not speak English.

She looked at him coldly and said evenly, "He is my father, asshole."

Warren just shrugged his broad shoulders and asked her out on a date, to which she replied.

"Are you serious?"

"Sure, why not?" he asked with an expectant look on his face.

"No, I don't think so" she replied without taking any time to think about her answer as she looked directly at me.

"Whoa Buddy, I'm down in flames, but you may be in the game," he said to me with a laugh.

I blushed and returned her look and smiled. She smiled back, and I drank in her face and skin, which was very pale and smooth. I was falling before I even found out her name.

Her name was Sylvain and she worked at the hotel front desk. We both fell hard for each other, and I never knew anything like the feelings I had for her. She had everything that I ever dreamed of in a woman. Her only flaw was a deep scar on her forehead, right below her dark, short hair. It looked like it was bad and was never pulled together with stitches. It only made her more beautiful to me. We spent every moment that we were not working together in my room. And then, she was gone. I looked all over for her. I tried to find out where she lived from the other receptionist, but she would not tell me. On the last day, she told me a few details of Sylvain's story. Sylvain was engaged and decided to leave me without saying goodbye. She couldn't face me, but she knew that I would never stay in Laplagne and that I would eventually leave her alone and go back to the United States. I would have given anything to see her one more time, talk to her, see her eyes... but it didn't work out that way. I realized that she was probably right, some things are just too good to be true, and you must leave them before the dream destroys everything that you have.

I returned to Paris on a night train with Warren nine days after arriving in the Alps. I stayed one night in the one bedroom Agency apartment with four other models. I slept on the floor behind the couch with a bed made up of most of my clothes. The next day I flew to Cyprus with Knut for the Wrangler campaign. It was a very beautiful island with the bluest water that I had ever seen. Knut shot pictures from the moment we arrived. I had no idea that Wrangler had so many shirts and jackets, as well as jeans. I dove off a cliff with my Wrangler Jeans and then went waterskiing the same day. Knut was very excited about the pictures and told me the pictures on the boat would be perfect for the cover of GQ. He said that he was sending several slides of me for the cover of GQ after we returned to Paris. He showed me a few of the polaroids of the shots that he was sending; they seemed like they would work fine on the cover. I was excited but also realized that they were only cover tries.

That night I was arrested by the Secret Service at the hotel pool. A few of the Turkish patrons at the bar told them that I was English military and that they heard me talking about assassinating the President of Cyprus, which was, of course, total bullshit. It took two hours for the Concierge to straighten things out, explaining that I was an American model. I was wearing a white t-shirt, had a crew cut and was wearing camouflage pants, so I looked the part.

We headed back to Paris after six days. I was tan, had my hair short and was ready to get back to American soil. I was tired and just wanted to go home and do a whole bunch of nothing for a week or two.

The next day an out of the blue campaign come in for Claude Montana with Arthur Elgort. It was two days in the studio with a beauty that was on a few episodes of Miami Vice. She was tall, blonde and a dancer. We took almost all of our pictures together. She was fun, but all business. The pictures were amazing, and Arthur was very happy with everything that we did in front of the camera. I thought that the pictures were different than anything that I had in my book.

I got booked for another job with an older model named Bruce Hulse for Kronenbourg in Nice. He was one of those "I've got it all figured out" types. He thought he was the man, superior to all living things. He treated me as if I were his understudy in a play, giving me unsolicited advice on everything from posing for the camera to ordering food at the restaurant; "Order the most expensive thing on the menu, let them know that you are worth the expense," he said with a wink and a smile. Or, they could kick your ass off the job for being a douche. I thought to myself. He ordered two lobster tails and a mixed drink with vodka. I ordered a chicken and rice dish and a cold beer.

I shot another campaign for Panchetti and another for Daniel Hechter with a new model that was just featured in a Versace campaign. His name was Jason Beghe; he was a muscular redhead with freckles. He didn't look like your typical model, but he was very funny and always had something to say to me. He told me he was a wrestler and was very friendly with more confidence than anyone that I had ever met, like he could do anything. I thought he was amusing and looked forward to his stories and sayings; he never seemed to run out of things to say.

As August quickly approached I started to ask Sophie if I could go back to the US. Most of the models told me that August was a month that everyone in France went on holiday, and I really wanted to get back home. Two months in Milan had quickly turned into three, then four and now I was heading into my fifth month away from home. Sophie said that I could leave in a few weeks after the Collections were finished. I agreed, reluctantly.

I was absently walking back to the apartment from my afternoon appointments on an overcast and muggy Monday. I was near the botanical garden that led up to the Louvre. I noticed a young model from the agency running across the road, barely avoiding getting hit by a fast-moving Citreon that beeped at him as he scooted to the safety of the curb.

"Hey," he called out breathlessly with a big smile.

"Hi," I said as we both walked towards each other.

"I'm Brian," he said as he offered his hand for me to shake.

"I'm Daryl," I replied as we shook hands.

"Are you going to the big Bruce Weber go-see?" He asked.

"No, I didn't even know there was one," I replied, a little confused.

"Well, it's huge. Bruce is meeting with almost every model that's in Paris at the Hotel Lotti today."

"Huh...maybe I should call Evelyn to see what the deal is," I said.

"Whatever. I'll wait, then we can walk over together," he offered sincerely.

I grabbed a five-franc coin and called the agency from a payphone on the corner.

Evelyn picked up the phone; "Hallo, First Agency," she sang out.

"Hello, Evelyn, is Sophie there?"

"Ah no, chéri, Sophie is on holiday," she responded with mock sadness.

"Oh. I'm here with Brian and he says there is an appointment at the Hotel Lotti with Bruce Weber, did someone forget to give me the appointment?" I asked.

"Ah, no Dareel, this appointment is not for you. Bruce is looking for brunettes, not blondes. Sorry chéri," she said with some forced sympathy.

"Ok Evelyn, thanks," I said as I placed the phone on the receiver.

I repeated the conversation to Brian and ended with "I guess I'm not supposed to go. Thanks anyway, man."

"Are you f-ing crazy?" he questioned with outstretched arms to add emphasis to his words.

"No" I replied with a slight laugh.

"Well, then come with me!" he insisted. "Forget Evelyn; this is Bruce-freaking-Weber, man!"

I replied with a shrug of my shoulders and said "ok" and followed Brian to the lobby of the Hotel Lotti.

We arrived at a large hotel lobby with oriental rugs placed on the marble floors. There were couches and tables with chairs scattered around, small gathering places for talking and meeting. There were forty or fifty models sitting on chairs, couches and a few were standing. They all looked nervous and were clutching either their backpacks or slick looking portfolios from their French agency. Brian and I seemed to be the last ones to arrive. I took a seat in the only open spot, near the archway that led to the wide staircase that curved to the second-floor balcony.

Soon a small man with a blue bandana covering his head walked into the lobby. He was wearing a white t-shirt and baggy jeans and sneaks with white socks. I thought that Bruce sent his assistant to look at our books. He looked around the room and said in an unassuming voice,

"Hi, I'm Bruce…who's first?"

I was a little confused, thinking that this could not be the great Bruce Weber. He looked more like a clown from the weekend rodeos in Missouri than a great photographer. I watched the faces of the models and thought that they all looked like they were holding their breath. After what seemed like five minutes, I got up and said to myself "nobody?" as I walked over to Bruce with my crappy book. Everyone watched me like I was going to do something amazing. I handed my crappy book to Bruce and sat down on the couch facing the chair that he was sitting in. He looked thoughtfully at my pictures and then paused and looked up at me.

"Can you dance?" he asked seriously.

"Yes, I can dance," I replied without giving it much thought.

"No, I mean really dance," he asked again, still looking at me. "Like this," he said as he held up my book and showed me the picture of me doing a transition jump for gymnastics.

"Yes, I was in dance show in high school, and I did ballet. I can dance...I'm not a professional, but I can dance," I said with some degree of confidence.

Bruce smiled broadly and paused for a moment.

"Good, can you stay around the lobby for a while? I want you to meet someone," he said quietly in a gentle voice, seeming that he did not want the others in the lobby to hear.

"Sure," I replied as I took my book out of his outstretched hand.

I went to another section of the lobby, near the front desk and waited. Bruce came over in about an hour after the last of the models had left the lobby. He asked me to follow him.

"You were a gymnast?" he asked as we walked to the elevator.

'Yes, in high school...I was a bit too tall by my senior year, but I liked it very much."

"That's very cool!" he said as we rode the elevator up to the fourth floor and went to room four hundred fifteen. The door was open and a few people were moving clothes from racks and laying them on the bed. Beautiful long dresses made from beautiful fabric.

"Hi Grace," Bruce said to a tall woman with red hair and perfect posture.

"Hello Bruce," she said with a British accent as she turned to face us.

"This is Daryl," he said. "I would like to use him with

Tracy for the collections editorial. Do we have a gray suit that we can try on him?"

"I think so," she said as she turned to a younger woman that appeared to be her assistant and spoke to her quickly and asked her to get a gray suit for me.

In a few minutes, she asked me to try on the jacket, it seemed to fit fine. She had a tailor make a few marks on the sides where it needed to be taken in and smiled broadly at me.

"This seems to fit well," she said to Bruce.

"Yes, I think it will work great," he said.

"I'll call your agency and give them the information. We're working at night, so that we can shoot the clothes that they need for the shows during the day. It should be Wednesday night at around eight. See you then!" Bruce said to me near the hotel room door.

"Ok Bruce, see you then," I replied, not sure what had just happened or what I would be doing in a shooting for the collections with women, but it was *Bruce- Freaking- Weber*. I didn't feel the same way that I felt with Knut and Fabrizio. Bruce seemed very excited to work with me, although I didn't feel he was interested in who I was, only interested in getting great pictures.

Night had fallen while I was in the hotel with Bruce and Grace. It was raining hard, and the cars were splashing through the newly created puddles along the streets. My shoes and pants got wet from the downpour. I arrived at the apartment around nine and rolled out some clothes on the floor and found an old blanket in the closet and went quickly to sleep before I could think about the day that I just had.

40

FALL FROM GRACE

I took the subway to 17 Villa Alesia. It was a factory type building with brick walls and concrete floors. The second story window looked down at the narrow cobblestone street below. There was nobody in the studio, so I sat at one of the picnic tables that someone had dragged up to the studio from a park somewhere. I took out *The Sun Also Rises* from my backpack and started to read where I left off...when *Jake and Brett* meet up with the *Count* in Paris. A thin black man with unintentionally baggy pants opened the bars to the service elevator and rolled in the same clothes rack that I saw at the hotel room a few days ago. He smiled tiredly at me. When I waved back and asked him how he was doing, he looked at the ground and shuffled back to the elevator without responding. Five minutes later a whole group came spilling out of the service elevator and into the studio. Bruce was in the middle of the pack, and two young girls were near him. Grace was close by, and a square looking man with square glasses and thin black and gray hair took up the rear of the group. He walked over to me and introduced himself in English; "I am Bernardo," he said with a big smile. "I driver," he said as he extended his hand for me to shake.

"I'm Daryl," I replied, as I smiled back at him.

He seemed pleased to have someone to talk to, so he sat across from me at the picnic table and started to tell me about the "group" that he was driving around Paris. Another male model named Nick showed up. He had black hair and a black beard at around nine PM. He was pleasant but seemed preoccupied. Either he did not want to be here, or he had other things to do that he thought were more important.

Bruce heel-toed it over to the picnic tables and gave us a few instructions.

"You guys are basically props for the girls. They will be wearing the dresses from the collections and you both will be wearing a gray suit with a white shirt and black tie. Very simple and elegant.

"Didier will cut your hair, Daryl...Nick, your hair is fine, just find a dresser to help you with your suit."

Bruce motioned for me to follow him to a corner of the studio near the bright lights and the seamless background, where we would be shooting.

"Daryl," Bruce said in that voice that seemed like he was holding back the urge to giggle.

"This is Didier, he is always with me and cuts everyone's hair.... Didier, can you cut his hair a little shorter on the sides and spike it straight up with some of that gel that you like."

I shook Didier's hand and he smiled at me without showing any of his teeth, as if they were discolored or missing. He was tall and thin and wore a crisp blue, open-collared shirt and a pair of perfectly fitted khakis and brown loafers with argyle socks. He was very soft-spoken and had an accent that I could not place, sounding Dutch and British, at the same time.

"Please, sit down," he directed me quietly.

I sat in a metal folding chair and put my backpack in the corner. Didier casually threw a small sheet over my shoulders to keep the hair off of me. He snipped at my hair with a very small pair of scissors that seemed very sharp. I kept waiting for him to break out the clippers, but he never did. He did everything with the scissors and a fifty cent plastic comb that he kept in his shirt pocket.

I went to the bathroom and then got dressed in my suit. They had no shoes for me, so Bruce lent me his black loafers to wear over the red socks that Grace had given me.

"I'm Tracy," a beautiful girl said to me, wearing an over the top dress with some very grown-up makeup. I think she was seventeen or eighteen. I saw her in the Ralph Lauren campaigns in the States. She was healthy and had broad shoulders that didn't go with her fancy dress. She had the best smile I had ever seen, perfect, warm and inviting.

"So you're the guy that they changed my hair color to match!" she said with her hands on her hips and a pretend scowl on her face.

"Oh, sorry," I said, not fully understanding why I was apologizing. "I'm Daryl," I finished as I reached out a hand for her to shake. She had a grip like a small vice, and it became apparent to me that Tracy was much more than just a pretty face.

We both smiled and walked over to the picnic table,

and I got her a cup of water from the cooler and we stood waiting to be called into action.

Tracy and I did five different dresses the first night. I had a hard time keeping awake while the other models were shooting. Nick was paired up with a very young latino girl from the Bronx named Talisa Soto. She was only fourteen years old. When she arrived, she was wearing a school uniform type white shirt and black pants. Her black hair was down to her waist and she had bangs that covered most of her face. Bruce told Didier to cut her hair short. Like Ingrid Bergman's in For Whom the Bell Tolls. It suited her. She looked like a completely different person. Tracy and I watched her turn from a very shy kid into an all powerful diva with sweeping gestures of her hands and dramatic lines in the collection dresses. She always covered her teeth with her mouth or her hand. They seemed to be very widely spaced and had calcium deposits like my teeth, only on every tooth, not just a few. Years later I saw her in the movie Mortal Combat and her teeth were completely fixed. Tracy and I were watching a star being born right in front of us.

Nick was gone by the third night. I think he struggled with the dancing part, and from that point on Talisa did all of her pictures alone. Bruce brought in four standard poodles to shoot with us. In one picture they all sat around us, as Tracy and I laughed and looked away. Grace seemed very happy with how the shooting was turning out and Bruce spent most of his time trying to get Tracy to have more fun and interact with me. He told Tracy to kiss me, and she kissed me on the cheek while I closed my eyes and smiled. Bruce only seemed to talk to me when we were shooting, not anything like Fabrizio, Knut and Arthur...they talked to me all of the time, whether we were shooting, eating, or traveling. They seemed to be genuinely interested in me.

"Hi Daryl," Bruce said during a break at two in the morning. "Have you heard of Calvin Klein?" he asked, as he sat down at the picnic table near me.

"Um, yes," I answered...who hadn't?

"Well, I'm shooting a campaign for Calvin and I think you would be perfect for it," he continued. "What do you think?" he asked. "We are doing a huge billboard in Times Square, too."

"Of course Bruce, that sounds amazing," I replied, not really believing what I was hearing.

"That's great," he said as he looked around the studio.

"Can we do some test pictures that I can send to Calvin? I think now is a good time," he said with feigned indifference.

"Sure Bruce, sounds good," I said, getting up from the table. I walked over to the seamless.

"Ok, can you take off your shirt? " he asked. "This is an ad for Calvin Klein jeans."

"Sure," I said as I took off my t-shirt and put it away from the backdrop on the floor.

I stood with my arms slack at my sides, and then I put my hands on my hips and smiled. I was not really sure what to do. Bruce was silent as he clicked away behind the camera in the dark part of the studio. I noticed Tracy and Talisa walk into the studio from the freight elevator. They were talking and looked briefly at what I was doing and then saw Bruce taking pictures, so they swung wide, away from that corner of the studio. Didier was watching with some interest from the area beyond the picnic tables by the kitchen. He looked like he was making a cup of coffee.

"Ok Daryl, can you take off your pants? I want to get some body shots for Calvin."

I hesitated for a moment and then pulled off my jeans and put them with my t-shirt. My briefs were not that clean and I blushed as I returned to the seamless. I never considered myself a body model, more of a face. I did not have a bad body, I just was not that confident. My skin was not as smooth and even toned as a guy like Brock. I could do body work in a pinch, like the underwear job with Warren in Brittany. Warren was definitely not a body model, but he didn't give a shit. He didn't care that he was hairy, barrel-chested with skinny legs and there was not a six pack to be found. Bruce continued with snapping pictures, remaining silent as he clicked away with the auto wind attachment.

"Why don't you hold Daisy?" he asked absently. Daisy was the smallest white Standard poodle of the group. I picked her up after calling her over to me and tucked her under my right arm, holding her by letting her sit in the crook of my arm. Bruce seemed to like this. I wanted to get dressed and get back to work. It's almost impossible to see anyone in the dark sections of the studio when the lights are flashing. It was very bright and I was feeling more and more uncomfortable. Daisy got too heavy for me to hold and I gently put her down on the concrete. She looked up at me with her big human eyes, as if she wanted me to hold her for a few more minutes.

"Can you take your underwear off?" Bruce said casually as he changed the body of his camera with one with fresh film.

"Excuse me?" I said as politely as I could, thinking that maybe I hadn't heard him correctly. He couldn't possibly want me to go buck naked in front of two young girls and the rest of the crew. Even Bernardo, the driver, was sipping his coffee at the picnic table. I looked around and it seemed that Grace was not there, for some reason.

"Um, can you take off your underwear," he repeated, "Don't worry, you won't see anything, the pictures will be tasteful.... I take pictures of everyone in the nude. Do you know Jeff Aquilon?" He said with a belief that it was already decided that I would pose nude on the seamless background for him and his little black camera.

Not see anything? What the hell was he talking about? They will see everything and the pictures will be graphic as hell. Bruce was like Ken Haak, only Bruce was the most powerful photographer, NO, he was the most powerful man in the fashion business, period.

I shifted my weight from my left foot to my right, looking down at my feet, I was still wearing Bruce's black loafers and red socks. I considered the impossible decision that I needed to make in an instant, alone on the seamless. I thought that my position as an up and coming model may offer me some protection from retaliation from Bruce and those that followed him, like the chosen one, simply because of his power and influence.

I looked up into the darkness from the circle of light that surrounded me from all sides and said in a small voice, "No."

"What?!" Bruce said, as if he hadn't heard me correctly.

"I said, no," I spoke evenly, without hesitation, in a steady and clear voice. I knew immediately that I was finished, but I couldn't go against the one person that I was stuck with for the rest of my life, me.

Bruce gave me one look that said it all, shocked and

amazed. He left the studio without saying anything to me. Didier nodded somberly in my direction as I picked up my pants and got dressed in the middle of the studio. I put my t-shirt back on and walked over to where Bernard sat with his cooling cup of coffee.

"Bravo, Monsieur," he said with sad eyes and a hint of a smile pulling at his lips. "Très gallant." I shook my head from side to side and sat down with my arms on my knees.

Bruce returned to the studio thirty minutes later and started shooting Talisa in a sweeping black dress that showed her bare, broad shoulders. Bruce did not speak to me for the rest of the shooting; he gave directions to Tracy when he wanted us to do something different. Grace showed up an hour later. She had no idea what had transpired in her absence. I took the subway back to my apartment at six AM, climbed the four flights of stairs and set up my bed behind the couch and pulled the drapes to the floor of the giant windows, hoping to block out the sunlight and sleep the day away on a day that I knew I would never forget. Sleep came easy and fast on the floor of the dusty living room.

EPILOGUE

The career that had held so much promise after working with the very best photographers and magazines in Europe, never came to fruition. After one trip with GQ to Santorini with Ricoh Pullman, I never worked for GQ again. Donald Sterzin, a close friend of Bruce Weber's, the Art Director of GQ made sure that I never appeared on the cover of that magazine after seven cover tries taken by three different photographers. Weber and I worked together in Bellport for the last time ever in September of 1982. It was a group shooting for GQ, an article on models and their brothers. He took some pictures after the main shooting of my brother Stokes and I without our shirts on. He used my picture for the cover of his first book, released in 1983. It was an untitled book with an all black front and back cover for $220.00. I did not even know that I was on the cover (or that the book even existed) and I never signed a modeling release. I found out when I saw the book in the window of Rizzoli's on St. Patricks Day, 1983. I asked Beth Anne Hardison (my Booker at Click) why I did not at least get a copy of the book or get invited to the opening, to which she replied;

"Bruce doesn't think that you trust him."

I replied that I didn't care if Bruce thought I trusted

him, or not. To which she replied, almost pleaded; "But you have to care, Daryl!"

I never did any campaigns for Calvin. When I met Calvin at a party a year later, he had no idea who I was. Click sent me on fewer and fewer appointments, until I was only seeing clients two or three days a week. Scott Copeland never represented me. He worked closely for years to bring Bruce new models.

When I complained to Beth Anne about how few appointments I was getting each week, Francis Grille overheard me and pulled Beth Anne aside and said to her, "If he doesn't like the way we are treating him, then he can just get the FUCK out of here. We don't need him!"

I went to meet with Dan Deeley at Wilhelmina men's agency the next day. By then, I was just another model with very few commercial clients. There was no buzz about me by this time. Dan tried to help, but my career was over before it even started in the United States.

I earned about 160.00 dollars per day for shooting with Bruce for three nights in Paris for British Vogue. I made 220.00 per day for each day of the two-day GQ shooting in Bellport. Bruce still remembers me to this day, and from the looks of pictures on the internet, I am one of the few guys that refused to allow Bruce to take full frontal nude shots of me.

In 1982-1983 Bruce had pictures in all of the editorial magazines, did ALL of the major fashion campaigns and was part owner of the Click Modeling Agency. If there was any industry that Bruce was not in control of in the fashion business, I was not aware of it. I never made more than fifty thousand a year for the two plus years that I struggled against the inevitable and left the modeling business to go back to school.

It seems there has never been a model that rose so quickly, only to disappear so completely. It seems that I was the David that was slain by Goliath. If I had it to do all over again; if the choice could be reversed and I would achieve all that my career seemed destined for and became a name that everyone knew, I would still have done the same thing. Who I am today is a product of that decision. My seven children now know that it is not only words when I say to them,

"It's never wrong to do the right thing."

THE END

ABOUT THE AUTHOR

D. L. JANNEY is a happily married father of seven children and lives in Connecticut. He was born in Moorestown, NJ. When he was three years old his family moved to Palatine, IL. At 17 he left home to attend Monmouth College in Monmouth, IL. He left college in the fall of his sophomore year and headed to New York City. After two years working as a professional model he returned to school at Boston University and obtained a degree in English literature with Distinction. He has worked as a carpenter and contractor for the past 25 years and spends time watching his children grow, writing and sleeping. He is currently writing a collection of short stories.

www.ingramcontent.com/pod-product-compliance
Lightning Source LLC
Chambersburg PA
CBHW022226010526
44113CB00033B/509